To all Brummies, wherever they come from.

01

First published 1994 by Birmingham City Council, Department of Leisure and Community Services, Libraries and Learning Division, Central Library, Chamberlain Square, Birmingham B3 3HQ.

First printed March 1994
Reprinted August 1994

British Library Cataloguing-in-Publication Data
CPI Catalogue Record for this book is available from the British Library.

ISBN: 0-7093-0202-9   (Hardback)
ISBN: 0-7093-0203-7   (Paperback)

Typeset, printed and bound in Great Britain by HE Jones Ltd., Birmingham.

CARL CHINN

BIRMINGHAM: THE GREAT WORKING CITY

GREATER BIRMINGHAM:
SHOWING MAIN ROADS, RAILWAY LINES, CANALS & DISTRICTS WHICH HAVE JOINED BIRMINGHAM SINCE 1838

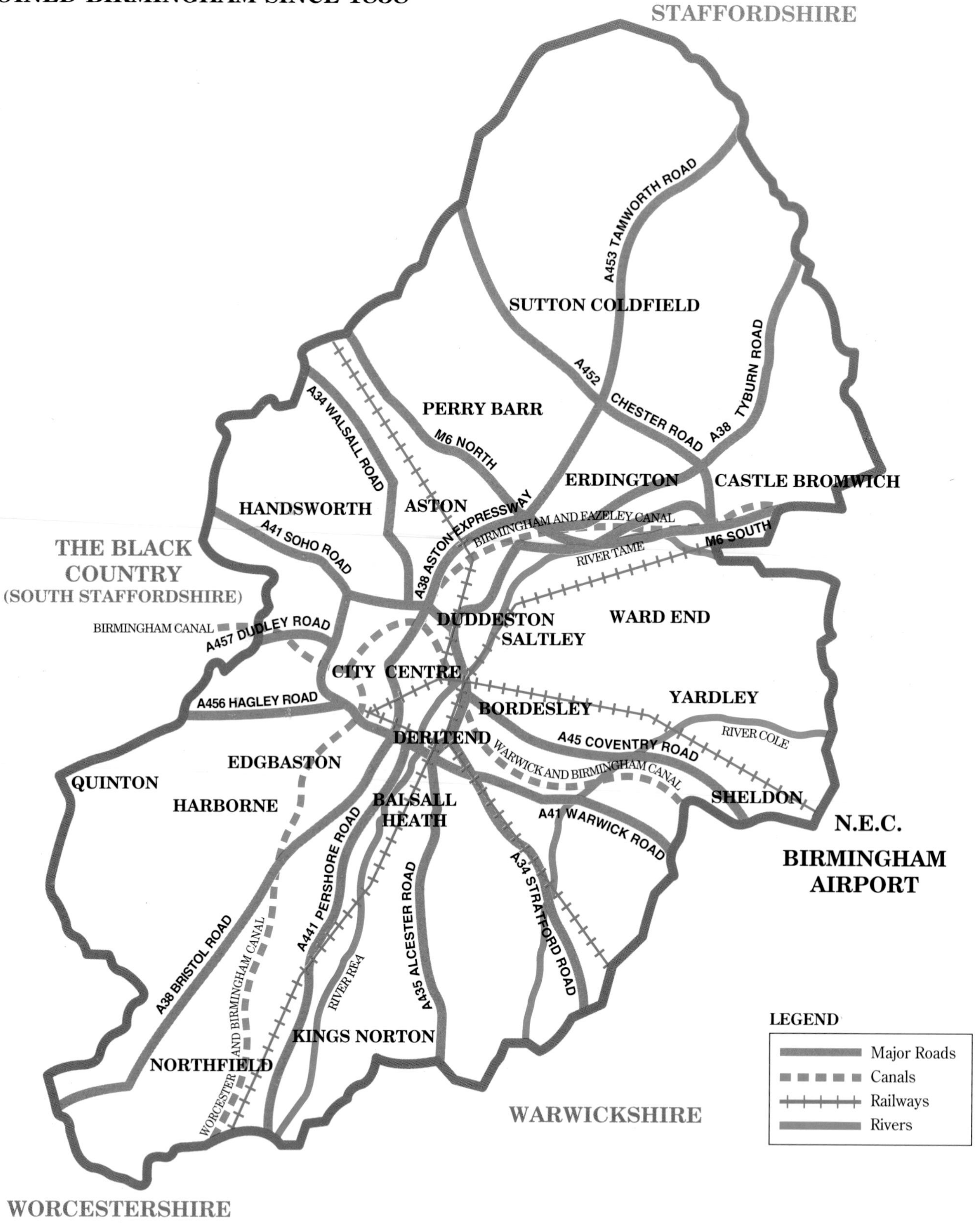

STAFFORDSHIRE

SUTTON COLDFIELD

A453 TAMWORTH ROAD

TYBURN ROAD

PERRY BARR

A452

CHESTER ROAD

A38

M6 NORTH

A34 WALSALL ROAD

ERDINGTON

CASTLE BROMWICH

HANDSWORTH

ASTON

A41 SOHO ROAD

A38 ASTON EXPRESSWAY

BIRMINGHAM AND FAZELEY CANAL

M6 SOUTH

THE BLACK COUNTRY
(SOUTH STAFFORDSHIRE)

RIVER TAME

DUDDESTON
SALTLEY

WARD END

BIRMINGHAM CANAL

A457 DUDLEY ROAD

CITY CENTRE

A456 HAGLEY ROAD

BORDESLEY

YARDLEY

RIVER COLE

DERITEND

A45 COVENTRY ROAD

EDGBASTON

QUINTON

HARBORNE

BALSALL
HEATH

WARWICK AND BIRMINGHAM CANAL

SHELDON

A41 WARWICK ROAD

N.E.C.

BIRMINGHAM
AIRPORT

A38 BRISTOL ROAD

WORCESTER AND BIRMINGHAM CANAL

A441 PERSHORE ROAD

RIVER REA

A435 ALCESTER ROAD

A34 STRATFORD ROAD

KINGS NORTON

NORTHFIELD

WARWICKSHIRE

LEGEND

———	Major Roads
- - - -	Canals
+++++	Railways
———	Rivers

WORCESTERSHIRE

CONTENTS

FOREWORD

Like so many citizens of Birmingham, I am not a Brummie by birth. It is 20 years since I moved from Worcestershire to live and work in this city. In that migration, I have followed in the footsteps of hundreds of thousands of other West Midlanders and of those from further away. Because of such movements, modern Birmingham is a multi-cultural city enriched by citizens who have come here from across the world, and I am delighted to be involved in a book which tells the story of all its people.

Over the last 25 years, history has moved from an emphasis on 'great men'. Our knowledge of the past has become more democratic as the actions and lives of those who have been hidden from view have been brought into light by social historians. This shift has been made possible by a variety of approaches to the study of history. They include the use of oral evidence to give the views of those who previously had no voice, the collection of photographs to show the lives of those who were once ignored, and the gathering of artefacts and memorabilia to indicate the hard work and toil of those who created wealth but often did not share in it.

Because of these changes in research, historians are increasingly aware of the contributions made to society by the working class, the poor, women, children, immigrants and the lower middle class. The voices of these people now reach us and demand that we take note of them. And if our interpretation of the past has became more open, then the study of history has also become more democratic. The past is no longer the preserve of the professional academic, it belongs to everyone. Throughout the year, Birmingham Central Library is packed with people finding out about their families and discovering more about their neighbourhoods and communities. They have realised that history belongs to all of us and is not the domain of the rich and powerful. At the same time, they have become aware that our present and our future cannot be separated from those who have gone before.

This book has been written in the light of these realisations. It is a people's history and it belongs to all Brummies wherever they come from. Through their words and their pictures, we can acknowledge the contribution made to our lives by those who have been called ordinary but who in reality were all extraordinary people.

Carl Rice
Chair, Leisure Services Committee
Birmingham, 1993

ACKNOWLEDGEMENTS

Many people have helped me greatly in the research and writing of this book. Some of them are mentioned in the text or in the Notes at the end of each chapter, whilst those who have let me use their photographs are acknowledged on the relevant page. But I should like to mention my appreciation of the input of a number of other relatives, friends and colleagues.

First of all, I thank my wife Kay and our children, Richard, Tara and Catríona for their support, understanding and enthusiasm for my work. As a Dubliner, Kay must get fed up sometimes with all my talk of Brum and I appreciate her tolerance!

Second, I acknowlege the part played in this book by our Mom and Dad - Sylv and Buck; Nan - Lily Perry; Aunt Win 'Mick' Martin; Grandads Arthur Perry and Richard 'Tim' Chinn; Uncles Georgie, Billy and Alfie Wood; Uncle Bernard Chinn; Great Uncles Wal and Bill Chinn; and Great Grannie Lil Wood and Great Grandad Bill Wood. Individually and collectively they passed on to me their loyalty to Birmingham and their pride in our city. Above all, through their stories and lives they made me realise that history is not just about the big names who are well known. Through their example, they taught me to respect the contribution made to Birmingham's history by their own kind - working-class Brummies.

That feeling was made more immediate by my relatives and friends of my own age group - all of whom grew up with a deep and unshakeable bond with Birmingham: Our Kid, Darryl - who has always been there for me; my aunt Lynne Baker, who is more like a sister; my big cousins Gail Gregory, and Billy, Johnny and Kenny Wood; and my mates, 'Big' Dave Evans, Sandra Chinn, Paul McCance, Christine Flaherty, Julie Walters, Barbara and Paul 'Branty' Brant, Lynne and Tony Martin, and Sandra and Malcolm Axon.

And for making me realise that Brummies aren't just English but are everyone who belongs to this city, I mention my Irish muckers Maggie and Billy Hughes, and Harry Gillan - all of whom have been in Birmingham longer than I have; my friend Carl Thorpe, a Black Brummie from Jamaica; my Mom's school mate Micky Volante, whose dad came from southern Italy; and Samantha Meah, a South Asian Brummie whose affection for the city is matched by few.

I thank also the following people who publicised my research: Tony Butler of Radio WM; Peter Leather and Steve Dyson of *Metronews;* Steve O'Neill and Pamela Wilkinson of *Birmingham Voice;* Ross Reyburn and Carol Ann Rice of the *Birmingham Post;* Bob Kane of the *Express and Star;* and Malcolm Stent. In particular, I appreciate the enthusiasm and encouragement of Bryan Bird and Carl Rice, and I am also grateful to the following people for their support: Professor John Grenville, Professor Richard Simmons, Dr Bob Bushaway, Dorothy Thompson, Professor Harvey J. Kaye, Peter Barwell, Harold Blumenthal, Fred Chapman, Brenda Newton, Matt Redmond, Renee Spector, Paul Tilsley, Bill Turner, Pat Coleman and John Dolan.

This book could not have been published without the active participation of Dr John Bourne and Dr Dick Holt who have read various drafts and have given me valuable advice. Nor could it have appeared without the essential work of those who have been involved in photographic research and support. These people are: from Birmingham Library Services, Richard Albutt, Community History Development Librarian - whose assistance has been essential, Pete James, Photographic Development Officer, Robert Ryland, Local Studies Librarian, and Philippa Bassett, Senior Archivist; from Birmingham City Council Communications Unit, Gillian Dunkerley, Council Design Manager; from Birmingham City Council Department of Planning and Architecture, Gareth Lewis; and from the Photographic Section, the School of Geography, The University of Birmingham, Geoff

Dowling and Simon Restorick. Geoff was also generous in allowing me to use photographs from his own collection, as were Peter Donnelly and Mike Tunnicliff.

In the production of the book, the following people have been vital: Dawn Wise, Promotions Unit, Birmingham Library Services; Mark Ansell, Graphic Designer; Keith Hughes, Print Manager, and Richard Graham, both of Birmingham Commercial Services; and Richard Ingham, Sales Director, and all the staff at H. E. Jones Limited. I thank as well Chris Meade, Arts Development Officer, Birmingham Library Services; Patrick Baird, Head of Services, Local Studies and History, Birmingham Library Services; and Des Workman from Birmingham Social Services.

Last but not least, I acknowledge the insights I have gained from hundreds of conversations I have had with Brummies old and young from across the city. Many have written down their memories for me, and Letter or Interview refers to information I have gained from such people. I thank you all. I hope you enjoy this book and that it does justice to all who call Birmingham home.

PREFACE

This book has been written by someone who belongs to Birmingham. I am a Brummie and I am the son of Brummies. I believe in my city and its people, wherever they come from. Because of this, I cannot claim to have written this work as a disinterested observer. I have an interest in Birmingham. I wish it to continue to be a great working city, in which all of its people have jobs.

Whilst researching this study, I realised that it would be an impossible task to cover every event which has been important to Birmingham's history. And I also became aware that I would not be able to mention all those who have influenced the city's past. Instead, I have focused on the issue which I believe is the most vital to the history of Birmingham - work. To tell the city's story in this way, I have addressed three questions. First, why did Birmingham become a great city and why has it remained one? Second, what are the industries which have affected its growth? Finally and most crucially, who were the people who laboured and created things and who made Birmingham a great working city?

This is not a blow-by-blow account of Birmingham's past. Nor is it a political, economic or municipal history. These can be found elsewhere. This book is a social history. It is based on the belief that Birmingham can be understood only if we have a feel for the city and its people. To achieve that is not an easy task. But through this book, I hope that I will have given readers the feeling that they have come to know and understand Birmingham and its citizens a little better.

INTRODUCTION

Modern Birmingham. Vibrant, dynamic, exciting, innovative. A city of constant change, adaptation and inventiveness. A great working town, sounding with the clash of machinery, echoing with the noise of transport, resonating to the voices of cultures from across the world.

Throw out those dated and demeaning clichés about bleak and philistine industrial cities. Modify those images of dark satanic mills and of a dismal, dreary and dank environment. Birmingham's picture is not grey and boring. It is bright and rousing. Dinginess and drabness have not brought people here. They have come looking for opportunity, they have arrived in hope of a better future, they have appeared in search of possibilities.

For centuries Birmingham has been a city of immigrants. Its people came from the squire-dominated villages of the Midland Counties; from the famine-ravaged Ireland of the 1800s; and from poverty-stricken Southern Italy. During the 1920s and 1930s, these Brummies were joined by Scots, Welsh and Northern English all seeking a life away from the depredations of the Depression. Since 1945, this mixture of cultures and experiences has been given new vitality by the addition of people from the Caribbean, from East Africa and Yemen, from Pakistan, Kashmir, Bangla Desh and India, from China and Vietnam, from Poland and Cyprus and by another wave of emigrants from Ireland.

Modern Birmingham is a fascinating and thrilling mixture of lifestyles, languages and beliefs. But all of its people are united by one deep bond. They have come to work in the workshop of the world. Adept at every manufacturing skill, its citizens have made a multitude of goods. From creating buttons to guns, from the design of jewellery to brass bedsteads, from the crafting of pens to cars, the workers of Birmingham are renowned for their prowess and their imagination.

They are distinguished as much by their independence, by their desire to be their own 'gaffer', by their thirst to have their own business. English-run workshops and factories, Chinese and Cypriot restaurateurs, Italian terrazo firms, Irish building contractors, Kashmiri balti-house keepers, Sikh and Gujrati shopowners, Caribbean entrepreneurs - the list is endless.

Ability and determination are matched by commercial expertise. Birmingham is a manufacturing city of the first order, but throughout its history it has been more than this. It thrived and grew because it was also a major financial centre, a hub for collecting and distributing products, and a focal point providing services for its people. Modern Birmingham maintains this intricate and essential variety of functions. It makes goods; it offers investment; it gives facilities for shopping, leisure and enjoyment; and it builds, rebuilds and builds again.

Birmingham is invigorating and it is vital. It lives through its people. Together they form an orchestra of talents and abilities, the diverse sections of which exhibit their own distinctive natures. But each contributes to the final performance - harmonious, energetic and creative.

CHAPTER 1
THE TOYSHOP
OF EUROPE

A Birmingham smith, about 1895, carrying on his trade in much the same manner as did the smiths seen by Leland in 1538. (Birmingham Library Services)

BIRMINGHAM INGENUITY

Late eighteenth and nineteenth-century Birmingham was remarkable for the multitude of wares which were made in its factories, workshops and homes. Even those who loathed industrialisation were forced to acknowledge the versatility and cleverness of the townspeople. As with the romantic poet Robert Southey, the detractors of manufacturing dreamt of a rural paradise and they drew back in horror from places like Birmingham which revelled in the making of things. Still, they were awe-struck at the 'display of human inegenuity' in the metropolis of the Midlands. More sympathetic observers were as overwhelmed by the massive amount of goods which were produced there. In 1888 it was computed that from the city's factories alone:

> **upwards of 20,000,000 pens are sent out every week to the markets of the globe. Guns are made to the extent of 8,000, buttons 150,000,000, saddles nearly 1,500, copper or bronze coins 6,000,000, bedsteads 9,000, cut nails 500,000,000, spectacles 25,000 pairs, eight tons of papier mâché goods, gold and silver jewellery of every description about £20,000 worth, wire in iron and steel 4,500 miles long, and perhaps the most astonishing figures are those in connection with the manufacture of wax vestas, more than 450 miles of wax being used. (Birmingham, *An Alphabetically Arranged Guide to the Industrial Resources of the Midland Metropolis*, 1888)**

Manufacturing was the predominant reason for Birmingham's growth and its accomplishment. It is not a port like Liverpool; it does not lie at the crossing of a great river, as does London; unlike York, it is not an ancient administrative or religious centre; and it does not share Edinburgh's strategic importance. Birmingham is a child of industry. But although its rise to prominence and fame came only in the eighteenth and nineteenth centuries, the seeds of its success were sown in the Middle Ages.

A MARKET FOR 'BERMINGEHAM'

Well placed in the middle of England, Birmingham is in an admirable spot for its triple role: collection point; manufacturing centre; and trading site. But location alone cannot provide the answer either as to why it became a great city or as to the failure of nearby towns and villages to match it. The success of Birmingham has to take account also of the verve and wiliness of its people - both native born and incomers. For many generations, the city has been a lode star for skilled workers not just because it is fortunately situated but also because it has given them scope and freedom. And the unskilled have flocked here as well, drawn in by the prospect of work, the glimmmer of improvement and by an open nature. Richard Holt has argued persuasively that Birmingham's magnetism was evident as early as the twelfth and thirteenth centuries.

The city's name is an Anglo Saxon one meaning the settlement of Beorma's people and since the Middle Ages it has been interchangeable with Brummagem - the form preferred by working class Brummies. According to the Domesday Book of 1086 the place consisted of just nine peasant households. It might have remained an insignificant hamlet had not its lord decided to ask the king if he could hold a weekly market there. Peter of Birmingham was given a charter to do so in 1166, almost one hundred years before competition arose in nearby settlements such as Solihull, Sutton Coldfield and Halesowen. The new market flourished because of its monopoly and also because it was accessible from a number of local routes - amongst them that which crossed the River Rea at Deritend. It benefited also from national factors. Throughout England, this was a period of expansion, population growth and greater commercialisation - all of which encouraged the rapid development of small towns and market centres.

There is little doubt that the positive inter-play of local and national trends had a profound effect on Peter's little village:

> **"the surviving evidence is unanimous in asserting that the market grant was followed by a period of rapid economic growth . . . In the space of a century, and probably considerably less, Birmingham changed from a small agricultural village to prosperous manufacturing and market town. It possessed bailiffs, borough court and a gaol guarded by professional gaolers. Craftsmen and merchants had settled there, and immigrants were being attracted from surrounding villages. (Richard Holt, *The Early History of the Town of Birmingham 1166 to 1600,* 1985)"**

Market Day, 1900. Seven hundred and fifty years after its market charter was granted, Birmingham's 'barrow boys and girls' were still gathering in the shadow of St Martin's Church. (Birmingham Library Services)

The increasing wealth of Birmingham was indicated by the expensive rebuilding of the parish church in 1250. Twenty-five years later, its swelling importance was made clear when its inhabitants were summoned to send two representatives to Parliament.

A TOWN ECHOING WITH ANVILS

Sustained by the rural economy of East Worcestershire and North-West Warwickshire, the inhabitants of Birmingham began to offer a number of services to the people of its agricultural hinterland. They dealt in cattle, corn and wool, they sold ale, bread and food, and they made goods. This can be seen from the details of an agreement which 16 of them reached in 1232 with their lord, William de Birmingham: two of them were involved in trade - one as a purveyor (a supplier of food) and the other as a mercer (a dealer in luxury goods); and six of them were craft workers - a smith, a tailor and four weavers. In the next century, another manufacture comes to notice when mention is made of 'Birmingham Pieces' - jewellery or ornaments which were well-known as far away as London.

By the 1300s, it is probable that the town was the third largest in Warwickshire, after Coventry and Warwick itself; but the first description of Birmingham was not made until 1538. In that year, John Leland came:

> **"through as pretty a street or ever I entred into Bermingham towne. This street as I remember is called Dirtey (Deritend) . . . There be many smithes in the towne that use to make knives and all mannour of cutting tools, and many loriners that make bittes (for horses), and a great many naylors. (John Leland, *Itinerary*)"**

J. Darwen & Son, saddlers of Edgbaston Street, a firm exemplifying a trade that was present in Birmingham from the Middle Ages. (William Hawkes Smith, Birmingham and its Vicinity, 1836)

Other occupations included tanners and fullers of cloth. But the future of Birmingham lay not with the textile or leather workers; it was in the hands of the fashioners of metal. One reason for this was cost; their tools were cheaper relative to the money which was needed to set up in other occupations. Holt pointed out that in the early 1500s, a man need pay only ten shillings for an adequate set of smith's tools, including an anvil, bellows and hammers. Leland added another cause of the preponderance of metal workers in Birmingham. An astute commentator, he noted that the smiths of the town received their iron and coal from the fields of Staffordshire. Since its rise as a major place, Birmingham has been connected intimately to the Black Country - not just by proximity but also by an inter-dependence. South Staffordshire was central to the town's later growth, providing many of the raw materials which its workers made up and sold to the world as finished goods.

Almost fifty years after Leland's description, William Camden (1586) was also impressed by the great number of smiths in Birmingham. He found it 'swarming with inhabitants, and echoing with the noise of anvils' on which were made scythes, cutlery and blades - many of which were for war-like purposes. As early as 1513, Birmingham ironmongers had supplied Henry VIII with weapons for his infantrymen; whilst in the English Civil War, local swordsmiths sold their wares to the Parliamentary forces. The partisanship of many of the town's people led the Royalist historian, Clarendon, to declaim 'Bromwicham, a town so generally wicked' and in 1643 it was attacked by Prince Rupert. Oral tradition names his base as the Ship Inn, which was at Camp Hill before it was knocked down; and it attributes the name of the area to the camping of the cavaliers. More prosaically, it is likely that Camp Hill is called after a local landowner, John Kempe.

The Battle of Birmingham was not a major one, but even small conflicts lead to death, wounding and destruction. Following the defeat of the outnumbered Brummies, much of their property was burned and many of them were robbed of their possessions by the victorious and vindictive Cavaliers. But pillaging was not a one-sided afair. The Middlemore family had their home at Edgbaston Hall taken from them by Parliamentary troops; whilst an irregular force of anti-Royalists besieged Sir Thomas Holte in the newly-finished Aston Hall. After three days, he was forced to surrender and made to pay a heavy ransom. The hall - which still bears the marks of the conflict - remains a magnificent Jacobean building in the heart of industrial Aston.

THE DEVELOPMENT OF BIRMINGHAM

Traditionally, Birmingham's growth from village to town was seen as a slow process. Holt's researches have shown this assumption to be incorrect. Birmingham was prominent locally from the time it was allowed to have a market; and already during the eve of the Middle Ages, some of its manufacturers had begun to sell their goods nationally and to acquire a wide reputation. This trend became more marked in the 1500s. The gathering momentum of trade is a probable reason for the sharp rise in activity in Birmingham from the last quarter of the 1600s. Lists of taxpayers show that in 1671 there were 69 forges in the town. Twelve years later, this number had swollen greatly to 202, nearly half of which were on the low ground approaching the River Rea - in Digbeth and Deritend. The town's population rise was as spectacular. According to its earliest historian, William Hutton, it was around 5,500 in 1666, reaching upwards to 15,000 by 1700.

Part of this increase was from natural growth, part was a result of immigration. Most of the newcomers came only a short distance into Birmingham. For the years 1686 to 1726, a list names nearly 700 of them. Of their total, 90% hailed from within twenty miles of Birmingham, with 500 coming from the three counties of Warwickshire, Staffordshire and Worcestershire. Birmingham was establishing itself as the magnet of the West Midlands. Its citizens consolidated its position and ensured its further growth by their forward-thinking. Not content with restricting themselves to their traditional forms of manufacturing, shrewdly they applied their talents to an increasingly wide range of industrial processes.

BIRMINGHAM GROATS AND GUNS

During the later 1800s, Brummies boasted that anything, from a needle to a ship's anchor, could be bought in Edgbaston Street, near to the Bull Ring. The astounding diversity of products made in Birmingham did mark it out as somewhere unusual. In particular, it was different from the cotton towns of the North-West of England, from the woollen areas of the West Riding of Yorkshire, and from the mining districts of Great Britain. All of these places relied for their prosperity upon the well-being of one industry. If that suffered, then local economies were laid waste and hard times befell all.

Of course, Birmingham was affected by slumps in trade and many of its people experienced poverty and irregular employment. But overall, the city was better able to ride out depressions than most of its rivals. It did so because its people were prepared and were able to diversify into new or different forms of manufacturing. The profound effect of this shift into multiform industry was recognised by Hutton who made it clear that:

W. Westley's East Prospect of Birmingham, about 1730: the River Rea is in the foreground, St Martin's in the Bull Ring is on the left, and St Philip's is in the background.

> **"the ancient and modern state of Birmingham,
> must divide at the restoration of Charles the Second.
> For though she had before held a considerable degree of
> eminence; yet at this period, the curious arts began to take
> root, and were cultivated by the hand of genius."**
> **(William Hutton, *History of Birmingham*, 1795)**

Chief amongst "the curious arts" were coin forming and gun making.

From 1609, copper pennies were issued by the Royal Mint, with copper ha'pennies and farthings following from 1665. The coming of these new forms of coinage gave an opportunity to unscrupulous metal workers to imitate them. Many of these deceivers were found in the Midlands, leading the poet Dryden to pen the lines 'Twas coined by stealth, like groats at Birmingham'. Forgers remained in the town for many years. As late as 1812, the 'notorious coiner Booth' was hanged after the military had been forced to attack his heavily fortified farm in Perry Barr. On his premises was found the huge amount of £3,000 in good notes, 200 guineas in gold, £600 in counterfeit silver coin, and a large quantity of forged notes. The presence and infamy of false minters have had a long-term and adverse effect on the reputation of Birmingham, its majority of honest workers and its goods. Just as many people in the late twentieth century have decried unfairly all Hong Kong products as cheap and unreliable, so too in the eighteenth century were the wares of the Midland town castigated as counterfeit and inferior.

The good name of Birmingham coin makers was rescued by Matthew Boulton. In 1786 he established in Hockley a mint for forming coppers. Soon after, he was supplying them to the British and other governments as well as to the East India Company. Boulton's business ceased production in 1850 and its machinery was bought by Ralph Heaton, a die sinker who had moved into the striking of coins in the 1820s. Now trading as the Birmingham Mint and part of IMI, the firm is one of the city's oldest and traces its origins to 1794 and a brassfounding business.

So successful was Heaton and his employees at minting coins, that in a seventeen-year period the work of his company included:

> **"about 2,000 tons of copper and bronze for our
> own country, 1,400 tons for India, 700 tons for
> Tunis, besides an aggregate of more than 1,000
> tons for other countries, including Turkey, China
> (Hong Kong), Hayti, Sarawak, Tuscany, Venezuela,
> Canada, Chili, &c... But this is not all. In 1861 and
> 1862 we struck 1,600 tons of bronze coin in Milan, for the
> new kingdom of Italy... the blanks being made in
> Birmingham, and sent out. A coinage of 750 tons was
> struck in Marseilles on the recoinage of France, after the
> re-establishment of the Empire. (Ralph Heaton,
> 'Birmingham Coinage', in Samuel Timmins, ed,
> *Birmingham and Midland Hardware District*, 1866)"**

Since 1860, the Birmingham Mint has operated at a factory in Icknield Street, and it has continued to be a progressive and creative operation. In 1992 it perfected the production of nickel-plated coins, so exemplifying the manner in which many of the city's traditional industries adapt and react to changing circumstances and to the new demands of consumers.

Like the striking of coins, the origins of gun making in Birmingham are hidden by a lack of evidence and by the distance of time. Samuel Timmins (1866) believed that the trade had existed in the town some years before 1689, when it first came to notice for the manufacture of small arms for the government. Whatever its early past, gun making became a major industry in Birmingham and from 1813 barrels were tested compulsorily at a proof house in Banbury Street. Between 1855 and 1864, 6 million weapons were proofed here and at the country's only other similar institution in London; 4¼ million of them were made in Birmingham.

The gun trade flourished on field sports, on the expanding British Empire and on wars like those in The Crimea and between the States in America. This connection meant that it was trapped in an unfortunate paradox. Peace and good times for the many brought hardship for gun workers.

> **"The extreme fluctuations in demand (for military weapons especially) makes it difficult for even the best established places to keep any number of hands in regular employment. It may happen in a slack time that their factories will be half empty of men for months together; then, on the reappearance of a 'flush', not only will the factories be speedily filled, but the work will run over into all the workshops of the locality. ('Pictures of the People Drawn by One of Themselves. No. vi.- How They Work. The Gun Trade',** *Birmingham Morning News,* **1871)"**

From its completion in 1862, the Small Heath factory of the Birmingham Small Arms Company loomed large over the gun industry. It was formed by a number of leading manufacturers to combat the Enfield works which was owned by the government and which was producing guns from 1858. The BSA occupied 26 acres between the Great Western Railway line and the Birmingham and Warwick Canal. During the First World War it was an enormous supplier of weapons, sending out 10,000 rifles and 2,000 Lewis guns a week; and it made a similar contribution to the country's efforts in the Second World War between 1939 and 1945.

Gun makers in Whittal Street, late 1920s. Frank Titteron, who worked on sporting guns, is sitting in the middle of the front row and wearing overalls. (Dot Leroux)

Despite its huge size, the BSA was unlike the Birmingham Mint. It did not enjoy a monopoly in its field of operations; nor did it make every part of its products, as did the state-owned operation at Enfield. BSA obtained many of its parts from small "gaffers". The Trades Directory of 1866 named 599 of them, most of whom were concentrated in a distinct quarter around Shadwell Street, Steelhouse Lane and Loveday Street. Their specific occupations reflected the wide variety of processes involved in the manufacture of a finished weapon. As well as gun makers there were those who made barrels, furniture, locks, nipples, implements, cases, waddings and stocks, whilst there were present also finishers and engravers. Albert Fenton grew up in Hanley Street, and he recalled that the gunsmiths:

> **"occupied a small area up a back-yard consisting of many small workshops each concentrating on the many different parts which together went up to make the sporting-gun. These guns were sold all over the world to famous people, like the Shah of Persia. Some rooms you walked up to from the outside on wooden stair-cases and each had a name-plate on the door. Inside the rooms were very cramped, with work-benches all along the walls. Some had little machines which ran by a motor with belts to drive them. The men were working on polishing gun-barrels or carving wood-stocks for handles. There were tools everywhere, hanging on nails and straps all over the walls and lying on the benches, you gradually became aware of it all in the dim shafts of light from the small windows. The men were very skilled at their trades which were handed down from father to son and I loved to watch them doing the elaborate engraving on the metal parts of the sporting-gun and shape the firing-mechanism. Noting all this at each of the different gun-smiths made me appreciate the immense skill that went into the making of guns, all hand-done... (Albert Fenton, *Albert's Story*, unpublished manuscript, no date)."**

Workers leaving the BSA, 1930s. (Birmingham Library Services)

Except for a few firms and a pub named after its former workers, little remains of Birmingham's Gun Quarter - although the council is attempting to revive this area. Only William Powell and Son (1802) and Westley Richards and Co. (1812) survive from the thriving number of gun makers who were trading in the early nineteenth century. This last firm was responsible for the invention of the breech-loading rifle, but as early as 1849 it had moved to a semi-rural spot on the outskirts of Birmingham in Grange Road, Bournbrook. Similarly, the BSA factory has been cleared and in its place stands a trading estate. For decades its huge building was a landmark, not just in Small Heath but in Birmingham as a whole.

Kynoch's workers outside a priming shed in 1889. (I.C.I. Magazine, 1929. Thanks to Roy White)

> **❝My father worked as a rifle-packer for the Armoury dept, later removed to the top B.S.A. in Armoury Road, Small Heath. Later that dept was moved to Enfield. First remembrance of B.S.A. factory.**
> **The gates were opposite the house we lived in, you could see through them, there were two cannon balls on each side of the gate, a one storey building with a small green on front, also a belfry built higher on buildings (and which) used to call workmen five minutes early before closing door to start work after final ring.**
> **I worked on munitions at the B.S.A., worked on grooving magazine centres for Lewis machine gun from start of World War I until the finishing years. Many the day the factory bell rang and I scraped in. No bell today on B.S.A. (Mrs M. Jones, *Letter*, 1992)❞**

An offshoot of the gun industry continues to prosper - ammunition production. BSA itself was involved in cartridge making, but it was the firm of George Kynoch which was associated most with the process. Formed in 1862 by a bank clerk from Peterhead in Scotland, the business first made percussion caps in Great Hampton Street. Its operations expanded when the Lion Works were opened at Witton, and alongside its cartridge huts Kynoch's established rolling mills. This feature led to its eventual takeover by ICI's Metals' Divison.

Now part of IMI, the Witton site has been transformed dramatically - both in its outlook and in its type of production. Of its 220 acres, half has been re-formed and landscaped as a business park filled with trees and bushes, whilst metal rolling no longer takes place. Low growth, over-capacity and substitution began to affect badly the non-ferrous business in the 1960s. This led IMI to abandon this side of its operations and to move into building wares, drinks dispensers, pneumatics, special engineering goods and melted titanium - of which it is the only producer in the United Kingdom. Ammunition making for sporting guns remains the only link with Kynoch's; and in the 1980s, IMI developed a revolutionary method of priming cartridge caps which was safer, easier to handle and possible to carry out in ordinary units of production and not in huts. (Keith Gascoigne, MDA Public Relations, *Interview,* 1993)

THE GENIUS OF INVENTION

By the later eighteenth century, Birmingham's manufacturers were shaking off the opprobrium which became attached to them through the activities of coiners. Their goods were becoming famous throughout the world; their skilled workers were noted for their prowess; and they themselves were earning renown for their industrial discoveries. According to the French traveller, B. Faujas de Saint Fond:

H.E. Jones Limited, fine lithographic colour printers, founded 1906 in High Street, Deritend. (H.E. Jones Limited)

> "From the activity of its manufactures and its commerce, Birmingham is one of the most curious towns in England. If any one should wish to see in one comprehensive view, the most numerous and most varied industries, all combined in contributing to the arts of utility, of pleasure, and of luxury, it is hither that he must come. Here all the resources of industry, supported by the genius of invention, and by mechanical skill of every kind are directed towards the arts, and seem to be linked together to co-operate for their mutual perfection. (B. Faujas De Saint Fond, *A Journey Through England and Scotland to the Hebrides in 1784*)"

John Baskerville was amongst the most celebrated of the town's manufacturing inventors. A native of Wolverley in Worcestershire, he came to Birmingham as a young man, earning his money by inscribing grave stones and by teaching others to write. About 1740 he set up as a japanner, and he was acclaimed as 'effecting an entire revolution' in the making of goods which were made black and glossy by a hard varnish.

A wealthy man because of his own endeavours, Baskerville sought to create an incomparable form of type for printing. He did so. In 1758 he published an edition of Virgil's *Poems* and he followed it with Milton's *Paradise Lost, The Bible* and other Latin and English classics. These artistic and manufacturing achievements were brought to the public by Baskerville's own presses and they were printed on his own paper with his own ink. The Whig historian, Lord Macaulay, exclaimed that his works 'went forth to astonish all the librarians of Europe', whilst Timmins enthused that:

> "Great as the triumphs of the art of printing have been, and numerous as are the laurels which Birmingham has won, there are few nobler chapters in our local story than those which record how... in a material and commercial age, John Baskerville made our town famous throughout the civilised world for the best and greatest works of man, in a style which has rarely been equalled, and even now, has never been surpassed. (Samuel Timmins, 'The Industrial History of Birmingham', in, Samuel Timmins, ed, *Birmingham and Midland Hardware District*, 1866)"

Baskerville died childless in 1775. No English buyers could be found for his type. Four years later it was bought by a Parisian literary society which used it to print an edition of the works of Voltaire. Printing did not make a significant comeback in Birmingham until the next century when the trade was stimulated by the rise in literacy and the increase in clerical jobs which required specialist stationery. Businesses which catered for this demand included E. C. Osborne Ltd begun in 1832; James Upton Ltd which started up 20 years later and today is a colour printers; and Henry Mills Ltd, a numerical printer established in 1855 and now a bookbinders and print finishers. Associated with the printing trade were firms like Arthur Holden & Sons which has manufactured surface coatings and inks since 1832, and wholesale stationers such as John Heath and Co. which began 20 years later.

Asa Briggs pointed out that nineteenth-century Birmingham was a place which had not only a wide industrial base but also an open social structure. He believed that these two factors were vital in the development of the town, giving craftsmen the opportunity - or at least the prospect of it - to improve their position. His argument could be applied equally as well in the 1700s, with John Baskerville providing a prime example for sustaining it. In a similar vein was Henry Clay, a former apprentice to the master printer.

Acclaimed by Robert K. Dent as 'another of the heroes of the workshop', Clay patented the making of papier-mâché (1772). This product was made by pasting several layers of paper upon each side of boards which were of a regular thickness. They were then moulded, dried on a hot stove and rubbed or dipped in oil and varnish. The material thus made could be sawn, planed or turned like wood, and japanned. It was used to form tables, cabinets, snuff boxes, tea trays and panels for doors, coaches and sedans. Until the middle of the 1800s, Birmingham was unrivalled as the world's leading papier-mâché centre. The industry's disappearance by 1900 was the result not of foreign competition, nor of bad workmanship but of changes in fashion.

BRUMMAGEM BUCKLES, BUTTONS AND PINS

Buckle making was an industry which was subject also to the fancy of the public. Like papier-mâché production, its prominence in Birmingham began in the late eighteenth century. Metal buckles were made for shoes, hats and knee-breeches and they were exported to America, France, Holland, Germany, Italy and Spain. But the prosperity and survival of the industry was short. Laces began to replace buckles on shoes. Trade dropped drastically and in 1791 the distressed workers petitioned the Prince of Wales to help them. He and the Duke of York ordered their gentlemen and servants to discard shoe strings. But their action was to no avail, and buckle making had almost died out before 1800.

> **For buckles then by high and low were wore,**
> **Nor were, by sprigs of fashion, deem'd a bore,**
> **A fatal epithet, however gloss'd,**
> **For thousands, by that word,**
> **their bread have lost. (James**
> **Bisset, *Magnificent Directory*, 1800)**

During the same period, nail making by hand was another trade which disappeared from Birmingham. Instead it became concentrated in outlying districts to the west, such as Harborne and Northfield where a few nailor's cottages remain standing. Writing in 1913, Tom Presterne brought to mind the lives of the nailmakers which he had witnessed as a young man. Both men and women worked very hard, from early morning until bed-time for five days a week. On Saturdays they would trudge to town with their wares in a coarse sack. They would sell them to a nailmaster and from him they would buy back a bundle of iron with which to make the next week's nails. By now, the hand-made nail workers of Harborne had been reduced to just a few. Their numbers had declined drastically from the 1840s when they came into competition with the mechanised nail industry of Birmingham. Here, in the 1860s, 15,000 to 16,000 tons of iron were cut into nails by a workforce of 1,200 men, women and boys.

No person should lessen the terrible hardships which faced the unemployed nailors and buckle makers of Birmingham; but the town's wide industrial base did give them opportunities for new employment. A constant theme runs throughout Birmingham's history: as one industry declined or disappeared, another expanded or emerged. So it was in the later 1700s when the waning of the buckle trade was matched by the waxing of metal-button manufacturing.

For many years, the leading industrialist in Birmingham was John Taylor - to whom Hutton declared that the town owed part of its riches, extension and improvement. Born in 1711, Taylor began work as a cabinet maker. When he died aged 64, he left a fortune of

Cutting out the blanks from shells for pearl buttons. (The Illustrated Exhibitor and Magazine of Art, 1852)

'not less than £200,000' - a colossal sum for his times. This wealth was founded on the gilding of metal buttons, a process which Taylor was believed to have introduced to Birmingham. By this action, the goods were covered with a thin layer of gold leaf, or were plated in a similar way with silver. Later in the eighteenth century, this procedure was rivalled by dipping, an operation which was cheaper because it covered buttons with a bare amount of precious metal.

Between 1770 and 1800, twenty-one patents were granted for improvements in the fastening of clothes: nineteen of them were from Birmingham alone. So closely was the town associated with the trade that its inhabitants were nicknamed 'Brummagem Buttons'. Unfortunately, like buckle making before it, the gilt metal-button industry was dependent upon the whims of style. It prospered so long as wealthy men wore fastenings on their long tail coats, tight buckskin breeches and gaiters; it diminished once these modes of dress were replaced by the more modest garments of the early Victorian period.

In a reduced market, some metal-button makers continued to make their goods for uniforms and 'fancy' wear - as they do still at one of England's oldest businesses, Firmin & Sons in Newtown Row (founded in London in 1677 by a Huguenot refugee). Others moved into the more popular end of the market, forming their buttons from glass, or covering them with cloth, silk, linen and 'Corozo Nuts' from Central America. A beautiful white colour, like that of ivory, these could be turned readily on the lathe and then dyed in a variety of shades. In 1865, about 6,000 people worked in the various branches of the button trade, compared to nearly 10,000 in gun making and over 8,000 in brass manufacturing. In the following years it lost its position as one of the leading forms of employment in Birmingham - although many people continued to work at the aptly-named factories of Buttons Limited.

Like the Birmingham Small Arms Company, this firm was set up by a group of leading manufacturers and for similar reasons. They were faced with increased foreign competition and they felt that the only way to respond to this was by bonding together. As a consequence in 1908, Buttons Ltd began operations at two works: the larger, in Portland Street, Aston; and the smaller, in Warstone Lane in the Jewellery Quarter. The company made its profits from cloth-covered buttons, but also it manufactured those from corozo, various metals, leather and casein (an early form of plastic made from milk and with a formaldehyde base). Robin Evans, the son and grandson of directors of the firm, remembered one other kind of button which was formed at Portland Street.

> **In the yard at the back, amid a jungle of scrap metal and rubbish, was a great pile of horn and hoof, newly arrived from overseas. The stench was appalling, the mass alive with maggots, while from an open doorway came a whiff of steam and the same pungent smell. I peered inside, and there sitting on a high stool stirring a bubbling cauldron of this obscene mixture, was an elderly woman wearing a man's cap. I turned away, nauseated, but realised that this process was necessary before buttons could be made from such material. (Robin Evans, 'Company Extraordinary: Buttons Limited 1908-1959', *The Birmingham Historian*, no. 3, Autumn/Winter 1988).**

Buttons Ltd closed in 1959, a victim of the coming of the real plastic button which could be made easily by anyone with a moulding press. Effectively, it meant the end for those manufacturers who prized the skill of their workers in fashioning buttons from diverse materials - amongst them shells.

In the mid-nineteenth century, one third of the trade's workers had been involved in this long-established method of production. It did not require either elaborate machinery or large capital. Consequently, it was dominated by self-employed artisans who practised their craft in workshops. At Villa Street, Lozells, George Hook and Sons was the last business of its kind in Birmingham. Their hand-worked buttons typify the artistic talents of many of the city's skilled workers. Now in Smethwick, the firm:

> 66 still manufactures buttons in the traditional way from Mother of Pearl, Abalone, and sometimes from 'good' Mollusc shells. Their preference is for the 'Yellow-lip' Oyster Shell which they import from the West Coast of Australia... These shells are enormous by our standards being up to 18" across and up to 2" thick. They are favoured because of the quantity of yield per shell and because the Yellow-lip, wherever cut, is full of iridescent colours when polished... cutting is by hand-guided trepan (used in a 'bench' drilling machine). The same machine is used to drill the buttonholes after the 'sticks' of material have been 'parted' into buttons on a traditional 'Button-Lathe'. Depending on the type and number, buttons are polished by tumbling-barrel. (Brian Henderson, *Letter*, 1991) 99

George Hook Senior and his son George Thomas Hook holding a shell to be worked into pearl buttons, March 1982. (Birmingham Library Services, Warwickshire Photographic Survey)

Like the gun trade, a feature of the button industry was the lack of control most workers had over making a product in its entirety. In the 1760s, it was calculated that one button would pass through fifty pairs of hands, and each of these would shift up to 1,000 fastenings in a day. Almost 100 years later, in the large factory of W. Elliott and Son, an observer reckoned that 'the sub-division of labour is too minute for us to follow'. Jobs included the punching of discs, the making and fixing of shanks, gilding, pressing and stamping.

The separation of production tasks amongst a variety of workers was as obvious in the making of pins. On the first page of his seminal work, *The Wealth of Nations,* Adam Smith

Woman and children chopping and bundling firewood in the one downstairs room of Birmingham back-to-back house. (Edward Cadbury, M. Cécile Matheson and George Shann, Women's Work and Wages, 1906)

alerted the world to the 18 processes which accounted for those which were made by hand in Birmingham. One person drew the wire used in their manufacture, another straightened it, a third cut it, a fourth pointed it, a fifth ground it and made it ready for its head, and so on. Smith stated that because of this situation, ten people could make nearly 50,000 pins each day. It was not until the mid-nineteenth century that mechanisation began to change this long-drawn out method of production. In 1831, two Birmingham men called Daniel Ledsam and William Jones patented machines for putting heads and points on pins; and they were followed by Mr Jenkins from Greet who devised a tool whereby these articles were stuck to the paper from which they would be sold.

By this period, the best known pin-making firm in the town was that of Thomas Phipson, a nephew of Samuel Ryland who was credited with starting the trade in Birmingham in the mid eighteenth century. Crucially, Ryland was also a wire drawer. This skill was essential in making pins, for they were fashioned from pieces of polished brass which were stretched into the right thickness on a drawbench. The amount of wire which could be made in this way was staggering. In 1866, it was reported that at the Birmingham factory of Edelsten and Williams a strip of brass three-quarters of an inch long was drawn so that it stretched for two and three quarters miles.

This firm made hair-pins, thimbles, eyelets and hooks and eyes. Like buttons, these latter articles were put onto cards by hundreds of poverty-stricken women and children in their own homes. Their wages were tiny. In the 1860s, Will Thorne's mother laboriously sewed 12 hooks and the same number of eyes onto a single card. For a gross (144) of these, she earned the pittance of ½d - out of which she had to buy her own needles and cotton.

This kind of badly-paid, exhausting and tedious home work was common in Birmingham until the 1940s and 1950s, although by then, it tended to be given out by smaller firms. Our Mom's family lived in Aston, and my Aunt Win told me that in the Depression of the 1930s, my great Granny Wood:

> **always had home work. Radiators from B's. There used to be a big brass rod and used to have to thread some square and some round. Gills they used to call 'em. You'd got to thread 'em on a rod till you'd filled it. And they hadn't half used to cut your fingers. Then they used to go to B's and all be welded together for a radiator. And we all used to help. Daytime and nightime. The factory was only a few doors away. We used to tek the pram and tek back what her'd done and fetch another lot. Cleaning as well, cleaning at a pub, perhaps of a morning. Hard working woman. And all the housework and such as if the grandkids wanted anything washed and ironed for a dance. It'd be done... (Winnie Martin, _Interview_, 1987)**

There is little doubt that by splitting up the manufacture of an article, employers speeded up and lowered the cost of its production. As a result, the division of labour was responsible in part for the growth of Birmingham and its prosperity. But it should be remembered that the general well-being of the town's citizens was bought through the lowly-paid and hard employment of tens of thousands of unskilled women and children.

TOYS

Buckles and metal buttons were part of that large class of manufactures which contemporaries called "toys". These were not the playthings of children, but were chiefly trinkets of every kind made from steel: purse mounts; brooches; bracelets; sword hilts; and chatelaines (sets of short chains which were attached to women's belts and from which were hung keys, pencils, watches etc.). The multitude of small articles made in Birmingham led the town to be dubbed 'The Toy Shop of Europe' by Edmund Burke, the late eighteenth-century politician and writer.

Trinkets continued to be manufactured in Birmingham at the end of the 1800s, and now included curling irons, sugar nippers, beef-steak tongs and nut crackers. However, by this time much of the trade had become absorbed into jewellery manufacturing; or else it had moved fully into the metal-badge and button part of the industry. Vaughtons Ltd is an example of this process. Founded in John Street in 1777, it operates today from Livery Street and makes badges, medals and masonic and civic regalia. Perhaps protected by the speciality of their business, other badge-makers also have long pedigrees: William Dowler and Sons of Brearley Street (1774); Thomas Fattorini Ltd of Regent Street (1824); and Morton T. Colver Ltd, also in the Jewellery Quarter at Hockley Hill (1868).

Soho, from Nineveh Road. (Drawn by F. Calvert, engraved by T. Radycliffe).

MATTHEW BOULTON:
INDUSTRIAL HERO

Amongst the toy makers of Birmingham was Matthew Boulton, later to be acclaimed by Timmins as 'one of the industrial heroes of the world'. Born in the town in 1728, his father was a prosperous manufacturer and so his prospects for business success were more favourable than those which had faced Baskerville, Taylor and Clay. But so were those of the sons of many industrialists, and few of them can lay claim to a place in history as can Matthew Boulton.

He began work at seventeen and he is credited with inventing the means of inlaying buckles, buttons and trinkets - many of which were exported to France. By 1759 he was head of the family concern. Three years later it had developed so much that it had outgrown its premises at Snow Hill, and new ones were built at Handsworth where Factory Road runs now. Although then outside Birmingham, the site was well positioned to receive coal from Wednesbury; it had a steel rolling mill; and the Hockley Brook gave it a good supply of water for power. In 1762 the Soho Manufactory was opened at a cost of £10,000 - a huge sum.

The Birmingham industrialist claimed that his building was the largest factory in the world. In 1774 it was described as consisting of:

> **"four Squares, with Shops, Warehouses, &c., for a
> Thousand Workmen, who, in a great variety of Branches
> excel in their several Departments; not only in the
> fabrication of Buttons, Buckles, Boxes, Trinkets, &c.,in
> Gold, Silver, and a variety of Compositions; but in many
> other Arts, long predominant in France, which lose their
> Reputation on a Comparison with the product of this
> place... The number of ingenious mechanical Contrivances
> they avail themselves of, by means of Water Mills, much
> facilitates their Work, and saves a great portion of Time and
> Labour. The Plated-Work has an apearance of solid Silver,
> more especially when compared to that of any other
> Manufactory. Their excellent ornamental Pieces, in Or-
> Moulu [gilded bronze], have been admired by the Nobility
> and Gentry, not only of this Kingdom, but of all Europe;
> and are allowed to surpass anything of the Kind made
> abroad; And some Articles lately executed in Silver-Plate,**

The orginal lathe used by Mathew Boulton, taken in Thornhill House, Handsworth. (Birmingham Library Services)

shew that Taste and Elegance of Design prevail here in a superior Degree, and are, with Mechanism and Chymistry, happily united. (M. Swinney, *Birmingham Directory*, 1774) "

Boulton had begun the plating of silver in Birmingham about 1766, but he also made wares with solid silver. So did other Birmingham smiths, but the trade in such goods was inconvenient because they had to be hallmarked and checked for their quality in Chester or London. In 1773, to remedy this situation, the Soho industrialist headed a petition which asked Parliament to allow the establishment of an Assay Office in their town. It did so. Situated in Newhall Street, the institution continues to test gold and silver and to mark good wares with its symbol of an anchor.

Despite the fame and popularity of the products made at Soho, the manufactory was an expensive operation. It was large; Boulton insisted on making quality goods - whether they were for the mass market or for select customers; and he paid high wages to bring in talented workers and designers. To help overcome the problems of finance, he took on John Fothergill as a partner; he mortgaged and sold property; and he secured many loans. But it was not just cash that was in short supply at Soho; so too was water. The imperative of finding new means of power led Boulton to another partnership. This was with James Watt, the Scottish engineer who developed the steam engine. From 1775 the two men manufactured many such machines. In the process they gave an impetus which was vital to the development of industry in Great Britain and throughout the world.

Boulton's contribution to manufacturing endeavour was comprehensive. He was a capitalist, an entrepreneur, a craftsman, an inventor, a factory manager, an engineer, a trader. And he was something more. He was an enabler. His backing and strength of character allowed James Watt to make his steam engines; and his support and employment helped another Scotsman, William Murdock, to perfect coal-gas lighting - a phenomenon which astonished and delighted the public when the Soho Works was illuminated with gas-lamps in 1802. All three men are buried at St Mary's Church in Handsworth where there are busts of them and a statue.

Both Scots were members of an informal group of industrialists, scientists, engineers, physicians and thinkers who met from 1766 at Boulton's house in Handsworth - now renovated. This collection of enquirers called themselves the Lunar Society, because they gathered monthly on the night of the full moon. Other members were John Baskerville; Samuel Galton, a member of the Quaker gun-making family of Steelhouse Lane; James Keir, formerly a manager for Boulton and latterly a manufacturer of chemicals and soap in Tipton; Josiah Wedgwood, the master potter of Etruria; Dr Withering of Edgbaston Hall, who ascertained that digitalis (extracted from foxgloves) could act as a stimulant for the heart; Dr Joseph Priestley, the Unitarian minister of the New Meeting in Birmingham, scientist and chemist; and Dr Erasmus Darwin, the botanist whose grandson found fame by propounding the theory of evolution.

It was Darwin who encapsulated the vivacity and intellectual questioning of these men when he wrote that at their meetings, 'what wit, what rhetoric, metaphysical, mechanical and pyrotechnical, will be on the wing, bandied like a shuttlecock from one to another . . .' (1778). But Birmingham's fame was due not just to the well-known and celebrated members of the Lunar Society. The town's distinction owed as much to the hosts of small gaffers and craft workers who innovated and created; and it was dependent upon the hard work, low pay and privation of the poor - men, women and children. History may have lost the names of these tens of thousands who made the wealth of Birmingham; but their immense contribution to the past of this city must be remembered and acknowledged. They and their kind turned Birmingham from the Toy Shop of Europe into the Workshop of the World.

NOTES

A number of people have discussed with me issues which I have written about in this chapter. I should like to thank them for their support. They include Richard Holt - without whose advice I would have remained ignorant about medieval Birmingham; Les Frith, Director, and R. A. Fisher, Development Manager, of Holford Estates; Dame Rachel Waterhouse - for her thoughts on Mathew Boulton; Joy Smith of MDA Public Relations; Sheila Fowler, for her work on the de Bermingham family; Shirley Brooks for sight of *Albert's Story;* R. G. Lancelott, Chairman 'Friends of St Mary's Handsworth'; Colin Pitt and Maurice White - whose fervent interest in Birmingham has matched my own; and Jill Wilyman, Bill Martin, Stan Glover, John Wright, Robin Brampton and Jim Caffrey for the copies of books on old Birmingham.

FURTHER READING

The following works are essential for anyone who wishes to learn more about Birmingham and they have been indispensible in my own researches.

Asa Briggs	*Victorian Cities* (1968)
John Thackray Bunce	*History of the Corporation of Birmingham, Volume 1* (1878)
Conrad Gill	*History of Birmingham. Volume 1. Manor and Borough to 1865* (1952)
Richard Holt	*The Early History of the Town of Birmingham 1166 to 1600* (Dugdale Society Occasional Papers, No. 30; 1985)
The Victoria History of the Counties of England	*A History of the Count of Warwick. Volume VII, The City of Birmingham* (1964)

I recommend also the following works:

George Barnsby	*Birmingham Working People* (1989)
Carl Chinn	*They Worked All Their Lives: Women of the Urban Poor in England, 1880-1939* (1988)
Margaret Gelling	'Towards the Rehabilitation of Brummagem', *The Birmingham Historian,* no. 7, Spring/Summer 1991
Eric Hopkins	*Birmingham. The First Manufacturing Town in the World, 1760-1840* (1989)
Tom Presterne	*Harborne Once Upon A Time* (1913)
Marie Rowlands	*The West Midlands Since AD 1000* (1987)
Victor Skipp	*A History of Greater Birmingham - down to 1830* (1980)
Victor Skipp	*The Making of Victorian Birmingham* (1983)
Jennifer Tann	*Birmingham Assay Office 1773-1993* (1993)

BRUMMAGEM

Sure a little bit of muck and dirt,
Fell out the sky one day,
And it settled down in Digbeth,
Beside the River Rea,
When the Corporation saw it,
It made them all exclaim,
They put some roses round it,
And they called Summer Lane,
Then they dotted it with Kynoch's,
Where I works with our Old Mon,
And they gave it Saltley Gas Works,
Where Our Albert carries on;
Then they gave it Nelson's Statue,
The Bull Ring and Big Brum,
Sure and when they had it finished,
Why they called it Brummagem.

(Words thanks to Len Booth and George McLeod;
sung to the air of 'Sure a Little Bit of Heaven').

View of Birmingham from Bordesley Fields near the Coventry Road; St Philip's, Christchurch: 'New Street' and the Town Hall are in the background, St Martin's is in the foreground. (William Hawkes Smith, Birmingham and its Vicinity, 1836)

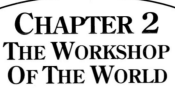

CHAPTER 2
THE WORKSHOP
OF THE WORLD

Right: Interior View of Aston Flint Glass Works of B. & W. Gibbins.
(Wrightson's Directory of Birmingham, 1818)

THE CLAMOUR OF
MANUFACTURE

If nineteenth-century commentators were struck by the quantity and diversity of Birmingham's goods, they were as impressed by the sound of their production. The French historian, Alexis de Tocqueville, exclaimed in 1835 that the town was 'an immense workshop, a huge forge, a vast shop' in which 'nothing was audible' because of the sound of labour; and twelve years later, Hugh Miller declared that nowhere else in the world were 'the mechanical arts more noisy'. But no writer bettered Charles Dickens in bringing to the ears of his readers this clamour of manufacture. He did so through the persons of Mr Pickwick and Sam Weller when they entered 'the great working town of Birmingham.'

> **"As they rattled through the narrow thoroughfares leading to the heart of the turmoil, the sights and sounds of earnest occupation struck more forcibly on the senses. The streets were thronged with working people. The hum of labour resounded from every house; lights gleamed from the long casement windows in the attic stories, and the whirl of wheels and noise of machinery shook the trembling walls. The fires, whose lurid sullen light had been visible for miles, blazed fiercely up in the great works and factories of the town. The din of hammers, the rushing of steam, and the dead heavy clanking of engines, was the harsh music which arose from every quarter. (Charles Dickens, *The Posthumous Papers of Mr Pickwick*, 1837)"**

It was the singing of metal and the hissing of water which had given rise to Birmingham's pre-eminence as a manufacturing centre. But the town's transformation into a place of international significance was effected not just because of the craft of its workers. It was also due to the willingness of its industrialists to invest in each other's inventions and businesses; and because they were able to send out their wares to the markets of the globe via a good transport system.

THE CANAL AND RAILWAY
HUB OF ENGLAND

It has become a commonplace assertion that the passage of merchandise was difficult, ponderous and costly before the cutting of canals in the later 1700s, and that these adverse conditions hindered the growth of industrial towns like Birmingham. This opinion has depended upon the view that English roads were ill-formed and inadequate for the needs of long-distance travel. But as Christopher Dyer has shown, this was not the case during the later Middle Ages when Birmingham and its region had good road communications and along which passed bulky carriers. From the east, merchants brought in fish from the Lincolnshire port of Boston; whilst from the west, drovers came with cattle from Wales. This latter trade was so important and long-lasting that by the 1500s, one end of the cattle market in High Street was called after the Welsh.

However, the continual growth in population and significance of Birmingham did come to place severe strains on the road system which served it. By the early eighteenth century, the townsfolk were importing large quantities of coal and iron from the Black Country; but communications with that district were hindered by the flooding of streams and by roads which were ill-formed and furrowed. The slowness of these routes led to higher payments for carriage and thus to greater production costs; whilst the finished goods became even more expensive because the outward highways from Birmingham were also sluggish.

In an attempt to improve the quality of the roads which served the town, turnpike trusts were set up. The first of these made a route from Birmingham to Wednesbury (1727), and by the later part of the century others went to Wolverhampton, Dudley, Walsall, Kidderminster, Worcester, Evesham, Coventry, Chester, Stratford and Warwick. Via these last two places, the town was connected to London in a coach-journey which took nineteen hours in 1784. But even though the turnpikes were better formed than previous roads, the passage of heavy goods on them remained much slower than that of coaches - dependent as it was on cumbersome wagons and straggling lines of packhorses. It was also costly, because of the tolls which were charged by the trusts. A cheaper and more effective means of transport for raw materials came with the building of canals.

In this development, the north-west of England had led the way with the cutting of the Sankey Brook Canal in 1755. Its success was outstanding and it encouraged Birmingham people to consider the building of a waterway which would connect them with the South Staffordshire coalfield. At a public meeting in 1767, the engineer James Brindley put forward his plans for the enterprise. Following an Act of Parliament, work on the £70,000 project began - financed by those who purchased shares at a price of £140 each.

The Birmingham Canal was finished in 1772, covering 22 miles from Paradise Street Wharf to Audley, near Wolverhampton. Here it joined the Grand Trunk system of waterways, so that now Birmingham had effective communications to the ports of Liverpool, Bristol and Hull and from there to markets around the world. This was not the only dramatic effect of the canal. It may have followed the contours of the land and so lengthened its passage, and its owners may have charged tolls, but compared to land travel it was cost-cutting. This was made obvious by the slashing of the price of coal - from 13s per ton by road to 8s 4d per ton by water.

Lifford Lane Wharf, facing Breedon Bridge, Pershore Road, early 1900s. The man leading the horse is probably J. Wilkes. (Birmingham Library Services, donated by Miss E. Hook)

Such obvious benefits led to a song called 'Birmingham Lads' written by John Freeth, a local coffee-house keeper and poet.

This day for our new navigation
We banish all cares and vexation;
The sight of the barges each honest heart glads
And the merriest of mortals are Birmingham lads,
Birmingham lads, jovial blades.
And the merriest of mortals are Birmingham lads

With pride every heart must be glowing
Stamps, presses and lathes shall be going;
The lads to the wharf with their lasses repair
And smile at the streamers that play in the air,
Play in the air, free and fair,
And smile at the streamers that play in the air.

Since by the canal navigation,
Of coals we've the best in the nation;
Around the gay circle your bumpers then put,
For the cut of all cuts is a Birmingham cut,
Birmingham cut, fairly wrought,
For the cut of all cuts is a Birmingham cut.

Other canals soon followed. By 1790, coal was coming in from North Warwickshire via Fazeley; the next year, a quarter of a century of work started on a waterway to Worcester and the Severn; and from 1799, the Birmingham to Warwick Canal was in full operation. These were not all. Around Birmingham, waterways were cut to Dudley and Stratford; and through unions with other canals, Coventry, Oxford and London could be reached. The

Saltley Dock, 1903, showing the building of 'The Egypt' in the foreground. Working on the boat from left to right were: R.A. Osborne; Mark Gould; J.W. Gould; a mate of Tom Cox; another mate of Tom Cox; and Tom Cox himself. (Birmingham Library Services and Kathleen M. Smallwood)

forming of inland navigations continued well into the nineteenth century. In 1824, Thomas Telford supervised improvements on the Birmingham Canal which shortened its passage to fourteen miles; and the celebrated engineer was responsible also for a quicker route to the Mersey when he led the cutting of the Birmingham and Liverpool Junction Canal (1835). Similarly, travel between the Fazeley and Warwick waterways was made faster by a connection in 1844, whilst in the same decade, the Birmingham Canal was extended along the Tame Valley.

Birmingham seen from the railroad near Saltley, about 1840. (Birmingham Library Services, Pershouse Collection)

By 1846, when a number of companies had amalgamated to form the Birmingham Canal Navigations, the town was the focal point of England's system of waterways. But not only was Birmingham surrounded by canals, it was criss-crossed by 33 miles of them. Not surprisingly, these 'cuts' had an obvious and drastic effect on the shape of Birmingham. They formed physical barriers which divided the town into distinct districts; they brought inland ports to the central area, as at Gas Street Basin; and because factories were built alongside them, they encouraged the spreading of Birmingham into adjacent localities. By the early 1800s, on just the two miles of waterway from Bordesley to Aston, 124 works and wharves were to be found.

In a similar way, railways left their indelible mark upon Birmingham. By 1824, there was talk of linking by locomotive 'the three great capitals of England - London, Birmingham, and Liverpool -'; and fourteen years later, this objective was realised following the completion of the Grand Junction and London and Birmingham Railways. Boarding at Curzon Street Station, travellers and goods could arrive in the metropolis in five and a half hours, compared to a trip of double that time by road and of three days by canal. Such a fast route appealed both to private travellers and to industrialists who were concerned with the swift and cost-effective dispersal of their products. As a result of its attractiveness, by 1841, the London and Birmingham Railway was bringing in annual receipts of £577,000 from passengers and £137,000 from the carrying of merchandise to set against its building costs of £5 million.

Just as England's canals focused on Birmingham, so too did the nation's railways. As well as the lines to Liverpool and the country's capital, there were those to Derby and from there to the North East of England (1839), to Gloucester and the South West (1840), to Oxford (1852), and to Wolverhampton (1854). The building of each of these was an enormous enterprise. On the link to London, 20,000 navvies individually displaced 20,000 cubic feet of earth in only five years. This line was so awe-inspiring that Peter Lecount, an assistant engineer to Robert Stephenson on the project, compared its achievement to that of the Great Wall of China. The resounding and widespread consequences of such massive works cannot be underestimated. In *Dombey and Son,* Charles Dickens likened a cutting of the London and Birmingham to an earthquake which had rent the whole neighbourhood of Camden Hill. Houses had been knocked down, streets broken through, deep pits and trenches dug, and enormous heaps of earth and clay thrown up.

But railway companies did not just destroy, they were also creative. In Birmingham, although it is no longer used as a station, the building at Curzon Street (1838) remains resplendent in its classical architecture and Ionic columns. Because it was too far from the town centre, it lost its pre-eminence to New Street Station (1852), the roof of which:

> **❝is of larger dimensions than any other in the world, being 1,080 feet long, with a span of no less than 212 feet across, unsupported by a single pillar on either side. The rib arches are each composed of three sections, and the weight of each rib is 25 tons. There are no less than forty-five of these in the roof, at distances of 24 feet apart; and yet notwithstanding their ponderous character, poised at a height of 75 feet from the rails, they look light and fragile. (cited in John Alfred Langford, *Modern Birmingham and its Institutions: a Chronicle of Local Events from 1841 to 1871, Volume 1,* 1911)❞**

Birmingham's other major railway station was at Snow Hill (1854), although there were smaller ones at Lawley Street, Camp Hill and in the suburbs. And it was not just these structures which impressed the onlooker. So too did tunnels, cuttings and bridges of all kinds. According to a contemporary, The Birmingham Viaduct was 'the most important and stupendous work', challenging comparisons with almost any ancient or modern art. Built of brick with stone groins and dressings, it was made up of twenty-eight segmental arches of 'upwards thirty feet span and thirty-two feet wide'. In length it was about one thousand feet, stretching out on a curve of three-quarters of a mile radius. *(The Rail Road Book of England, 1851, cited in Victor Skipp, The Making of Modern Birmingham, 1983)*

The impact of the railways on the continued prosperity and development of Birmingham is incalculable. Still, an indication of their effect on the town's trade is given by the expanse of goods' yards: 120 acres alone in an eastern triangle around Bordesley, Duddeston and Saltley. Their presence often proved a boon to poorer working-class families in the 1920s, as James Whelan of Fazeley Street pointed out.

❝On the other side of the road was the rear entrance to The Birmingham Home For Lost Dogs and the big factory Clifford's Rolling Mills. One could get used to the animals barking, not so the frequent escape of sulphur fumes from the Rolling Mills. Activity in the streets, Monday to Saturday lunchtime was quite brisk. Horse drawn vehicles predominated mainly centred from the L.M.S. Goods Yard in Curzon Street & Lawley Street. Stone sets were the surface of the roads obviously for the horses. A fallen horse happened often, always attracted a lot of on-lookers. Horse manure was in plentiful supply. Pilfering from carts was not unknown - whole carcass of Canterbury Lamb did disappear sometimes. (*Letter*, 1989)❞

Some idea of the extensive trade carried on from these two goods yards can be gained from Alice Smith's recollections. Her father was in charge of 301 railway horses which were based at the Lawley Street depot alone. (*Interview*, 1987).

Celebrations in Wilton Street on Coronation Day, 1953. John Thomas Voice, general dealer in scrap metal, tea chests and second-hand cartons, giving a ride on his cart to his daughter Maureen, on the left at the front, and other Summer Lane children. (Maureen and Victor Cox)

More goods' stations were at Hockley and Brookfields, whilst there existed numerous private sidings. For just as canal banks had acted as magnets to industry, so too did the land adjoining railways lines: the BSA factory was built at Small Heath along the Oxford connection; whilst Tangye's, producers of hydraulic rams and pulley blocks, left their small factory near the town centre for a suburban site of eleven acres which was between two stations - at Handsworth and Soho.

Locomotive transport had a positive effect on employment in a more direct fashion. The railway companies themselves had large workforces, as did the nationalised British Railways after 1947. Under the general heading of railmen could be included train drivers, guards, clerks, stokers, signalmen, line maintenance workers, engine and cleaning shed men, electricians and others. These workers and their families tended to live in areas close to the main goods' yards or engine sheds, as in Saltley, Tyseley and that part of Nechells around Inkerman Street. In this way, these districts came to be regarded as dominated by railwaymen.

The spectacular rise of railway transport did not signal the end of canal-usage. In a 50 year period from 1848, the tonnage carried on the BCN rose from 4½ million to 8½ million - a total which was about 22% of that carried on all the inland navigations of England. However, unlike the early years of the waterways' system, this latter period was characterised by the short-distance movement of goods. There were exceptions to this rule. Into the 1930s, dates and Italian tomato purée for the HP Sauce factory were brought from London, via the Grand Union canal, by the famous carrying company of Fellows, Morton and Clayton. Still, over half the tonnage on the BCN was coal. Most of this was transported just eight miles to canalside factories, although some of it came to wharves from where it would be sold to coal dealers or else to local working-class people - as it was in Winson Green.

> **"Every Saturday morning I would go to the Coal Wharf to fetch 1 cwt (hundredwight) of coal in a barrow. We would watch the men unloading it off the barge. They weighed it on big scoop scales and tipped it into the barrows. They charged us 3d a barrow. When we took it back we used to put a sheet of paper in the bottom and sit the baby of the family in it for a ride. (Polly Chew, *Letter* from Tony Chew, 1992)."**

Overall, railways may have dominated the long hauls of goods, but the waterways of Birmingham remained an economic way to move products locally. The resultant inter-dependence between the two forms of transport was reflected in the building of 550 private railway basins along the canals.

Until the 1960s, the BCN continued as a feeder for the rail system through its carriage of coal to power stations. By then, both forms of transport had entered into decline, eclipsed by road haulage. But if trains continued to be of some use to manufacturers, canals became useless. Forgotten and neglected, many Brummies remember cuts with distaste as lifeless, dirty stretches of water along which floated dead dogs and cats, and into which were dumped tyres, bits of cars and other rubbish. This depressing view began to change in 1982 when a Canal Improvements Programme was launched - funded by Birmingham City Council, The Department of the Environment, the British Waterways Board and the West Midlands County Council. Since then, over £6 million has been spent on improving and landscaping Birmingham's canals and in creating fourteen miles of walkways along them. Their industrial purpose may have gone, but they have been brought back to life as facilities for leisure and recreation. Similarly, the Harborne Walkway follows the old railway line to Dudley Road, and it is to be hoped that other redundant routes can be used in the same way.

INVESTING IN INDUSTRY

The banking hall of the Midland Bank, New Street, 1920s. Now Dillons Bookstore, the building's architect was Edward Holmes and it opened in 1869. (Midland Bank Archive, Midland Bank plc)

William Hutton made it clear that whilst the Birmingham Canal loaded its proprietors with wealth, their investment also increased the general prosperity of the town. This inter-play between the private and public interest is a recurring theme in Birmingham's history. Unlike some industrialists elsewhere in Britain, many of those in the 'toyshop of Europe' did not run away from the place which had benefited them. Instead they re-invested much of their profits within their town, a tendency exemplified by the actions of John Taylor, 'the button king', and Sampson Lloyd, an iron merchant of Edgbaston Street.

In common with other local manufacturers, both men had loaned money to their fellows in trade before they set up as bankers in a formal way in 1765. With a capital of £8,000, they opened premises for the transaction of their business and they began to print their own notes. Their success was swift and within five years their capital had increased to £20,000 and they had started a branch in Lombard Street, London. Encouraged by this example, others followed Taylor and Lloyd. Amongst them were the gun maker Samuel Galton (1805) and the partners Richard Spooner and Thomas Attwood - both of whom were involved in the iron trade. Their bank was described by an acquaintance:

> **The inconvenient old office, with its rows of leather buckets, and its harmless array of antiquated blunderbusses; its old-fashioned desks, dark with age, and begrimed with ink splattered by successive generations of bygone clerks; the low ceiling and quaint elliptic arches; the little fireplace near the counter, where Aurelius Attwood, with his good-humoured face, used to stand warming his coat-tails, and greeting the customers as they came in, were all so much in harmony with the staid, gray-headed clerks, and the quiet, methodical ways of the place...**
> **(Eliezer Edwards, *Personal Recollections of Birmingham and Birmingham Men*, 1877)**

At the time of the English financial crisis of 1825-6, Birmingham had six private banks all of which had been started with profits from commerce and industry. Only one of these failed in that period of banking instability, but the trend turned now to institutions which were of the joint-stock type. These were based on the disciplines of accountability to shareholders, the election of directors, statutory meetings and audit, and systematic record-keeping. One such bank was the Birmingham and Midland, which was the inspiration of its first manager, Charles Geach. Previously, he had worked at the local branch of the Bank of England and he maintained strong links with this organisation. 'The Midland' held its banking accounts there and instead of its own notes, it issued those of his former employer.

By 1874, the bank had total deposits of £2.5 million, making it the second largest in Birmingham and the twentieth, in terms of capital, in England and Wales. In the following years, it continued to grow in size as it acquired rivals such as the Union Bank of Birmingham (1884) and the Central Bank of London (1891) - through which the Midland became a member of the London Clearing House. Seven years later, after it had taken over another competitor in the metropolis, its headquarters were moved to the capital. By 1918, the former Birmingham-based bank was the largest in the world, with deposits of £335 million. Because it is now owned by the Hong Kong and Shangai Banking Corporation, it is part of the world's leading bank group outside Japan.

As in the past, a leading British rival of 'The Midland' is the bank founded by Taylor and Lloyd. After 1852, the button-maker's family had no further association with this institution, but it was not until thirteen years later that Lloyds' ceased to be a private firm and changed into a limited liability company. In the same year, it acquired the successful bank of Moillet and Son - started by a Swiss-born exporter of Birmingham wares. Its chairman was Timothy Kenrick - of the West Bromwich family of iron founders and hardware manufacturers whose business was begun by a Birmingham bucklemaker. Like the Midland, Lloyds entered into a period of expansion, although it moved to London at the earlier date of 1884.

Over one-hundred year's later, Lloyd's is established firmly as one of the 'Big Four' of British banks. Both the others, Barclays and National Westminster, have strong connections with Birmingham also. The former developed out of the Birmingham District and County Banking Co. Ltd, established in 1836; whilst the latter includes in its forerunners Rotten and Scholefields Bank, formed in Bull Street in 1806.

Offices of the Birmingham Banking Company in Bennetts Hill designed in the Corinthian syle by Thomas Rickman, now the area office of Midland Bank plc. (William Hawkes Smith, Birmingham and its Vicinity, 1836)

'REMARKABLE INGENUITY'

Birmingham's rise as a manufacturing centre pre-dated the canal, railway and banking systems which served its manufacturers in the 1800s. But all three facilities were essential in stimulating the further growth of the town. They did so by providing the infrastructure and encouragement which allowed the industrialists and workers of Birmingham to develop their traditional strengths of skill, inventiveness and adaptability. These qualities are made apparent by the granting of patents for new manufacturing ideas. Up to 1849, people from Birmingham had gained a total of 667 patents, compared to the 508 given to citizens of Manchester and Salford jointly. A large number of the patents for the Midland's town related to the button industry, and as R. B Prosser put it in 1881, they 'indicated the remarkable amount of ingenuity which has been expended in the production of an every-day article'.

Most of these grants were not revolutionary in their implications. They were given to craftsmen who had improved existing techniques of production by making small but effective adjustments and alterations to machines and tools. Still, if Birmingham people led the field in patents, many advances in manufacturing craft went unrecognised. The skilled workers of the town were accustomed to making their own tools for their trade. Through doing so and through their use, craftsmen became aware of modifications which could help them in their jobs. George Holyoake was an example of these innovators. As a child in the 1820s, he worked at the Eagle Foundry in Broad Street. In this casting shop, metal was moulded into shapes required by other manufacturers, whilst heavy iron goods were also made. Watching his fellow workers, Holyoake was impressed with their care and thought for their products. His pride in making things was reinforced by his attendance at the Birmingham Mechanics' Institute, founded in 1825 for artisans and others to be instructed 'in the arts they practice'.

> ❝ By the time I was thirteen or fourteen I made a small bright steel fire-gate, with all the improvements then known, as a chimney ornament for my mother. All the drilling in the foundry was done by hand: as this was very laborious, I devised a perpendicular drill to be worked by mill power. At that time I had never seen one. My delight was in mechanical contrivance. Not being able to buy mathematical instruments, I made two pairs of compasses for pencil and pen - one with double point and slide, hammered out of bits of sheet iron. My tutor being pleased with them caused them to be laid on the table at the annual distribution of prizes

Fred Sutton, an apprentice tool turner at Tubes Ltd, Rocky Lane, Aston, 1915. (Fred Sutton).

at the Mechanics'
Institute. This led to my being publicly presented with
a proper case of mathematical instruments, given by
Mr Isaac Pitman, the inventor of phonography. Mr
Lloyd a banker in
Birmingham, caused George Stephenson, one
night when he was in the House of Commons, to put
my name down on his staff of young engineers. I was
very proud to have my name on his list, though
nothing came of it . . . (George Jacob
Holyoake, *Sixty Years of an Agitator's Life,* 1900) "

There was one worker at the Eagle Foundry for whom Holyoake had the most respect. He was 'a tall, lean man' who forged wrought-iron goods for kitchen ranges and black iron stoves. His pliers and tongs 'were the most perfect of anyone's' and everything he forged was 'excellent in fitness and finish'. This deep pride in their work has continued to mark out the skilled people of Birmingham. Born in 1898 in the city, Fred Sutton still has the tools his father made, and he recalls well his own days as an apprentice tool turner at Tubes Limited of Rocky Lane, Aston. Here an older colleague 'taught me ever such a lot and when there wasn't much work about he'd say "Hey, sit down and read this", engineering books he'd give me to read.' (*Interview,* 1989).

MAKING BRASS

In the eighteenth and early nineteenth centuries, the most important tools in the manufactures of Birmingham were lathes, drawbenches, stamps and presses. These latter two pieces of machinery were essential if a producer wished to make a large number of identical articles such as coins and buttons. In these trades, the press was used for cutting out blanks from a sheet of material, after which a stamp would imprint a pattern on them so as to form the finished product. Their use in Birmingham was prominent by the later 1700s, during which period they began to be noticed in the town's brass trade.

Metal-working had been crucial to the prosperity of Birmingham from its early days. In the seventeenth century, the national demand for the town's products led to the wealth of ironmongers like John Jennens, who both supplied the local smiths with bar iron and marketed their wares. By the early 1700s, steel was also in use as a material, in particular for ornamental work which needed to shine and not rust. The production of this metal is remembered in Steelhouse Lane which takes its name from the steel houses of the Kettle family.

Brass is an alloy of zinc and copper and it too was suitable for fancy work, although it was fashioned into mundane products as well. By the later eighteenth century, its use was of growing importance, and the brassfounders of the town were desribed as 'ingenious artists who make an infinite variety of articles'. To cater for the high local demand for the raw material, a brass house was set up in Broad Street in 1781. With production of the alloy in the town, its price fell dramatically from £84 to £56 per ton. This drop invigorated the making of brass wares. In 1818, *Wrightson's Directory* named 79 people who were involved in the trade, and they were outnumbered only by button makers, platers and those connected to the manufacture of jewellery and toys. The range of goods which they produced was wide. It included lamps, cabinet furniture, picture frames, coffin furniture, telescopes, hearth brushes, toasting forks, tubes for umbrellas, dog collars and nails.

Brass wares received a further boost from the introduction of gas and paraffin lighting - the former of which needed pipes as well as light fittings; and the Penny Post - which led to a demand for letter-weighing machines and plates for letterboxes. By the 1860s, about 10,000 people were engaged in the brass industry, so that it could be said that 'what Manchester is to cotton, Bradford in wool, and Sheffield in steel, Birmingham is in brass'. By this time, the trade itself could be split into nine divisions: brass casting; cabinet, bell and general brassfoundry; cock-making and plumber's brassfoundry; stamped brassfoundry, finished and in the rough; rolled brass, wire and sheathing; tube manufacturing; lamp making; gas fittings; and naval brassfoundry.

Like their fellows in most other Birmingham industries, many of the early brass workers toiled in houses which were converted into workshops. But by the mid-Victorian period, there was a marked trend towards factory production. This move was influenced by a technological process which enabled brass to be made more quickly and by the increased use of steam power. Prominent amongst these brassfounding establishments was the Cobden Works of Samuel Heath and Sons in Leopold Street.

"The premises occupied are extensive in their construction, and very conveniently arranged. These large works are occupied by great numbers of workpeople. The employés number many hundreds and the little army of men are always busily engaged in the execution of the many orders which are continually received. The trade controlled is of a very extensive kind, and a large connection is influentially maintained both at home and abroad. The productions of this firm are of a world-wide reputation and they invariably give every satisfaction; composed of the best material, and made in the most careful and experienced manner, they are perfections of manufacture throughout. The business is most comprehensive in its detail, and comprises an extensive manufacture of brass bedsteads (of which Messrs Heath & Sons are patentees), Mounts, also Lock furniture, Finger plates, Ashpan and Range knobs etc... In addition to the foregoing they are substantially established as Stampers and Piercers. Altogether this eminent establishment ranks among the most important of its kind in the kingdom. (Cutting supplied by Samuel Heath and Sons PLC)."

Bedstead workers at Hoskins Ltd, Upper Trinity Street, late 1950s. (Mr Falck, Hoskins Ltd)

By 1900, the company gave work to about 2,000 men and women. It does not employ so many today, but it remains a significant Birmingham concern of which the managing director is the great, great grandson of the first Samuel Heath. It is certain that this man was in business by the 1830s, and he was well placed to take advantage of two innovations which 'revolutionised the efficiency of bedstead making'. The first involved the chilling of castings, a technique which was patented by Dr William Church, an American who had settled in Birmingham. This allowed dovetail joints to be cast in moulding boxes, so enabling them to be fitted around the intersections of the tubular frame members of a bed. Such a method was only effective after 1841 when a patent was granted for a method of making taper brass tubes. The originators of this idea were Church and Jonathan Harlow - a partner in the Bordesley business of Peyton and Harlow.

Within a few years, there were twenty firms in Birmingham turning out 5-6,000 brass bedsteads a week. An increasing number of these were sold to private purchasers for use in their own homes, but many were bought wholesale for soldiers' barracks, workhouses and hospitals. A firm which continues to specialise in this last market is Hoskins Ltd of Upper Trinity Street, Bordesley. Founded in 1846, it later took over the business of Peyton, Hoyland and Peyton - a company which had a long list of credits: it had patented the ornamentation of brass bedsteads and the japanning of those in iron; and at the Paris Exhibition of 1867, it gained the only medal which was given for the making of metallic bedsteads.

Like most manufacturing endeavour, work in the brass trade was hard and often low paid. And if the youthful George Holyoake revelled in the forge and the foundry, Vere W. Garratt did not. Before 1914, he worked in a small smelting shop where old gas meters were melted down in cupolas (furnaces) and cleansed before they were recast to be made up again. His vivid description of its operations emphasise that the wealth of Birmingham was paid for by the ill health and early death of many of the town's workers.

> **"The brass shop was a whirling mass of machinery, where the men worked in deafening noise and dusty atmosphere with very inadequate ventilation. Worse still was the iron foundry, in which the rough castings of meters were filed smooth by hand and machine and where a thick haze of filing dust was inevitably breathed in by the men. When I first saw the foundry in the misty glare of the gas-lights and met the bloodshot eyes of men with perspiration running down blackened cheeks as files and hammers screeched and dinned through the polluted atmosphere, I thought that hell itself would be a preferable place to work in. But I managed to get a better look at that infernal abode by visiting the polisher who worked in a kind of 'box-room' over the revolving brushes that threw into his face a poisonous cloud of particles from the metal he polished. The irony of his job was that while he brightened the brasses he blackened his lungs in the process and made periodical visits to the sanatorium for treatment. A married man he told me he was condemned to an early grave. (V. W. Garatt, A Man in the Street, 1939)"**

Polishers were not alone in suffering because of their job. Factories were and can be dangerous sites. Powerful and fast machinery has to be attended by alert employees, but also it must be guarded properly so that accidents can be minimised and made less frightful. The importance of safety legislation cannot be diminished and it is made relevant by personal experiences of injury and mutilation. At the age of 14 in 1871, Will Thorne worked at Abraham's metal rolling and ammunition works in Adderley Park Road. One of his jobs involved taking annealed bars of metal to pickling tubs where a strong vitriol solution was used to clean them. He described how the biting acid would splash his hands and eat the flesh to the very bone. Only 'by washing my hands in milk was the excruciating pain eased and the effect of the vitriol killed'. (Will Thorne, *My Life's Story,* 1925)

My own Nan, Lily Perry, lost her right index finger when she was operating an unguarded milling machine at Shelley's in Aston in the 1950s. She had a bandage on her finger because she had a big blister and it was this 'that took me through' into the cutters.

Pickling shop at Joseph Appleby Limited, press workers, Tower Road, Aston. (Arthur Wilkes)

> **I walked the entire length of the shop and I says to our foreman, who was the other end of the shop, 'Oh, look what I've done'. And he fainted he did. Then they took me into the ambulance room and the ambulance come and they took me the General.**
> **It took me index finger. It took me thumb. They stitched me thumb back on. And it took the end of the finger next to me index finger. I had 47 stitches. Went through me hand as well and all me guides. I went back into the General and they took me guides out of me right foot to see if this could do it. But they never could. (*Interview,* 1993)**

In an earlier period, Albert Fenton's granny lost all her fingers on a power press. This was when she worked at Hamson and Stokes in Hanley Street. She was left with 'little stumps and her thumbs, yet she could still do deaf and dumb language' which 'must have been very useful in a noisy factory'. (Albert Fenton, *Albert's Story,* unpublished manuscript, no date).

Despite her maiming, our Nan continued to work in factories and she enjoyed both her work and the companionship it provided. Of course, many mechanical operations are repetitive and boring and they can be 'soul-destroying'. But factories are not necessarily places of dspondency and disillusionment. My great-uncle Wal Chinn worked at 'The Gunners', the B.S.A., before 1914 and he recalled that:

> **A good spirit and a sense of humour seemed to prevail in the workshop, where a joke or sing song would boost the morale. Some budding Caruso that felt 'on song' could start a solo effort with an old favourite verse and chorus, to become infectious and taken up with gusto by the surrounding workers on machine or bench . . . The approval at the end of the chorus was usually a barrage of applause from hammers and other tools, tapped out on anything handy. Encouragement would be accompanied with all sorts of wisecracks... (Walter Chinn, *From Victoria's Image,* unpublished manuscript, no date).**

PEN SHOP OF THE WORLD

If Birmingham was the centre of the brass trade in Britain, then it was also the 'pen shop of the world'. This title was achieved chiefly because of the success of one man, as was made plain by Elihu Burritt, the American Consul in Birmingham during the 1860s.

> **It is doubtful if any article of such wide fame and universal use ever was so identified with one man's name as is the steel pen with Joseph Gillott, of Birmingham. Even the pens manufactured by others sent abroad there**

The Prince of Wales, later King Edward VII, watching the process of slitting pens in Gillot's Pen Manufactory. (The Graphic, 7 November 1874)

❝suggest his name and fame. In ten thousand school-houses scattered over the American continent between the two oceans, a million children are as familiarly acquainted with Joseph Gillott as with Noah Webster. The primer of the one and the pen of the other - twin pioneers of civilisation - are making the tour of the western hemisphere together, and leaving behind them a wave and wake of light. Gillott's manufactory is a kind of central celebrity in Birmingham to visitors from America and other countries. (Elihu Burritt, *Walks in the Black Country*, 1868)❞

Like Baskerville before him and Kynoch afterwards, Gillott was an immigrant to Birmingham, coming from Sheffield when he was a young man. At first he worked as a buckle maker, but with the downfall of his trade and in about 1829, he began to make steel pens on a hand press in the attic of his house. His business flourished. Gillott's pens were of a good quality and there was an increasing demand for them. This was because more middle-class people were writing letters or using pens in their jobs as clerks, whilst growing numbers of the working class were benefiting from education - in Britain and abroad.

Through his innovations and use of machinery, Gillott set the pace in steel-pen manufacturing and soon he was based at the Victoria Works in Graham Street. Here, at one of the largest factories in Birmingham, presses cut out pens from sheets of plain metal. After this, the individual products were subjected to other machines which gave them slits, added tubes, and polished them. This mechanisation had an astounding effect on the price of pens. In the late 1830s they were sold wholesale at 5s per gross (144); by the mid 1860s their cost was as low as 1½d for the same number.

During this decade, Gillott's was not the only major manufacturer of pens in Birmingham. Altogether there were 12 firms which used ten tons of steel each week to produce 98,000 gross of pens. Amongst their workforce, there was a preponderance of women over men in a ratio of 2050 to 360. To their number could be added those who made the paper-boxes and other accessories of the trade. Their labours are forgotten often, but their endeavours were essential not just to the packaging of pens. They were vital to most of the city's industries. When she left school at the age of 12 in 1901, May Golding and a friend started work packing small items for a budding entrepreneur in Greet.

❝In the room were a small table and two chairs, packages on the floor with very small cardboard boxes, an urden bag, and a small pair of scales with a little brass weight. The man placed the scales on the table, put the weight on the scale, then opened the bag containing the 'small items'. Tipping the bag open, thousands of tin tacks spread across the table. We were astonished at first, then he explained what we had to do. He took two tweezer-like tools out of his coat, put a number of little boxes on the end of the table, filled one little box on the scale until it balanced, tucked in the flap on the box, and stood back... We had to fill as many boxes as we could at a time, pack them in cartons which held twelve, and later put the dozen cartons in a bigger box which held a gross. We worked from about 8 o' clock until 6.00 p.m., with an hour for dinner from Monday to Friday... and we were rewarded with one and sixpence... The boxes of tacks were sold in general stores for a halfpenny each. (Tom Golding, *96 Years a Brummie*, 1889-1986, 1986)❞

ART AND INDUSTRY

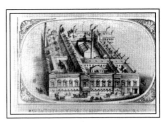

Elkington's factory in Newhall Street, now the Museum of Science and Industry. (Cornish's Visiter's Hand Book Through Birmingham, 1853)

As renowned as Gillott in the pen trade was Josiah Mason, from Kidderminster. As a boy, he had hawked fruit and vegetables, after which he had tried his hand as a shoemaker, blacksmith, carpenter and painter. When he settled in Birmingham, he became involved in the jewellery trade and he invented a machine which bevelled rings. After this venture, he set up making pens - at the same time as his rival and friend, Gillott. With his fortune made, Mason paid for the establishment of almshouses, an orphanage, and a college which was the forerunner of The University of Birmingham. And like so many manufacturers who had preceded him, he financed the technological researches of others, in particular those of the Elkington cousins.

From a family of toy makers, H. and G. R. Elkington realised the importance of the manufacture of plated ware. This trade involved the soldering of silver or gold onto copper and it had gained prominence with the products of Mathew Boulton. By the early years of the nineteenth century, the leading firms like Rylands made 'articles used for the table, in dinner, breakfast, coffee, and dessert services'.

Much of the work was intricate - some candles were made of up to 20 pieces - and it was time-consuming. An ingot of copper had to be planed and filed to make it ready for the silver which had been rolled into the right thickness and then cut into a suitable length for the final product. After this, the two metals were laid together with wires, placed on an anvil, covered with a heavy piece of iron and struck with a sledge hammer until they were 'bedded'. Then a solution of borax was spread around the edges of silver to help with fusion and the plated ingot was put into an oven to bake. When the plater saw a bright line around the fringes of the precious metal, he knew that the copper and silver had become united. Once the ingot had gone cold, its sides were filed and it was rolled to make it ready to be shaped by 'hammering', 'raising', 'stamping' or 'spinning'.

Finally, the finished article was burnished by female workers. They washed it in water, and, in sections, they rubbed it with soap. Each such area was pressed backwards and forwards with a bright steel tool - dipped constantly into a basin of soap suds - so as to close the pores of the silver. Last of all, the product was brightened and made smooth and clear by the use of a blood-stone burnisher.

This whole operation was made obsolete by electro-plating – a fast and effective means of coating a base metal with that which was precious. Its origins owed much to the scientific inquiries and patents of the Elkingtons and their associates, Alexander Parkes and Dr John Wright. The new method of plating involved the use of nickel which had been cast or stamped into the shape of an article. This was then dipped into a vat in which there was a solution of nitrate of silver or cyanide of gold. The nickel was suspended by copper wire through which an electric current was passed. This separated the precious metal from its solution and fused it to its base counterpart.

In 1850, ten years after their main patent was granted, Elkington's factory in Newhall Street employed 500 people; by 1880, the workforce totalled 1,000. Of this figure, a large number were men who were allowed to develop the skills of designing, modelling and chasing - and over 50 of them attended classes in science and design at The Birmingham and Midland Institute. A few employees were artists of renown. Amongst them was Morel Ladeuill. He won a gold medal at the Paris Exhibition for what were described by Burritt as 'specimens of exquisite conception and execution.' But the article which most affected the American was an example of raised work. This was a large silver vase on the outside surface of which craftsmen had lifted the silver into representations of 'all the leading inventions of the century, in all the allegorical metaphors and symbols that were wont to delight the classical imaginations of ancient times'. It is fitting that since Elkington's was absorbed into a large group, that its factory is now the site of the Birmingham City Council Museum of Science and Industry.

Elkington's was not the only Birmingham firm which was famous for its art work. As celebrated was the glassware of Osler & Co. of Broad Street. In 1851, this concern made a magnificent fountain of glass for the Great Exhibition - itself inspired by previous industrial exhibitions in Birmingham; and at a later date, Osler's formed the candelabra which provided the lighting for the tomb of The Prophet Muhammed at Medina. The making of glass products in Birmingham dated to at least 1762 when a Mayer Oppenheimer set up a house for that purpose in Snow Hill; and by the early nineteenth century, Osler's was one of a number of glass works. Their existence is recalled by the pub of that name on Broad Street, the actual building of which belonged to Abraham Cutler. Today the firm of Pearce and Cutler operates as glaziers and manufacturers of aluminium and upvc windows. This particular business dates its beginning to 1815 when Smith and Pearce were glass and lead merchants in Cannon Street.

An associated trade was the painting of glass. During his employment at Soho, Francis Egington had achieved a high reputation in this art form. Amongst his commissions were those for St. George's Chapel Windsor, Salisbury and Lichfield Cathedrals, and Magdalen College, Oxford. In Birmingham itself, he painted windows for Aston Parish Church and for the east side of St. Paul's in the Jewellery Quarter. After his death, his art was continued by his son and others, but it came to be superseded by the stained glass work of John Hardman.

In 1837, this Birmingham man struck up a strong friendship with Augustus Welby Pugin, an architect who was a devout Catholic. Pugin was determined to revive the building forms of the Middle Ages and two fine examples of his work are St. Chad's – the first Catholic cathedral to be built in Britain since the Reformation - and St. Joseph's in Thimblemill Lane, Nechells. He was as keen on designing works of metal and glass and which also adhered to 'strict medieval principles'. Hardman set up in business to achieve these objectives. From works in Newhall Street which employed up to 100 people, his firm produced 'Birmingham Gothic' ecclesiastical and civic regalia; but it became most famous for its stained glass windows. It continues to have an international reputation in this field, although its workforce is much smaller than in the nineteenth century and it now operates from Lightwoods House.

Crescent Wharf, looking from the Birmingham Canal towards Broad Street, close to the present site of the National Indoor Arena, early 1800s. (Birmingham Library Services, Pershouse Collection, after David Cox)

Artistic work was not the preserve of the electro-plating and glass industries. It was present in the medals of Sir Edward Thomason, which he struck to 'celebrate great occasions and to commemorate great people'; it was obvious in the enammelled coins of William Henry Probert and Edwin Steele; and it was also evident in much of the work-a-day manufactures of Birmingham like the copper ware of Lee & Wilkes Ltd, founded before 1780, and suppliers of miniature metal articles for the Queen's dolls' house. As a whitesmith, George Holyoake proclaimed that 'good, well- contrived, well-finished machinery always gives me as much enjoyment as a good painting'. The close connections between art and manufacturing were enhanced by insitutions like the Birmingham School of Arts and Craft - now part of the University of Central England - and the Birmingham and Midland Institute. This was founded by Act of Parliament in 1854 and its members were in the forefront of advanced education which was industrial and general. A major supporter of the B.M.I. was Charles Dickens. In 1853, he raised funds for it by reading *A Christmas Carol* in the Town Hall, and he became its sixteenth president.

Such institutions and the pride of the crafts people of Birmingham give the lie to those intellectuals who denigrated industrial cities as souless places. They were not. They were brought to life by their people, by their workers and by their wares. As a writer, J. B. Priestley shrank away from Birmingham in 1933 as a place 'of big profits and narrow views, which sent missionaries out of one gate and brass idols and machine guns out of the other'. So it was. The making of money was a major impetus to the people of the city.

And it cannot be denied that the guns of Birmingham were instrumental in gaining an empire. More than this, the city's wealth was gained at the expense of the ill-health, early deaths and poverty of thousands of its people. But to see the city as the site only of money-grubbing war mongers is not just one-sided, it is unfair and smacks of the snobbishness of those who are accustomed to a comfortable life. Birmingham depended for its existence on the making of goods which people wanted. It made its mark in an ever-changing and competitive market. But that did not mean that its wares were empty of care and devoid of artistic talent. They were not. From the humble pearl button to the sculptures which could be reproduced by electro-plating, the workers of Birmingham took pride in their work and in how it looked.

CARRIAGES, WIRE AND TUBES

Samuel Heath, Joseph Gillott and the Elkingtons were not the only large employers in Birmingham. By 1884, there were 1,100 workers at the 'Met', the Metropolitan Railway Carriage firm at Washwood Heath. A similar number made the same product at Brown, Marshalls and Co. nearby. Both were amalgamated in 1902. Later named the Metropolitan Cammell Carriage and Wagon Company, the business continued to provide work for a huge number of men until well after 1945. Now Metro-Cammell Ltd, the firm maintains its high reputation internationally, but with the drastic shrinking of Britain's railway system, it has had to make redundant many skilled workers. Unfortunately, this decline in the train network has meant also that the railway sheds in Saltley and Tyseley are no longer the hives of activity which once they were.

Another large concern which has disappeared into a bigger group is that of John and Edwin Wright, rope makers of Garrison Street. Their firm was begun in 1770, but it came to prominence for two reasons: their patent for making ropes of wire and hemp; and the use of their wire ropes in the Atlantic telegraph cable of 1866. This product was a fine example of co-operation between two innovative Birmingham businesses, for the cable itself was made up by Webster and Horsfall of Hay Mills. Begun in the 1840s as a manufacturer of musical wire, the company expanded its operations after 1854. This was when James Horsfall patented a method of hardening steel wire which led to his

Nicklin & Son wireworkers of Bradford Street. (Wrightson's Directory of Birmingham, 1818)

partnership with the Websters of Penn Mills. The new product was lighter, stronger and more versatile than its softer predecessor and it was used for needles, fish-hooks, small springs and umbrella frames. It could be applied also to the manufacture of ropes for mines and engineering works. These continue to be produced at Latch and Batchelor in Hay Mills, whilst the parent company of Webster and Horsfall remains a leading British wire drawer.

One other long-established firm with its origins in wire-drawing is G. and J. Swingler which was founded in 1786. Its present trade is making chains, an unusual manufacture in Birmingham despite its reputation as a centre of metal-bashing. More common was the production of tubes. These were essential to the success of many of the town's trades, for they were used in the making of brass-bedsteads and guns; whilst at a later date, they were essential for motorbikes, cycles, motor cars, oil piping, and aeroplanes. Originally, tubes were made by hand. A strip was cut from a sheet of rolled metal and was then bent round an iron rod which was the size of the inside of the tube needed. Next, the rounded ribbon was bound with wire whilst borax and solder was placed on its seams. After this, it was fused in a forge fire, and when it was cold, the wire and surplus solder were removed and the tube was hammered into its final shape.

By the 1860s, thanks in part to the discoveries of Sir Edward Thomason, tube making had become mechanised. Revolving or circular shears cut out the strips of metal and they were drawn into shape by other machines, as described by Lily Need. She worked at Serck Radiators in Greet. During the 1930s:

> **The job involved the use of ten foot long solid steel rods, solid steel chains two cubic inches thick, dies weighing eight pounds, and two sets of large rollers, one to pull the large chain along its track, the other to draw out the tubes, the whole machine being about sixteen feet long. At the end were two heavy metal wheels, each of which was about six feet in diameter.**
> **The modus operandi was to ease brass tubes onto the steel rods. The end of the rod was pushed into the die by hand and fed through the one set of rollers. It was then caught in the jaws of a large pair of pinchers called a dog, presumably because it had a solid steel tail the shape of a hook, and about the size of a young wire haired terrier, which took the links of this clattering chain and, moving along with it, pulled out the brass tube to twice its length. The rod was then swung backwards onto a long table and eased off the bright burning tubes with the aid of greased pads smelling nauseatingly of rancid animal fat. These tubes used to cover ships' taffrails. The slightest mark made them scrap and we didn't get paid for them. (Lily Need, *Struggling Manor, Inner City Birmingham in the 1920s*, 1993)**

In the nineteenth century, the leading manufacturer of tubes was R.W. Winfield whose factory in Icknield Port Road gave work to about 800 people in the 1860s. This firm gained world fame for its fine brassware, designed by people like W. C. Aitken, and its owner was renowned locally for the school which he set up in working hours for boys whom he employed, and for his high rates of pay to skilled men. After Winfield's death in 1869, his business declined until its disappearance by the end of the century. Still, tube making continued in Birmingham at the aptly-called Tubes Limited of Rocky Lane - now operating in Oldbury; Earl Bourne & Co. of Dudley Road, which as Delta Tubes is based today in West Bromwich; and T.I. Reynolds, now makers of aircraft engine rings, hollow extrusions and cycle frames in Tyseley. This last firm is unusual in that its offices are in

Hay Hall, a centuries-old house which has been restored by its present occupiers with the help of Birmingham City Council.

POWERING INDUSTRY

The growth of large factories in Birmingham was tied in closely to the increased use of steam power from the 1840s. Unlike the cotton towns of Lancashire, Birmingham was not associated with the widespread use of large steam engines. Even though James Watt's developments of such machines had taken place locally, the town's industries were characterised by tools which were driven by the endeavours of men, women and children. When their power was insufficient for a purpose, then it was provided by the many water mills in the region.

Cutting rods for brass bedsteads at Fisher Brown & Co, Lionel Street, 1902. (Birmingham Library Services)

Some of these specialised in the grinding of corn, as did Sarehole Mill in Wake Green. This was the home of Mathew Boulton the elder in his last years, but from 1858 it was owned by the Andrew family. They continued as corn millers until 1919 and their former home is now a working museum which highlights the significance of agriculture in Birmingham's recent past. But the mill is remarkable not just for the longevity of its working life. J.R.R. Tolkien lived nearby in Wake Green Road from 1896 to 1900, and as a child his imagination was affected deeply by the miller, his property and the countryside which surrounded it. These influences are obvious in the writer's fantasy novel *The Lord of The Rings,* and they linger yet in Moseley Bog. Before the 1890s this was the site of a supplementary storage pool for Andrew's mill, but now it is an enchanting urban wetland where rare plants are found and in which wildlife thrives.

For a short time metal was smoothed and rolled at Sarehole Mill, but these tasks were not its mainstay as they were at those mills at Bournbrook, Dogpool (on the River Rea at Stirchley), Duddeston (also on the River Rea) and Trittiford (on the Chinn Brook), as well as at Thimble Mill (on the Hockley Brook at Nechells) and at Lifford Mill (by the River Rea). Bromford Mill (close to the River Tame) and Hay Mill (on the River Cole) were wire mills - and the latter is used as such today by Latch and Batchelor Ltd; whilst paper was milled on the Hol Brook and River Cole. Altogether in the early 1800s, there were 45 working water mills in the Birmingham district. By the latter part of that century, most had disappeared as steam began to be used for powering heavy machinery.

This driving force had a great attraction to inventors such as John Inshaw. Born in 1807, 'as a lad he lit his father's house with gas, and utilised heat from retorts for driving a steam engine in 1821'. At a later date he became known for his:

> **"steam clock, and this name was given to his tavern in Morville Street which he kept, 1859-86. Here he exhibited many working models and mechanical devices. The twin screw propeller was invented by him, also electric clocks, whilst his water indicators were employed on all Corporation water carts. At one time George Stephenson consulted him on the subject of wheels for locomotives . . . It is said that the first portable engine was made in his workshop.**
> **Aston Manor paper mills was founded by him in 1879, while at various times he was engaged in tube making, metal rolling and cut nail making. He also effected improvements in the making of mineral water. (*Letter* from J. C. Garratt, from newspaper cutting supplied by G. Inshaw, 1993)"**

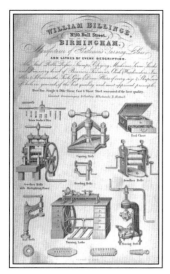

William Billinge, general ironmonger, lathe and tool maker. (Wrightson and Webb, Directory of Birmingham, 1839)

Despite the avid interest in steam power by people like John Inshaw, engines for this force were not common in Birmingham before the mid-nineteenth century. In 1815, there were just 15 of them in the town; by 1830, they had increased to 120, and eight years later, their number had doubled to 240. Compared to Manchester, this was not an outstanding figure, nor was the use of steam engines in Birmingham widespread. Most were involved in the metal industries where they were used to roll brass and copper, draw wire and to power forges and foundries. In these manufactures, steam was a powerful impetus to mechanisation and large units of production; and from the 1840s, it had the same effect on the steel-pen and glass trades of the town.

THE TOOLS OF INDUSTRY

Steam engines themselves were made close to Birmingham at the Soho Foundry of James Watt & Co. in Smethwick, near to which was Tangye's Cornwall Works. One of the first large orders of this firm was for jacks used in launching the *Great Eastern*. At the time, this was the largest ship in the world, and it is believed John Inshaw was the person who suggested the use of Tangye's machinery. These included hydraulic lifts, presses for the cotton and wool industries, and machines for punching and shearing. By the 1850s, the firm had been joined by other machinery manufacturers. Amongst them was Joseph Taylor who made all kinds of presses. As Taylor and Challen, the business which he founded continues in Hockley making power presses and those for coins.

By 1913, Birmingham was a major centre for the production of these machines, as it was for those which were used for drilling, milling and lathe work. Still, much machinery was manufactured actually 'in house', details of which were kept quiet by industrialists who feared that rivals might poach their ideas and processes. In particular, smaller tools were made on the premises, and most large factories had a room for this purpose However, a few firms specialised in their production. As early as 1740, Thomas Newey had set up making augers, tools for boring holes in wood, and gimlets, another form of instrument for boring. His firm remains in business in The Jewellery Quarter making hand tools and ticket nippers.

An important instrument for industry and society in general was the rule, and by the 1860s its production was concentrated in Birmingham and London. The chief companies in the Midland's town were I. & D. Smallwood, started in 1810, and that of Michael Rabone. This began in 1784, and as Rabone Chesterman it continues to make measuring equipment in Hockley. The business has kept many of its records, and they indicate that at least until the 1830s some payments for their wares were made in kind: in 1818, they received spirits from one client; four years later, they were given Irish linen worth 3s 5d by another; and in 1835, a Wolverhampton purchaser passed over 30lbs of cheese valued at 7d per pound.

In the same decade, John Rabone introduced steam-driven machinery to his business, which by now made 164 patterns for 'All sorts of Rules for Gauging, Navigation, Surveying, Drawing etc . . . Likewise all kinds of Foreign Rules'. However, the company's moves towards mechanisation were met with staunch opposition from their workers who feared that the end of hand-operated tools would lead to their loss of jobs. So great was the antipathy of one man that it led him to violence. He stabbed John Rabone in the breast and back after his employer had rebuked him for not carrying out a process on a powered machine. Although few workers went so far, it is certain that throughout Birmingham there were many who worried deeply that steam power would make them useless and unemployed.

Despite the determined antagonism of their workers, Rabone's was mechanised fully by the 1870s:

> **❝In few manufactories that we have inspected is the principle of the sub-divisions of labour carried to a greater pass than in the Hockley Abbey Works. Some idea of fact may be gathered from the statement that every rule in process of completion, if only a few pence in value, has according to its kind to pass through 40 or 50 different machines, and undergo from 60 to 100 distinct operations. Hence the premises to carry on such a trade are very extensive. (newspaper cutting, about 1876, cited in Douglas J. Hallam, *The First 200 Years. A Short History of Rabone Chesterman Limited,* 1984. My account of Rabone's is based on this book)❞**

Mrs Allen's paraffin shop, Herbert Road, Small Heath, about 1897: Florence Naylor, Harriet Naylor, Lizzie Naylor, Mrs Allen, neighbour and child. (A.E. Hay)

The reporter was astonished that even the small brass pins of rules were made by self-acting machinery. A coil of wire was placed in a revolving cylinder. One end of this roll reached into an automatic drum which pointed and made the pins at a rate of 800 per minute. It was made clear in another article that one beneficial consequence of this mechanisation was a rise in the wages of the workforce.

WOMEN IN BUSINESS

After Michael Rabone's death in 1808 and until at least 1835, his wife Elizabeth was listed as an 'ivory and box-rule maker'. The running of artisan and other businesses by women was not unusual in this period before the cult of domesticity had driven upper working class and middle-class females out of public life. In 1818, *Wrightson's Directory* listed a number of them. They included: Ann Fluitt, a bridle bit and stirrup maker; Lucinda Evetts, a brass founder; Ruth Worrallo, a file maker; Elizabeth Gill, a manufacturer of guns; Mary Dowler, a candlestick maker; and Susannah Parkes, a producer of gilt toy and watch chains.

Some of these women in business were widows who carried on their husband's craft and often added '& Son' to their trading name. But it is likely that these females were skilled in their own right; and it is certain that the actual number of women who had companies was greater than is indicated in trades' directories. This is because many of their operations were hidden at home, as in the case of Catherine Holyoake.

> **❝In those days horn buttons were made in Birmingham, and my mother had a workshop attached to the house, in which she conducted a business herself, employing several hands. She had the business before her marriage. She received the orders; made the purchases of the materials; superintended the making of the goods; made out the accounts; and received the money; besides taking care of her growing family. There were no 'Rights of Women' thought of in her day, but she was an entirely self-acting, managing mistress. (George Jacob Holyoake, *Sixty Years of an Agitator's Life,* 1900)❞**

A number of thriving concerns were started by women. The national firm of jewellers, H. Samuel, is named after Harriet who began business in 1863; and fifty years later, 'the high-class' Lansdowne Laundry in Sparkbrook grew out of the operations of a woman who took in washing for affluent clients. It should also be acknowledged that whilst the great majority of firms were headed by men, the success of many of them owed much to the work and knowledge of wives. A prime example of this phenomenon was Elizabeth Cadbury. The researches of Catherine Hall have shown that whilst this woman was not trained formally, she helped her husband substantially in the draper's shop in Bull Street which he opened in 1800. Her separation from the business, and that of her daughters, came only when the family ceased to live on the premises of their shop.

Richard Cadbury was one of a growing number of prosperous shopkeepers who were making their homes in middle-class districts like Edgbaston by the 1850s. But this residential move was impossible for those smaller retailers who gained their incomes in working-class neighbourhoods They continued to live above and behind their shops; and the involvement of wives in these businesses remained crucial. Mary Parson's mom and dad were of this kind. Between 1926 and 1933, they had a business in King Edward Road, Ladywood which:

> **" consisted of a small general shop, with a milk round attached, my father taking out the pony and trap with churns of milk each day, to make deliveries in the area, while my mother stayed at home to look after the shop. We sold all kinds of groceries and sweets, most of which were unpackaged and had to be weighed out on small balance scales. Bacon was sliced by hand with a carving knife, slabs of toffee were broken up with a small hammer and weighed in small quantities often costing only ½d or 1d. Boiled sweets were kept in tall jars, a selection being displayed in little dishes in the window, a large crock of milk stood on the counter, covered by a cloth and customers would bring in their jugs to buy just half-a-pint at a time. These small shops have been called 'the poor man's pantry' because the customers were too poor to keep a stock of food, but just bought small quantities as they were needed, in halfpenny worths or pennyworths. Our shop was open all day until eight o' clock at night, except on Sunday and early closing day, but even after closing time, there would sometimes come a knock at the back door and a request for some urgently required item of food... My mother had had previous experience of working in a shop, her parents having once kept a newsagent's in Aston. (Letter, 1993)"**

The Lansdowne Laundry, Studley Street, Sparkbrook, about 1939. The women in the foreground are sorting the laundry, those on the right are putting it through a calender to smooth it after it has been cleaned. (Lily Need, information Kitty Bell)

Small shops have remained a prominent feature in modern Birmingham. Since the 1960s, many have been run by South Asian Brummies, people whose origins lie in Kashmir, Gujrat in India, the Punjab in Pakistan, Bangla Desh or in East Africa. Some of these businesses were set up to sell the foods which were needed by Pakistani and Indian immigrants; but many were on the site of long-established businesses. In these, the sale of ethnic products is combined with the retail of those goods which are required by English, Irish, Scots and Welsh Brummies. As in the past, these small shops are vital facilities within working-class areas. They are 'open all hours' and they are especially important for the shopping needs of old people, single parents and those who are disabled.

Irene May Franklin in her family's general store at 11, Prince Albert Road, about 1954. (Maureen Murphy)

An example of a general storekeeper who is embedded in his local community is Mr C. Singh of the Washwood Heath Road. Like many Sikhs, he does not live and work in an area dominated by his fellows. Instead, he provides a service for customers of differing ethnicities. His shop sells 'stera' (sterilised milk) to English people, as well as sweets to their children and to those whose parents come from Kashmir, Pakistan and the West Indies. Each morning, he opens his doors at 5.30 for the passing trade and for the sale of newspapers. And like the English corner shopkeepers of the inter-war years, he allows a little credit to those customers whom he knows well and whom he trusts. Similarly, he takes pride in his usefulness to the local community and he is keen to point out that in his neighbourhood, 'they all know Mr Singh'. (*Interview, 1993*)

SMALL GAFFERS

During the Middle Ages, Birmingham and the surrounding villages was an 'area of free peasants and light seigneurial control'. According to Christopher Dyer, the absence of large landlords and the relative liberty of local people meant that they 'could get on with what they wished to' and this freedom helped the development of industry. Such an independent spirit was as evident in the nineteenth century and has remained obvious in a city which now has 25,000 businesses. For if small shops have remained common, despite the rise of large supermarket chains, then so too have the works of small gaffers, in defiance of the emergence of factories and large manufacturers.

In 1866, Joseph Chamberlain - later a famous mayor - wrote that almost all Birmingham trades had sprung from little beginnings. He noted that fifty years before, there had been very few factories of 'great size or importance' locally. At that time, most businesses were carried on in part of a dwelling-house or in small premises, 'shopping', which were attached to a home. But Chamberlain observed that this type of concern was on the wane. Because of the introduction of machinery and the 'universal employment of steam power', a substantial amount of capital was needed to start up and maintain a manufacturing business; whilst huge mills had emerged which were 'specially adapted to the wants of each trade.' The result of these developments was that large units of production had emerged with 'extraordinary rapidity'.

Chamberlain welcomed the onset of the factory system. He believed that its advantages were 'healthier work-places, regularity of hours, economy of labour, increased demand, lower prices, and at the same time higher wages'. His views are unsurprising. He was a partner in the screw-making firm of Nettlefold and Chamberlain - which is recalled in the huge modern combine of GKN (Guest, Keen and Nettlefold); and his great wealth was made from a highly mechanised factory in Broad Street. This and others in Birmingham turned out 130,000 gross of screws each week. Given the superior social and economic benefits which he believed were conferred by factories, Chamberlain declared that they would soon dominate the industrial structure of the town. He envisaged the 'extinction of the small manufacturers as such' and their 'employment as overlookers, or foremen in large establishments'. This assumption was incorrect.

Wedding of Joses Downing and Gladys Irene Eggison, 22 October, 1922, taken at 11, Tennyson Road, Small Heath. (Kaye Downing)

There is no doubt that big factories were more and more visible in Birmingham, and for the reasons which Chamberlain had given. But the variety of trades in the town and the independent nature of many skilled men and women ensured that numerous medium and small manufacturing businesses continued to be set up in the 'classic way'. This phenomenon was exemplified by the tin plate works of Thomas Brough, started in 1889 at his home 15-16, Loveday Street. Here, he and his wife raised their family amidst the production of tea urns, coffee pots, lanterns and potato mashers. Similarly, the wire-working business of William Small was begun in 1871, at 71, Moseley Street where he lived with his wife and six children. Over time, the firm expanded and took over the adjoining houses from numbers 72 to 75. Today, the company of F. L. and E. Small continues as wire fabricators on the same site. The façade of the dwellings has been preserved and some of the original interiors remain as offices.

Further evidence of enterprising workers who confounded Chamberlain's prediction is provided by the family engineering business of John Bradley. This was founded at the turn of the twentieth century.

> **The money which my grandfather put into the company to start with was partly won in a court case against a large national engineering company. My grandad was an engineer and millwright (gas engines, oil engines that powered machinery in factories etc & reciprocating engines or nodding donkeys) which one sees in the working of small oil wells. He had an inventive mind, & designed a method for bending steel pipes & patented it. He found out that a large firm was using this method without consulting him. My father was working for John Bradley. He also was an engineer. My father was sent to check if the larger company was contravening JB's patent & found out that it was so. Hence the court case and the award of damages. (William John Bradley, *Letter*, 1993)**

John Bradley's business prospered so that by the 1930s, in just one shop in the factory, there were 28 machines. The firm continued until the early 1980s when it was taken over by a larger company.

Below the medium-sized businesses such as this one were a multitude of small manufacturers. Some employed a few workers, others were 'one-man bands'. The Downings were members of a family which seemed to typify the versatility and skills of many of the small gaffers of Birmingham. They also exemplified the manner in which manufacturing and art overlapped with each other and were not divided sharply. In the late eighteenth century, Thomas Downing was a jobbing smith, someone who did whatever kind of work he could. Unlike him, his son Joses was a specialist and carried on a business as a wood carver and smith making wares which were based on medieval styles. In turn, his son, Thomas, became a well-known Birmingham artist who married Emilie Harris, a professional singer and teacher. Her mother was a pianist, her father was a piano tuner, but her paternal grandfather was a timber merchant.

The son of Thomas and Emilie was another Joses Downing and his wife was Gladys Irene Eggison, the daughter of a commercial traveller. On her mother's side, her grandfather was a weaver's male manufacturer, and her great grandfather was a cabinet maker and timber merchant; whilst her father was the son of William Eggison - a man who was catholic in his business interests. He was a brewer and publican at 'The Roebuck' on Aston Road, he carried on as a wholesale coal merchant nearby at Chester Street Wharf, and he was also a lamp manufacturer. Descended from artists and manufacturers, the daughter of Gladys and Joses continued into the late twentieth century the traditions of her family. As a designer at Dunlop Tyres, Kaye Downing highlighted the essential connection between art and industry.

That bond was as obvious in the careers of those who moved from the professional middle class into business, a trend epitomised by Charles Gabriel. The son of the vicar of All Saints, he served an apprenticeship with Tangye's before buying a small brass foundry in A.B. Row in 1884. Beginning with 13 workers, Gabriel's firm flourished and started to specialise in the manufacture of fittings for trams, buses and trains. In 1914, the business was boosted by its owner's development and patenting of a new alloy called 'Clarus's Metal' which was 'as light as aluminium, but stronger than brass'. Today, Gabriel's remains on its original site and whilst its brass and aluminium foundries have closed, it has acquired a high reputation in the design and production of steel handrail systems for buses and coaches, and for stainless steel castings, hygienic pipe fittings and tubular assemblies. (*Gabriel & Company Ltd 1884-1984, Centenary,* 1984; my account is based on this booklet).

Of course, not all small businesses prospered in this way. There were many which failed, whilst there were large numbers which had insufficient capital and were carried on in dilapidated premises. In the Hurst Street of the 1920s and 1930s:

> **"The street to me then seemed a busy little hive of industry. In some of the back yards among the people living there were small factories originally I suppose they were houses. The men workers made tin kettles, saucepans, and draw tins to draw the coal fires alight to enable the women to cook on the black ranges. The conditions were deplorable, not protected by any factory rules. You climbed rickety wooden steps to get to the factories and the noise was awful. No one complained because it was work, for money was hard to get. Some factories did Poster Signs, Engraving, Etching, watch making & repairs. (Mrs V. Connor, *Letter,* 1993)"**

Of all the Birmingham manufactures, the jewellery trade was that which was associated most with small gaffers, craft workers and Dickensian conditions.

THE JEWELLERY QUARTER

In the later 1700s, silver was a vital material locally in the making of buckles and in the plating of wares. Gold was utilised to a lesser extent by platers, although there were a number of specialists who worked it into seals, keys and watch chains. However, by the middle years of the nineteenth century, its use had increased greatly. This was because of a combination of factors. First, in 1824, the Birmingham Assay Office was allowed to mark articles made from gold. Second, from the 1840s, its supply became available more readily through the mines of California and Australia. Third, articles made with precious materials were becoming more popular because upper and middle-class people had greater sums of money to spend on luxury items. In itself, this affluence had resulted from the spectacular growth in the wealth of England and which had been gained from the nation's industrial and imperial supremacy. Fourth, electro-plating led to better quality products. Finally, gold jewellery became more popular because of the public's growing 'desire for personal adornment'.

Birmingham and its workers were in a good position to take advantage of this wish because it had a large number of skilled people who were 'inventive and artistic'; and they were able to set up as master jewellers without a great capital outlay. In 1866, J. S. Wright stated that all they needed was 'a peculiarly shaped bench and a leather apron, one or two

Silversmith at Adie Brothers, manufacturing silversmiths of Soho Hill and Great Hampton Street, about 1930s. (Birmingham Library Services)

pounds worth of tools (including a blow pipe), and for material, a few sovereigns, and some ounces of copper and zinc'. A gas jet was essential, but this was provided by the gas company on credit; whilst cheap premises were found in the top-room of the jeweller's home, in the small buildings over the communal wash-houses which were common in the poorer neighbourhoods of Birmingham, or in houses which had been sub-divided. Once established in this way, the self-employed small gaffer could make scarf pins, studs, links, rings and lockets which he would sell to a factor (dealer) who came round on a Saturday.

Almost 100 years later, these features continued to mark out the jewellery trade. Gwen Sly's dad was an engraver who worked mostly in gold and 'he derived enormous pleasure in creating designs on ladies' brush sets, powder compacts, cigarette casks, etc.'. In the 1940s he was self-employed and:

> **The house in which my father rented a room was in Augusta Street and had been built around 1830. It must have been a prosperous dwelling in its day where the jeweller lived two up and two down with 'shopping' at the back where he plied his trade. When my father moved in there was a watchmaker in one room, a diamond setter in another, a polisher in a third, and a stamper in the shopping. To this little hive of industry which was repeated all over the 'Quarter' porters from the various factors used to fetch and carry all the work to be done or completed . . . These porters who appeared to me to be about 100 years old but were probably in their 60s, bent with rheumatism, would shuffle round the streets pushing a basket carriage containing parcels of silver and gold goods. No-one expected they might be mugged... Even the slightest push would have knocked them over. At the end of the day they would wend their way to the Post Office and despatch their valuable cargo to customers not only in this country but all over the world. I wonder if the wearers of this jewellery ever realised how many craftsmen, each working in his five-bob-a-week room, had been involved in producing a work of art from the raw material within that fascinating area 'The Jewellery', (Letter, 1993)**

Like all industries, the jewellery trade was susceptible to slumps in the economy; but because its products were luxury items and not basic commodities, it is likely that recessions affected its workers more harshly than most. Frank Sly was unemployed for part of the 1920s, as was Eric Armstrong's gem-setter father. His son recalled that during his dad's frequent lay-offs from work, he was sometimes taken on as an outworker. On these occasions, 'my parent's bedroom would be converted into a temporary workshop complete with jeweller's specially shaped workbench, leather apron to catch the precious metals filings and scrap, hand drills spun back and forth with leather thongs, and other tools of the jeweller's trade'. (Eric Armstrong, *On the Sentimental Side,* unpublished manuscript, 1992)

Despite the vagaries of demand, the manufacture of jewellery was one of the biggest sources of jobs in Birmingham. Its importance was acknowledged locally, as was the connection of its prosperity to high-quality work. In the late eighteenth century, this had not been the case. Like the minters of coins, some of the precious metal workers of the town had been associated with inferior products. This was reflected in an old saying which went 'Give a Birmingham maker a guinea and a copper kettle and he'll make you a hundred pounds of jewellery.' Opprobrium such as this came to be dispelled because of the stringency of the marking of the Assay Office and because jewellers recognised that they had to make sound and attractive wares if their long-term employment was to be secured.

It was for this reason that the School for Jewellers and Silversmiths was established in Vittoria Street. This was managed by a committee drawn from the Birmingham School of Art (from 1912, part of the local education authority) and the town's Jewellers' and Silversmiths' Association. This latter body also made an annual grant towards the maintenance of the school, and with the education committee, it paid the fees of its students who attended night classes and some in an afternoon. Today the school is part of the University of Central England.

Shoppers watching the making of jewellery in a small workshop in the Jewellery Quarter, 1980s. (Birmingham Library Services)

Skill in making jewellery depends on good eyesight, steady hands and a flair for artistry. As a result it is a trade that is difficult to mechanise. Still, by the turn of the twentieth century some powered machinery had been introduced which allowed the manufacture of standardised products for a mass market. Although, as Thomas Anderton put it in 1900, this did not lead to 'large factories with tall towering stacks, powerful steam engines etc', it did encourage the emergence of big workshops. Amongst them was that of James Harrison. He began his business in Tenby Street in 1880 with a capital of £50, and whilst his firm later sold jewellery to retailers, its main business was making rings and other jewellery for wholesalers. James retired to London as a wealthy man and the firm was taken over by his sons Francis and Wilfred, later by his grandson Trevor, and more recently by his great-grandsons, David and Colin. Having moved to larger premises in Warstone Lane after 1945, they employed 70 people in their workshop, offices and on the road as representatives. Despite the sale of the business in the late 1980s, members of the family remain active in the jewellery trade.

Another large manufacturing jeweller's was the firm of Smith & Pepper. Like that of Harrison's it was situated in the Jewellery Quarter - that part of Hockley which became the centre of the trade in the 1830s. The works of Smith and Pepper in Vyse Street opened in 1899 and closed down in 1980. The departing owners and workers left behind them their papers, benches, tools, equipment and machinery. These lay undisturbed until funding from the City Council allowed a working museum to be established. The award-winning Jewellery Quarter Discovery Centre is surrounded by the workshops of craftsmen and women and by over 100 jewellery retailers - an indication of the continuing significance of Birmingham's jewellery trade.

WOMEN WORKERS

As in most Birmingham manufactures, women were prominent in the making of jewellery. They were employed in great numbers as outworkers, and they were present also in large workshops like that of Smith and Pepper. By 1911, they constituted 35% of the total workforce in the jewellery trade - although that was an official statistic which did not take into account part-time and irregular employment. Like other occupations, many women in jewellery making were kept from the most skilled work by the prejudices of male employers and workers. The former feared that it was uneconomical to train women to a craft because they would leave work when they married or became pregnant; the latter opposed the passing of skills to females because they feared that women would work for less money than men - and that this would lead to male joblessness. And of course, many men believed that the rightful place for a woman was in the home and not in the workplace.

Kathleen Dayus had to contend with these attitudes when she worked in The Jewellery Quarter just after the First World War. After a number of different jobs, she settled to 'learning to enamel brooches and badges and motor plates at Fray's in Tenby Street North'. The work was interesting, although 'all I was doing was learning how to "lay on"; that is, apply the powdered glass on the metal prior to firing in the kiln'. Feeling that she wanted to stretch herself, Kathleen Dayus sought to learn 'all the aspects of the process from grinding the enamel to firing, filing and polishing'. But she was prevented from doing so by 'an informal apprenticeship system' which aimed to stop the small gaffers having competition.

This operated by slowing down the passing on of skills. Workers had to spend three years at laying on before they could move on to another part of the job, 'and at that rate I would be middle-aged before I was expert in all the processes of enamelling'. Astutely, the young female worker left her position as soon as she had gained her skills in laying on. At her next job she made sure that she was trained in a different aspect of enamelling - and once again moved on. In this way she learned all of the operations to do with enamelling. By the Second World War she was able to set up on her own and she built up a thriving business. (Kathleen Dayus, *Her People,* 1982, and *Where There's Life,* 1985)

In spite of the bias with which they had to contend sometimes, women made a vital contribution to the prosperity of the jewellery trade. In the process, some of them did pick up certain skills and came to enjoy their work. One of them was Kate May Argyle. At the age of 14 in 1922, she began work at Broughton's in St Paul's Square.

66When she had her first day there she liked it so much that when she got home she was eager to get back in the afternoon. She made 'Alberts' which were men's watch chains . . . When my granny was making the chains, she had a few links that were loose that she joined together by soldering but the one thing was she had to be careful that they did not roll up into balls when they were too hot. When she first got there it did not matter if it happened because she was learning. She had silver to start with, not gold. They had to be twisted, then after that they had to be taken to the foreman, and if they broke the foreman 'didn't half look at you'. The foreman twisted them to see if they would break and then she'd have to go back and redo them if they broke. She also made women's necklaces which were tedious and very tiring to make. She had to pick up two pairs of pliers and she picked up the link to solder them together. She soldered it and picked up another one

Women workers making Mills hand grenades in the Bridge Street West factory, 1916.
(Birmingham Library Services)

and soldered it and picked up another one and carried on.
(Victoria Allen, 'My Granny in the Jewellery Quarter', by a
pupil at Colmore Road Junior School,
in Sue Cook, Sue Fenoughty & Erica Pounce,
compilers, *The Child's Vanishing Landscape*, 1993) ”

Women workers were so important in Birmingham, that in 1857 one commentator exclaimed that many of the town's manufactures would be 'annihilated' if their labour was suspended. Their jobs were extensive. In the Gun Quarter, females were employed as stock-barrel smoothers, whilst at the B.S.A. they worked as machinists; in the brass trade, they were lacquerers, solderers and burnishers and they operated presses and stamps; in minting, they sorted and wrapped the coins; and in rope-making, they were spinners. Many of these women were married and were paid low wages. Some were widows, others were abandoned by their partners, and a lot were married to unskilled men whose incomes were insufficient to support their families. In a period when there was no welfare state and when the spectre of the workhouse haunted the lives of so many working-class people, large numbers of married women 'collared' because their earnings were crucial to the survival of their families. They were unfortunate not to receive the recognition or remuneration they deserved; but in Birmingham, unlike the mining districts and shipbuilding towns, at least there were industrial jobs for married women. In this respect, the city had similarities with Manchester, the cotton towns of the North-West of England, the woollen districts of West Yorkshire, and the East End of London.

LABOUR RELATIONS

In a further difference to areas which were dominated by heavy industry, Birmingham was not a place where acute class conflict characterised social and economic relations. Indeed, the city seemed to be marked out by the moderation of its workers, the conciliatory attitudes of its employers and the political co-operation between the working and middle classes. Asa Briggs has attributed this phenomenon to the multiform industrial base of Birmingham. Both the varieties of trades in the city and the importance of hand crafts encouraged the proliferation of small gaffers. Formerly, these had been skilled men and this meant that there was not a wide gulf betewen them and their workers. At the same time, the small gaffers were examples of social and economic mobility: in times of plenty, they had set up in business for themselves; when trade slackened, they might slip back into the ranks of the employed.

These features of Birmingham life were commented on favourably by national politicians like Richard Cobden, by celebrated authors such as George Eliot, and by local observers like Samuel Timmins and J. Thackeray Bunce. They were noticed as much by foreign writers. In 1895, P. de Rousiers visited a small workshop. Depending on the state of his trade, the gaffer gave employment to between 10 and 20 skilled men. He had begun life as a worker and had prospered through 'self-help and perseverance'. Alongside his employees, he worked a 55 hour week, although often he did more because his workshop was in the same premises as his house. Having once been employed himself, he was seen as a harder master than were some big factory owners, but 'he knew all his men by their names, and social relationships were direct and personal.' (P. de Rousiers, *La Question Ouvrière en Angleterre,* 1895, cited in Asa Briggs, *History of Birmingham. Volume II. Borough and City 1865-1938,* 1952)

The small gaffers of Birmingham made a bridge between the skilled workers of the city and its larger employers. Many of these were imbued with the ideas of the Civic Gospel. This was preached by Non-Conformist ministers like George Dawson and R. W. Dale. It held that wealthy citizens had a duty to make Birmingham a healthy place in which to live

Samuel Heath presenting long-service awards to Wal Mason of Studley Street and Nelly George, 1950s. (Samuel Heath, managing director, Samuel Heath & Sons plc)

for all of its people. This belief was taken on board enthusiastically by a number of Unitarian and Quaker families like the Nettlefolds, Kenricks, Beales and Cadburys. Led by Joseph Chamberlain, they adopted the idea of municipal socialism. As capitalists and employers, they argued that certain utilities were essential to the well-being of the inhabitants of Birmingham. Because of this, they proposed that these utilities should be controlled by the elected representatives of the people. Accordingly, after they took control of the council in the early 1870s, the adherents of the Civic Gospel municipalised the city's water, gas and electricity supplies. This commitment to the beneficial power of local government continued into the twentieth century and was made clear when Neville Chamberlain established the Birmingham Municipal Bank - the only example of its kind in Britain.

Throughout the city, many employers adhered to the principle that they ought 'to put something back into the community'. In 1845, the Quaker corn dealer and politician Joseph Sturge was influential in setting up Severn Street School where men and women were taught to read and write early on a Sunday morning. Its teachers included many leading Birmingham businessmen: Cadburys, Albrights the chemical manufacturers, Lloyds, Wilsons the india-rubber producers, Tangyes, Southalls, and Hoylands the bedstead makers. The success of the Severn Street School was so great that it led to similar institutions outside Birmingham, and in 1884 together they formed the forerunner of the Midland Adult School Union which continues to operate.

But not all philanthropic employers were councillors or Quakers. In the early 1920s, the Jewish businessman Bertie Samuelson shared out 100 guineas each Christmas to 50 families who were in poverty; whilst his co-religionist, Leon Salburg, was renowned for raising money for good causes. He was the principal proprietor of the Alexandra Theatre which was 'freely at call for charity concerts' arranged by the Rocket Club - of which he was a member - 'and thousands of pounds had thus been raised' by 1947.

Anglican industrialists were as concerned at playing a wider role in the community. In 1860, James Horsfall paid for the building of a school room at Hay Mills where the children of his workers could be educated, and fourteen years later 'his liberality' led to the opening of St Cyprian's Church. The Heaths were also committed to the neighbourhood of their factory, and they remain proud of their continuing employment for men and women of all ethnic groups who live there; whilst Bellis and Morcom, partners in an engineering factory in Ladywood, organised annual Christmas parties for local children of the poor. (Victor J. Price, *Birmingham Yesterday: its places & people,* 1991)

Today this business is part of a larger group, N.E.I.-A.P.E., as is the works of Ephraim Phillips in Bissell Street. Now owned by Bauer & Schaurte Karcher Ltd, it was started in 1874 by another gaffer who was close to his employees. Arthur Hunt's father worked in this factory which made screws and nuts, and he told his children:

> **❝of travelling by horse bus to work in Bissell Street... He rose to become a foreman toolmaker and when he retired there was no pension scheme, but his employers gave him 10/- a week and Mr Phillips came to his house just before Christmas every year until he died (age 89) with a hamper of 'goodies'. (Letter, 1992)❞**

Close to the factory of Ephraim Phillips was the head office of Harry Payne, another businessman who was well known for his concern with the welfare of his workers. In the later nineteenth century he had left Northampton to start as a shoe maker in Highgate, and by the 1960s his firm had 80 branches in and about Birmingham. The success of each was due greatly to good relations which resulted from the active participation of employees within the firm as a whole.

As with the record of employers in Birmingham, that of the city's workers' organisations is generally one of moderation. This feature is epitomised by the career of W. J. Davis, leader of the Brass Workers. His paternal grandfather was 'a brass fender maker in a small way', whilst his mother's father was a jeweller and electro-plate manufacturer. Despite these family connections, Davis experienced poverty as a child, and by the age of nine he was at work. Four years later, he was in the brass trade and in 1872 he became secretary of the newly-formed Brassworkers' Society. He remained in this post until 1921, and he became a strong advocate of conciliation and arbitration. Indeed, to facilitate these objectives, in 1896 he demanded that the employers form an organisation with which his trade union could deal effectively.

The tradition of trade unionists like Davis is evident today in the attitudes of Bill Jordan, the Brummie General Secretary of the Engineering and Electrical Workers' Union. But it would be foolish to believe that there were no conflicts between capital and labour in Birmingham. There were. Arthur Chamberlain was an employer who was a member of a family which was held up as an example of caring factory owners, but he was staunch in his antagonism towards trade unionism. There were others who shared his antipathy and some who were harsh in their dealings with their workers.

> **“We used to have to work in the days. When I was at Giles and Ward… time was 7 o' clock in the morning and at twenty past seven, I worked with this feller Jack Smith, and he says 'mek a can of tea, Bill'. So, of course, we hadn't got the canteens like they got today, hadn't facilities, 'cus it was a casting shop. So I had to go down and hot one of the cans of water in one of the old castings, you know, and old Giles come through and he says to me, 'Chinn, what're you doing!' He could see what I was doing, mekking a can of tea. 'Go and put your coat on'. That was twenty past seven in the morning. When I went back up into the shop, I was… putting me coat on and the foreman come to me, old Sammy Savage, and he says, 'What's a matter, Bill?' I said, 'I got the sack.' He said, 'Got the sack? What for?' I said, 'The gaffer's come down the bottom shop, copped me mekking a can of tea, he's told me to go and put me coat on'. (William Chinn, *Interview*, 1979)”**

Striking railway carriage and waggon workers with their strike boxes in High Street, Saltley, 1908. (Birmingham Library Services)

Children in yard of back-to-back houses in Unett Street, about 1964. (Birmingham Library Services)

A few years later and along with other workers, my great uncle Bill was locked out of the B.S.A.. At that time, the gaffer was reputed to have said 'put the chains around the gate, when they've got empty bellies, they'll come into work'. My Grandad Perry also lost his job through a lack of consideration of the rights of workers. He was a band-saw operator in a small die-casting shop in Highgate, and after 29 years employment he and other long-serving workers were laid off with no redundancy or severance pay. According to Our Mom, 'it broke his heart, but he got a job the next day as an attendant at the Art Gallery'.

If relations between employers and employees were not always typified by co-operation and conciliatory attitudes, neither was Birmingham a place from which poverty had been banished. The manufacturers of the city relied greatly on the low-paid employment of women, teenagers and unskilled men. These people could afford to rent only the worst-quality housing. This was of the back-to-back type, and in the 1930s one in five Brummies lived in these tiny three-roomed structures.

> **❝I was born at my grannie's house at 79, Cheapside. There was not any water, gas or electricity in the house at all. The water and toilet was at the back courtyard, where also was the communal brewhouse. Neighbours took turns to do their washing in the boiler, which was fuelled by old boots, slack, wood etc. The neighbours also shared outside toilets. The lighting in gran's house was candles, and an oil lamp. Cooking was all done on the fire with ovens at the side. I don't remember my mother who died age 24 yrs in 1926. I was the eldest of 3 children who were all born in the attic by candlelight. (J. Hill, *Letter*, 1992) ❞**

THE CITY OF A THOUSAND TRADES

Under the direction of Joseph Chamberlain, Birmingham gained the reputation of 'the best-governed city in the world'. But behind the façade of improvements like the Corporation Street shopping thoroughfare, there was a Birmingham of deprivation, ill-health and early death. Notions as to the prosperity and comfort of the city's working class have to be challenged. What cannot be disputed is Birmingham's title as 'the city of a thousand trades'.

By the end of the nineteenth century, goods 'made in Birmingham' were to be found across the world. Whether 'sleeping or waking, walking or riding, in a carriage, or upon a railway or steamboat' the town's wares could not be avoided. Its axes, hoes, shovels, spades, hatchets and crowbars were to be found in Brazil as in Egypt, the West Indies as in the East Indies; its saws were used widely in India; its saddles were bought throughout Australia and South Africa; and its rice bowls were popular with Arab peoples. Some of the town's products were those which Brummies today feel ashamed of, such as slave manacles and collars. But most Birmingham articles were a source of pride for the people of the town, and they remain so. We may decry the poverty, unhealthiness and dirt that were associated with so many of our manufactures, but we remain staunch in our attachment to the making of things. This adherence is centuries old and it is evoked in the inscription on the tombstone of John Dowler, a blacksmith:

> **"My sledge and hammer lie reclined,**
> **My bellows, too, have lost their wind.**
> **My fire's extinct, my forge decayed,**
> **And in the dust, my vice is laid;**
> **My coal is spent, my iron gone;**
> **My nails are drove, my work is done."**

(John Dowler's epitaph, Aston Parish Churchyard, 1787)

Paper mills of Smith, Stone & Knight, Landor Street, 1895. (Birmingham Library Services)

The people of Birmingham take as much satisfaction from the astonishment of commentators like Robert Rawlinson. In 1849, he wrote that there were about 2,600 varieties of occupation in Birmingham; and by 1870, *Kelly's Directory* was listing 953 types of firm in the town. We proclaim to the outside world that we were the 'City of a Thousand Trades' and we wish that we could still make this boast. For we took it for granted that a variety of jobs were available for us to choose from. In the words of Ada Theay:

> **"being born in Fisher Street, 1913, when starting work,**
> **one had the choice of Perries Pens. I gave that a go. The**
> **Button factory in Potter Street. The Cabinet Maker's. I got a**
> **job putting together coggs for the three wheeling bikes.**
> **Then went to the paper works in Moland Street. I was 16.**
> **After getting married the first house I had which mother got**
> **me was being caretaker to the paper mills in Moland**
> **Street, and it was Smith, Stone and Knight. (*Letter*, 1993)."**

NOTES

In the research for this chapter, I have been helped by the following people: Professor Christopher Dyer, School of History; The University of Birmingham, Dr David Ingram, School of Geography; The University of Birmingham, David Perry, Corporate Banking Area Manager of Midland Bank PLC; Samuel Heath, Managing Director of Samuel Heath & Sons PLC; Eric Falck, of Hoskins Ltd; M.D.H. Johnson of Martineau Johnson Solicitors, for sight of his unpublished manuscript, *Josiah Mason;* Mrs Philips of John Hardman; Margaret Probert - for the information on W.H. Probert; Guy Horsfall of Webster and Horsfall, Latch and Bachelor Ltd; Kaye Downing - for her family tree; Mrs R. Brain, for her information on the Brough family which is included in, *I Remember,* unpublished manuscript (1989); Ron Eamonson, managing director F. L. and E. Small; Mike Olley for the material on Gabriel's; Roger Minifie of the Jewellery Quarter Discovery Centre; Mary Ford of Local Studies and History Section, Birmingham Central Library; Leslie Hill of the Midland Adult School Union; Brian Watkeys and Jack Payne; Audrey Green, for the booklet on the Unitarians of Birmingham; Trevor Hancock and Ivor Sankey for the book on the Rocket Club; Kate Jenns for information on women in business; and Joan Gumsley for the maps of Birmingham.

FURTHER READING

The works recommended below are in addition both to those given in full in this chapter and to those mentioned in Chapter 1.

Asa Briggs   *History of Birmingham, Volume II, Borough and City,* 1865-1938 (1952)

This book should be added to the list of works which I have found indispensable.

Thomas Anderton	*A Tale of One City* (1900)
Emily Bushrod	*The Birmingham Unitarians 1692-1973* (no date)
R. A. Church	*Kenricks in Hardware. A Family Business 1791-1966* (1969)
William A. Dalley	*The Life Story of W.J. Davis* (1914)
Catherine Hall	'The butcher, the baker, the candlestickmaker: the shop and the family in the Industrial Revolution', in, R. J. Morris & Richard Rodger (eds), *The Victorian City. A Reader in British Urban History, 1820-1914* (1993)
Douglas J. Hallam,	*The first 200 Years. A Short History of Rabone Chesterman Limited* (1984)
Olly Hill and Micky Fraser	*The Rocket Club. Being the history of a unique Birmingham Institution* (1949)
Geoff Hitchman	'Rookery House', in, *Bygone Birmingham,* December/January, 1993, Volume 1, no. 4
A. R. Holmes and Edwin Green	*Midland. 150 Years of Banking Business* (1986)
John Morris Jones	*The Cole Valley South (The Millstream Way), the history of a Birmingham River* (1989)
Hugh Miller	*First Impressions of England and its People* (1847)
J. B. Priestley	*English Journey* (1934)
R. B. Prosser	*Birmingham Inventors and Inventions* (1881)
Barbara Tilson (ed)	*Made in Birmingham. Design and Industry 1889-1989* (1989)
A. de Tocqueville	*Journeys to England and Ireland* (1835)
William White	*The Story of the Severn Street and Priory First-Day Schools, Birmingham* (1895)

CHAPTER 3
MOTOR CITY

The Aston Expressway approaching BirminghamCity Centre. (Roy Peters Photography)

FORWARD

There is one constant in the history of Birmingham: change. The survival of the city as a great centre of population has depended upon the ability of its citizens to adapt, to adjust, to move on and to transform their trades, their streets and their buildings. In 1983, Beryl Bainbridge imitated the English journey which J. B. Priestley had made 50 years before. She wrote that everywhere she walked, 'buildings were either going up or coming down, or else roads were being widened to take yet more cars'. She shrank from this 'endless process of construction and destruction'. Like many people, she castigated Birmingham as a 'hell'. But in common with most such attacks, her denunciation was based on a short stay in the city and it showed a lack of understanding for the historical processes which had made it 'a great working town'.

If Birmingham is to continue as a workplace and if it is not to decline into insignificance, then its people must continue to be sensitive to changes in society and to new demands for goods and services. At its most basic, Birmingham grew from a hamlet to the workshop of the world because it provided jobs for those who were born there and who came to it from other parts. The future of the city lies with this elemental connection with work. It is because of the recognition of this harsh reality that the citizens of Birmingham greeted the coming of the car. For this reason, we are as proud of our title as 'motor city' as we were of that of 'the thousand trades'. Those who denounce manufacturing as dirty and uninspiring ought to remember this.

Our affection for cars does not mean that we ignore the mistakes that were made when planners redesigned our city centre for the benefit of motor vehicles. We agree with Dervla Murphy that this led to the building of 'weirdly coiling concrete car-parks'; and we concur that the Inner Ring Road was a disaster. It collared the shopping district of 'town', cutting it off from the rest of Birmingham with a wide circle of buses, lorries, cars and fumes. It brought underpasses for walkers which are 'all sullen and soiled and drab even on a bright midsummer day'; and it gave us 'wind-swept pedestrian bridges high above the whine and roar of racing traffic'. (Dervla Murphy, *A Tale of Two Cities,* 1985)

The council is now set on freeing us from these monstrosities. On the Inner Ring Road, it is putting transport below ground and people above it. But the problems associated with cars do not make us regret their arrival. Mostly, we welcome the motor vehicle. It has brought us jobs and it has democratised travel. And with the presence of the car industry, we recognise the continuing importance of our manufacturing heritage. For the making of motor vehicles has benefited from the skills of Birmingham workers as much as it has gained from the willingness of local manufacturers to welcome scientific advance and to adopt new sources of power.

GAS ENERGY

Although Birmingham was not renowned for its use of steam, it was associated with the development and utilisation of gas power. The first works for this purpose were built in the aptly-named Gas Street in 1817, and within a few years most of the town was lighted by this form of energy. After 1875, the private suppliers were taken over by the Corporation and by the early twentieth century, it was selling gas in great quantities to householders for cooking and lighting purposes. At the same time, the use of this energy had become more widespread in manufacturing, so that by 1913 over 20% of gas sold in the city was for these purposes. It was utilised for annealing, hardening, tempering, welding, lacquering, japaning and glass making; it was especially helpful in the melting of metals; and it provided industrial heating and lighting.

The city's main gas works were at Nechells and Saltley where, in the 1870s, Will Thorne obtained:

> **❝the means of earning my bread by wheeling away coke from a gang of stokers in the retort house. The work was hot and very hard. As the coke was drawn from the retort on to the ground we threw pails of water on it, and the heat, both from the ovens and the clouds of steam that would rise from the drenched coke, was great.**
> **Once cooled the coke had to be wheeled away and pitched on to a big heap. For this we used a great six-pronged fork. It was gruelling work. The place was running night and day. We worked a twelve-hour night for two weeks, and then a twelve-hour day for the next two weeks. The change-over from day work to night work was dreadful. Ordinarily the work was agonising - twelve hours a day in heat and steam, and exposed to draughts; bending and straining the back and arms, taxing the muscles until they became numb - but the change-over multiplied this.**
> **We would start work at six o' clock on a Sunday morning, the last day in a two-week shift, and work the twenty-four hours right through until six o' clock on Monday morning. Every extra hour after the first twelve seemed like a month, and when these twenty-four hour stretches came to an end, I used to be absolutely exhausted in body and mind. (Will Thorne, *My Life's Story*, 1925)❞**

Thorne was determined to change this pattern of work and he convinced his fellow workers to stand out for the abolition of Sunday shifts. After he approached the management, the Gas Committee of the council visited the Saltley Works. Led by Joseph Chamberlain, its members agreed to the demand of the men. After this victory, Crooks tried to form a union and he led a strike. Whilst he was 'out' he went to London where he later founded the Gasworkers' Union and became a Labour M.P. for West Ham, although his birthplace in Farm Street is recorded by a plaque put up by Birmingham Civic Society.

The aftermath of the great gas explosion at the Gas Works in Duddeston Mill Road, 10 October 1904.
(Birmingham Library Services)

GENERATING ELECTRICITY

Laying the electricity cables in Berner Street Lozells, 1905. (Garth Luckuck, Head of Distribution Maintenance, M.E.B.)

Because of the ready availability of gas and because its sale was an efficient municipal enterprise, the demand for electricity was low in Birmingham. It was not until 1892 that a private company began to generate and supply this alternative source of power. Five years later, from its stations in Dale End and Water Street, it had 916 customers in the town centre, Edgbaston and Hockley. There was a growing call for electrical power elsewhere in the city. Encouraged by this, the council purchased the operations of the Birmingham Electricity Supply Company at the end of 1899. The price was £420,000 but this was recouped because of the massive growth in the number of electrical units sold: in 1901 these stood at 3,042,822, by 1913 they totalled over 63,000,000. A third of this figure was accounted for by the city's tram system, but a significant part of it was responsible for the running of machinery.

In 1947 the city's gas and electricity departments became part of nationalised industries, but their contribution to the powering of the city's factories before that date was great. This is indicated by the change in the driving force of the machines of one firm. The Birmingham Battery & Metal Co. Ltd, founded in 1836, manufactured brass and copper wares at its Digbeth factory. Heavy machinery was powered by steam, but by 1900 at new premises in Selly Oak, a gas engine had been introduced to the tube mill. Within the next 26 years, the factory was all electric. Working at Burman's, where the factory remains in Ryland Street, Arthur Williams recalled how this force was utilised by manufacturers:

> **"In factories today all the machines are powered separately, but then machines were powered by one large electric motor which worked a shaft which extended the whole length of the machine shop. Over each machine was a counter-shaft and so via pullies on the main shaft and counter shafts and leather belts the power was transferred to each machine. (Arthur Williams, *A Pre-Amble on Life as it Has Been for Me,* unpublished manuscript, 1986)."**

ELECTRICAL ENGINEERING

The expansion in the generating of electricity stimulated the making of dynamos, motor magnetos, pumps, meters, transformers and other machinery which depended upon or which catered for this type of power. It also gave a boost to electrical lighting, heating and cooking products. In response to this demand, many Birmingham brassfounders extended their range of goods to include switches and light fittings and firms like Best and Lloyd have gained a high reputation in this field; others moved fully into making electrical products. An example of this trend was William McGeoch and Company. Founded in 1832 by an ironmonger and brassfounder, it now trades as an electrical enginering manufacturer, as do a number of businesses which were formed specifically for this purpose. In 1901, the General Electric Company opened a factory at a 240 acre site in Witton where it made heavier electrical plant, fans and carbon batteries. At a later date, another works at Landor Street was the place at which were manufactured electrical goods for the household; whilst the associated firm of Chamberlain and Hookham made electricity meters at a factory in Bartholomew Street.

By the inter-war years, G.E.C. was employing over 10,000 people in Birmingham and was one of the world's largest suppliers and installers of electrical engineering products. It was not the only such business in the city, for in Tyseley there was the Midland Electrical

Manufacturing Company. Along with GEC, it remains a major local employer, as does Lucas Industries. Like many other firms of significance in modern Birmingham, this company is rooted in the city's past and in the skills, innovations and hard work of its people.

Joseph Lucas was born in Carver Street in 1834. His father was a plater and it is believed that the son himself worked at Elkington's. After a period of unemployment, he earned a living by selling paraffin from a basket carriage as he travelled around Hockley. From 1860, he was also merchandising hollow ware - buckets, shovels, scoops and galvanised chamber pots. Lucas was a small gaffer who did well and instead of retailing his goods he began to sell them wholesale to such effect that in 1869-70, one customer purchased oil to the value of £100.

An early advertisement for a Lucas paraffin lamp. (Thanks to Roy White)

Within the next few years, the enterprising Lucas had added to his business the making of a type of oil lamp for ships. These were called Tom Bowlings and the rights for their manufacture were bought from Isaac Sherwood, a lamp and chandelier maker of Granville Street. A friend called George Thomas recalled how Lucas set about their production.

> **One day Joseph sent me a message: 'Come down and see me this evening, George, I've got something that will interest you. 'I went to 209 Great King Street and there he showed me a ship's lamp. 'I want to make it,' he said, 'but how am I going to get the men to do it?' 'Leave it to me', I replied, and the next day I went down to Elkington's as the staff were leaving and I picked five of their best men. They all agreed to join Joseph Lucas if he could find a workshop. He did, a place round the corner in Little King Street, which he called Tom Bowling Lamp Works after the name of the lamp, and these five men were the first people to work there. I joined him as works foreman. (cited in Harold Nockolds, *Lucas. The First 100 years. Volume 1: The King of the Road*, 1976. My account of Lucas is based on this book.)**

During 1878, Lucas added to his products a bicycle lamp which was called the King of the Road. This proved a successful move. The riding of bikes was becoming very popular, so much so that councils had begun to pass bye-laws which required cyclists to have a light on their machines when it was dark.

From these beginnings, the firm of Joseph Lucas and Son expanded greatly. A new and larger factory was built in Great King Street and a full range of bicycle accessories was produced. Further growth was stimulated by the needs of the motor trade and Lucas began to supply car makers with horns, pumps, girder wrenches, tyre repair kits, lifting jacks and lamps. At first, these latter were fuelled by oil, then by acetylene and finally by electricity. The production of such lamps led Lucas into electrical engineering and by the inter-war years, the company had become one of the major suppliers of electrical goods for the motor industry. It had also started to make products for aviation companies.

Since then, Lucas Industries has become 'a leading international manufacturer of aerospace, automotive and industrial sytems' - although recent recessions have led it to move away from its former core businesses. The electrical factory in Shaftmoor Lane has been sold to the Italian firm, Magnetti Marelli; nearby, in Formans Road, batteries are made in partnership with the Japanese company Yuasa; and the firm's headquarters have been transferred from Great King Street to Solihull. Elsewhere in this overspill of Birmingham, Lucas plants specialise in 'high technology systems and equipment for all military and commercial aerospace and defence applications'.

During the 1930s, wireless engineers and radio manufacturers also were based in Birmingham. One of them was Telsen Electric Company Ltd. This started business in

New Austin Assembling Section for engines, North Works, Longbridge, late 1950s. (Birmingham Library Services)

1924 on the Aston Road and later had other premises in this district, the last of which was on the corner of Phillips and Thomas Streets. The firm closed down in 1934 amidst rumours that 'someone milked the Telsen and did a runner to Mexico'. (C. Aldridge, *Letter,* 1993)

Another wireless business was the Monitor Radio Company of Stechford which was housed in the building of Parkinson Stoves now Parkinson Cowan and based in Erdington. In the Second World War, Monitor was involved in the design, manufacture and assembly of clandestine equipment like 'the AP5 Transmitter/Receiver, 50 Watt Amplifiers (big in those days) and "EUEREKA BEACONS"'. The radio sets were produced under the guidance of Polish technicians and were used by British Intelligence Services to maintain contact with European Resistance fighters who had the beacons to guide Allied bombers to their targets; whilst the amplifiers were utilised for the direction of landings in enemy territory. (Frank Flanner, *Clandestine Radio in WW2 Birmingham,* unpublished manuscript, 1992)

CARS

Despite its recent shift towards the aviation industry, Lucas Industries remains connected to the motor trade and its rise would have been inconceivable without this link. In 1895, Birmingham was the place where F. W. Lanchester built the first British car which was four-wheeled and driven by petrol, but as in the electrical engineering field, he was not a lone pioneer. At the Wolsey Sheep Shearing Machine Company, Herbert Austin was responsible for making a two-horse power car with three wheels and a horizontal water-cooled engine. The firm itself was founded by an Australian, and following Austin's success it added to its business the production of motor vehicles. This side of its operation was sold in 1901 to Vickers Sons and Maxim Ltd.

At their Adderley Park factory, the company made marine and aero engines and petrol-driven buses as well as cars. In 1927 the works changed ownership again when it was acquired by Morris Commercial for the production of 30 cwt trucks. It was here that in 1936 one engineer, Fred Ormrod, devised an electrically-powered track which made the assembly of re-conditioned lorry engines quicker and more efficient.

> **❝ But the first job was the feller who fitted the cam shaft in and he'd got all the trimmings you see, and the right fit, and he used to check each one… the centre bearing, front and rear and so forth. Then fit the fly wheel on and all of that. Next feller, cam rods and pistons. Then the next feller, the gears, cam shaft so and so, oil pump so and so. Next all the rest, the sump and everything. And then it was tipped up with a line and then… put in the springs, everything. Tapits set for the right clearance etc., cylinder head so and so and then eventually lowered off and come onto a truck. (*Interview,* 1993) ❞**

The manufacture of cars under the name Wolsey continued at Drews Lane in Washwood Heath, a plant which also became part of the Morris group. As a child in the 1930s, Nora Ward remembered 'the "bull" blowing and the rushing tide of humanity spilling out of the factory gates'. (*Letter,* 1990). Today, the Wolsey is the site of Leyland Daf, a producer of vans. Recently, this firm has been bought by its management after its Dutch parent company went into receivership. Many jobs have been lost, but the company has a skilled workforce and a good-quality product and it is to be hoped that it will prosper and increase its number of employees.

Wolsey cars sold at the middle end of the market, whilst at the lower end were the products of Herbert Austin. Although he became chairman of the Wolsey Sheep Shearing Company, in 1905 he also set up his own car plant on a two and half acre site at Longbridge. Five years later, the firm produced an annual total of 576 Austins with single cylinder engines; by 1914, 2,000 workers had increased the annual output to 1,500 cars. This success was because Austin resembled Boulton and the other Birmingham innovators who preceded him. He did not restrict his involvement in industry to one field, instead he was eclectic in his talents.

Publicity shot of an Austin Seven, July 1922. Francis Malachi Hands is loading the car with groceries outside his shop on the corner of Chatham and Bristol Roads, Northfield. (Dorothy Hargest)

> **❝...Austin may be described as a designer. He was an engineer who, in addition to expressing a strong social purpose in extending car ownership, possessed an acute visual sense, and regarded the act of drawing and intuitive problem solving as more significant than the act of mathematical calculation or written description. Speaking of the period he spent as a youth in Australia, where, incidentally, he attended art school, he later reflected, 'it seems that I was then - as I am now, best able to express myself by means of the pencil.' (Roy Church and Chris Mullen, 'Cars and Corporate Culture: The View from Longbridge 1905-1989', in, Barbara Tilson, ed, *Made in Birmingham. Design and Industry 1889-1989*, 1989).❞**

During the inter-war years, the Longbridge works expanded hugely following the launch of the Austin Seven in 1922. This was advertised with the slogan, 'Cheaper than Taxis - Shopping a pleasure'. In a seven-year period, 100,000 of these vehicles were sold to an eager public. Their popularity was fuelled by the growing affluence of the British middle class. In part, this was accounted for by a falling birth rate, and the question was posed 'What was more important to middle-income families? A baby or a baby Austin?'.

Longbridge continued to grow after the Second World War. Prosperity brought the ownership of cars within the range of many members of the working class, and the demand for low-cost utility vehicles was high. As part of the British Motor Corporation, Austin catered for the preferences of a mass market, particularly with the production of the Mini. This model was initiated by Alex Issigonis, a man who prided himself on designing a whole car, and it sold in great numbers. For 23 years it was amongst the top six best-selling cars in the United Kingdom. One of those who produced the model was Arthur Williams, a tool turner at the Austin for 30 years. While he was there:

> **❝I was surprised to find that nothing seemed impossible. For instance, let me explain, if an engine part was being made at the rate of ten per week and then a hundred per week was required, in no time at all, extra machines were brought in and the extra quantity required were soon produced. It was amazing.**
> **It was in 1951 that the Spares Machine shop moved to the East Works (this is the factory where planes were built during the war). It is a vast factory about one third of a mile long and was empty. Winter was approaching and as you can quite imagine heating a factory of that size was quite a problem, so much so, that on many occasions the men worked in overcoats . . . It was here that I was priveliged to be one of the men who produced the first engine components for the famous Mini.' (Arthur Williams, *A Pre-Amble on Life as it Has Been for Me*, unpublished manuscript, 1986).❞**

During the late 1970s and early 1980s, the Longbridge works were beset by severe problems between management and workers. At the same time, competition from Japan made it seem that there was little future for the British car industry. Thankfully, this gloomy scenario has not taken place. Longbridge is now part of Rover which in turn was bought by British Aerospace and is now owned by BMW. Its highly-trained workforce is setting record levels of productivity and is turning out well-designed cars for which there is a clear public demand. Unfortunately, the success of the Birmingham car industry has not been matched by that of its motorbike manufacturers - a trade which was connected intimately to bicycle production.

BICYCLES AND MOTORBIKES

Although the modern bike was a product of the ingenuity of Coventry people, by 1914 Birmingham was the chief centre of its production. Almost 10,000 people were engaged in making bicycles in the city, and their numbers grew in the inter-war years as this form of transport became popular for travel to work and for recreational purposes. Famous firms like James Cycle in Tyseley and Hercules of Aston were based in Birmingham. By the mid-1930s, this latter was the largest bicycle factory in the world with a workforce of 4,000 people producing 750,000 machines each year. However, by 1960 the bike trade was dominated by Tube Investments via the British Cycle Corporation. Since then, rationalisation has led to the closure of Birmingham bicycle factories and the concentration of production in Nottingham. One business which has not been swallowed up is Kirk and Merifield, founded in 1892 in Bradford Street by George Lewis. His grandson is the present managing director and with a workforce of 43, the businesss continues the tradition of bike-making in Birmingham. Another to do so is Dawes Cycles of Tyseley.

In Coventry, the bicycle trade tended to be integrated with the making of motorbikes and there was a similar situation at the James and at the Rocky Lane works of the Hercules. But locally there was one major company which specialised in the manufacture of these machines. This was the Norton which began in 1889 with the making of the 'Energette'. The firm gained a high reputation and like many Brummies, I grew up aware of the

The bicycle shop of O.W. Hopkins, Great Lister Street, Nechells, about 1928. The business now trades in Hall Green. (Jack Hopkins)

prestige of its models and of the daring and skills of its racing team rider, Geoff Dukes. Based at Bracebridge Street in Aston, the Norton had regular Grand Prix victories in the inter-war years. For many motorbike enthusiasts, the owning of one of these machines was the pinnacle of their ambition. As Micky Volante remembers, B.S.A. bikes were best for reliability, but for speed the Norton was in pole position. (*Interview*, 1993). Bevan Laing had the same opinions.

John Hobson showing a Norton motorbike to Gilbert Voisseur and Maurice Puille, Parisian policemen, 1958. (Birmingham Library Services)

> **With enough money to make a dream come true I bought my first motorbike from Coles near the Central fire station. That first dream was a BSA Bantam, but after about six months of being left standing by bigger machines I bought a Norton 500. (*Letter,* 1990)**

BSA was not as unlikely a maker of motorbikes as it may have seemed. The company's managers had found that when trade was slack in the gun industry, much of its machinery was suitable for the production of bicycle frames. In turn, this move encouraged an interest in motorbikes. During 1903, the BSA produced its first frame for this kind of transport; whilst within seven years it was making complete motorcycles. The continuing expansion of BSA in the trade led to its acquisition of a local competitor, Ariel Motors of Selly Oak. After 1957, the bicycle part of BSA was sold to Raleigh (part of Tube Investments); and within the next 20 years, it had ceased to manufacture motorbikes.

The death of the Birmingham motor-cycle industry arouses strong passions. Some people blame the competition from Japanese companies who made small capacity machines - an area of production which was neglected by British firms; others find management culpable because of its complacency and lack of investment. Certainly, by 1968, Japan was exporting the phenomenal total of a million motorbikes a year. In the same decade, production at the BSA in Small Heath peaked at 43,000 machines. These were made largely by hand and by craftsmen, and although they remained in demand, the motorbike market was swamped by cheaper, production-line makes from abroad.

In a forlorn attempt to continue in business, BSA joined with its British competitors to form Norton Villiers Triumph in 1973. Two years later, the Small Heath factory closed and was knocked down, whilst Norton, too, seemed set to disappear. In 1953, it had become part of Associated Motorcycles Ltd - as had the James three years before. Within ten years, the Bracebridge Street factory was shut down and the making of Norton machines was transferred to London. However, after the collapse of the British motorbike industry, production returned to the Midlands when a small group of designers and craftsmen set up in Shenstone. The firm continues to make big machines and it has maintained a high reputation for its products.

COMPONENTS

In 1913, the secretary of the Birmingham Chamber of Commerce noted that the city's mechanics had 'acquired a peculiar skill in the production of articles for which mathematical accuracy was needed'. G. Henry Wright noted that these qualities were gained because of a varied experience in the manufacture of miscellaneous engineering products. Amongst these was a 'widespread activity in the production of component parts, fittings, and accessories' for those businesses which made cars, commercial vehicles, motorbikes and cycles.

The importance of components' firms has increased since these observations were made. By the 1950s, Birmingham based J. B. Brooks was providing 60% of the saddles for Britain's cycles; whilst the Midland Wheel in Avenue Road, Aston, continues to brace and true bike wheels as it has done since 1896. Components' firms were as important to the motor industry and during the 1950s, Fisher and Ludlow was employing 14,000 people in making car panels. This operation had begun in 1849 as a tinsmith's, and although it branched into the making of kettles and mess tins, it had a workforce of just 200 before it began to supply the motor trade. Fisher's later became part of the British Motor Corporation and now it is owned by Jaguar.

Originally, Fisher's was based in Bradford Street, but after 1945 it moved its operations to a factory at Castle Bromwich. During the Second World war this had produced aeroplanes and one of those who was employed there was Frances Crockett, whose father came from Tipperary in Ireland. She remembered that the workforce was under pressure to produce quickly as many planes as they could to help in the war effort.

> **"I lost my fingers working on the machines - we were doing these for the planes to go up that night, they were so in urgent need of them. And all my fingers were cut off, they went poisoned the next day... I nearly lost my arm. We went to the General Hospital, that had been bombed, they'd no gas, no nothing, so I had to be sewn up without any gas or anything, there was nothing there to relieve it at all. (Karen Garry and Frances Hayes, *Reflections. The Irish Community in Birmingham*, 1991)"**

Tyres are another crucial component for cars and an Irish family played a significant role in bringing their production to Birmingham. The patent for a pneumatic tyre was taken out by Mr Dunlop in 1888, and the next year, the first factory for its manufacture was opened in Dublin with funding from William Harvey du Cross. When it moved to a new locality, there were complaints about the noxious smells it gave out, and operations were moved to Coventry where there was a large pool of skilled labour. The tyres were made with rubber, but the Du Cross business had little control of the supply of their raw material. This changed when contact was made with Frank and Fred Byrne. Their father had worked as general manager for J. Kirby & Son of New Street, manufacturers of gutta percha (a substance made from the latex of trees in Malaysia). About 1871, Thomas Byrne set up his own business and 20 years later, all his sons were involved in the making of rubber. In 1896, Du Cross took over their operation in Lichfield Road, which also made tyres, and in this way, Dunlop gained access into the production of rubber. (This account is based on Joan Skinner, 'Dunlop in Birmingham: The Making of an Industrial Empire', in, Barbara Tilson, ed, *Made in Birmingham. Design & Industry 1889-1989*, 1989)

By the outbreak of the First World War, the accommodation at these works had become too cramped for the growing Dunlop business. A huge new factory was built on the outskirts of Birmingham, and as with the Austin, it was responsible for the spreading of the city into areas which had once been rural.

> **"My father was then with the Dunlop Rubber Co. which was centred near Aston Cross - (Manor Mills), but Fort Dunlop had been built during World War I and the transfer was taking place to the Erdington site. Special houses had been built to house the Dunlop employees. These still stand in Holly Lane, Kingsbury Road, Firtree Road and a few in Bracken Road which included the Co-op Grocery shop which for several years was the only shop in the area other than those in Erdington Village (High Street). (Fred Smith, *Random Recollections of Erdington in the Twenties*, unpublished manuscript, 1991)"**

By 1927, Dunlop was employing 12,000 people in Birmingham. Although tyre production has now ceased at the Fort Dunlop building, it continues on the surrounding site with the firm of S.P. Tyres U.K. Ltd – a major local employer.

CHEMICALS AND PLASTICS

The motor trade demanded not only components which were made specifically for cars, but also it needed long-established products such as paints and varnishes. Indeed, the paint manufacturer Croda Ltd traces its origins to 1797 and Samuel Thornton, a varnisher. Products made by firms like this were used by many industries in Birmingham, especially in the hollowware trade and in the galvanising (coating) of iron goods. However, the new industries of the twentieth century required advanced kinds of paints and varnishes, the development of which was dependent upon advances in chemical engineering and the provision of speciality chemicals. Firms like W. Canning catered for these demands. This was founded in 1787 by a drysalter - someone who dealt in dyes, drugs and oils - and it continues as a chemical supplier and distributor of electronic components.

Birmingham's most notable experimental chemists were Joseph Priestley in the late 1700s and Alexander Parkes of the mid-nineteenth century. The son of a locksmith, the latter was exceptional in his widespread scientific interests and in his large number of patents. He was involved deeply in the discoveries which led to electro-plating, he gave his name to a process wich desilverises lead, and he produced Britain's first plastic - Parkesine. This was modified by an American and it achieved fame as celluloid. Plastics were to become crucial in the production of cars and other goods, and factories were set up to provide this material. One of the largest was the Bakelite works in Tyseley.

This firm was the result of a merger between the Damard Lacquer Company of Bradford Street and a London competitor. In 1931, it moved to purpose-built works in Tyseley and it became Britain's leading producer of phenolic materials and industrial laminates for the electro-telecommunications industry. The closure of the business in 1985 has been described by Barbara Tilson as an example of how 'the seemingly mighty, too, can fall victim of industrial evolution, corporate "smash and grab" and unfortunate government policies'. (Barbara Tilson, 'The Plastics Industry in Birmingham and Design in Bakelite, Beetle and Melamine', in, Barbara Tilson, ed, *Made in Birmingham, Design and Industry 1889-1989,* 1989)

W. Canning & Co. at the corner of Great Hampton and Kenyon Streets, about 1850.
(Birmingham Library Services)

The BSA Laboratory. (Birmingham Library Services)

In particular, Bakelite was harmed by a regional policy which was adopted by both Conservative and Labour administrations. This discriminated against Birmingham by preventing successful firms from expanding in the city. Such businesses had grown precisely because Birmingham had both a multiform industrial base and a large number of skilled workers, but this vital link was ignored by governments which forced local companies to move their operations to the North of England and Scotland. Wolsey, for example, had to site a factory in Knighton; whilst in 1954, Bakelite's management had to build a new plant in County Durham and not in Tyseley as it had wished.

Before the Second World War, another major plastics concern in Birmingham was that of Edwin Elliott which employed 700 people in Summer Lane. This business began in 1903 when the proprietor started to import imitation stones which were used in cheap jewellery.

> **"Just before the outbreak of the First World War, he took on the import agency for a synthetic resin product called, romantically, Galalith. It was marketed in the jewellery quarter to replace the bone that had been in standard use for cutlery handles.**
> **It was also excellent material from which to make cheap beads. Edwin imported it in sheets and blocks. He rented a room at six shillings (30p) a week and installed a circular saw to cut the material to any size required by the trade.**
> **He soon realised that he could mould the handles more cheaply himself with the right machinery. He acquired a press and pump and became, almost certainly, the first man in Birmingham to enter the compression moulding field as a manufacturer of plastic cutlery handles. (Frederick Whitehead, 'My Midlands', *The Birmingham Post*, 15 March 1980, information provided by Miss Margery Elliott)"**

Edwin Elliott added to his interests a small business which made lenses for spectacles. This became the British Optical Lens Company and it was members of this firm who developed a technique for grinding and polishing a special type of green glass, through which British soldiers in the First World War looked down their gunsights. In the next global conflict, the plastics company produced millions of anti-gas eye shields. This firm is no longer in existence, but the spectacle business is now part of the Birmingham Optical Group plc Archer-Elliott of the Moseley Road which operates as a wholesaler and manufacturer for opticans.

THE THOUSAND TRADES

Edwin Elliott's rise as a businessman was typical of that of many Brummies. His father was an incomer to the city and he worked as the manager for the Broad Street engineering firm of H. J. T. Piercy & Company. Edwin himself had variety of jobs before he became self-employed: factory machinist; jewellery worker; and office boy for a German importer-exporter of fancy goods. His willingness to try different types of work, his keeness to adopt new techniques and his desire to have his own firm were features which he shared with many people in Birmingham. The Hall family have exhibited them for over two hundred years. In 1767, William was living in Moor Street, producing curry combs (used for brushing horses); by 1819, James was in Weaman Street making guns and pistols; 26 years later, Samuel was based in Great Hampton Street where he turned out fancy leather goods and cases; by 1887, Frank had moved the business to Warstone Lane; and today as D. H. Hall & Co. Ltd, the firm is involved in the manufacture of spectacle cases in Freeth Street.

Despite Birmingham's reputation as the hardware capital of Britain, the city has always boasted producers like the Halls, those who are unassociated with the metal trades. They include many long-established businesses: Salt and Sons - since about 1701 makers of surgical appliances; Arthur Gossage Ltd, a packing case producers which dates back to 1780 - as does Joseph Harris Ltd, dry cleaners and industrial textile renters; Thurston, which makes billiards equipment and which started in 1799 when Thomas Padmore operated as a cabinet maker and a turner of wood and ivory; and Newman Tonks Group plc, makers of architectural furniture which dates its origins to 1750. Others in the catholic world of Birmingham manufacturers are Stuarts Industrial Holdings, which began in 1840 as a granolithic company specialising in making concrete from crushed granite; Coaney Catering Equipment, which started in 1844 as a retailer of corks and bottles; and Frederick Restall which makes contract furniture and seating for sports stadiums and which was founded in 1864.

There are many other businesses like these, and as much as the metal-working firms their presence was responsible for Birmingham's reputation as a city with a broad manufacturing base. As late as the 1930s, there remained over 1,500 trades in Birmingham ranging from the toy makers Chad Valley to Joseph Gilman & Son Ltd, distributors of janitorial equipment; from the manufacturer of carrying cases Samuel Groves & Co. Ltd to Philip Harris Medical Ltd, pharmaceutical wholesalers; and from P. L. Wilcox, specialists in ferrous and non-ferrous machined products to Margoschis, stamp dealers. Despite the importance of the car industry and its suppliers, the city remained a place which was extensive in its type of producers. Amongst them were brewers.

VINEGAR AND BEER

In 1946 the locally born novelist, Walter Allen, wrote that 'it would be possible to fix one's whereabouts in Birmingham, even though blindfold, simply by the prevailing smell: malt and vinegar signify Aston, rubber the Tyburn side of Erdington, gas Saltley, cocoa Bournville and Selly Oak, amyl acetate - the smell of pear drop and nail varnish - the jewellers' quarter'. Our Mom would agree with him. When she married Dad and came to Sparkbrook from Aston, she missed the smells of Nechells Gas Works, Ansells Brewery and the HP Sauce factory. It was this latter firm which gave the fourteen-year old Hilda Hughes her first employment.

> **"One of the jobs I did was to put cork rings on glass stoppers & then put them in the bottles as they came down the line before they went round the machine which pressed them down. I quite enjoyed it & we had a good laugh, but my clothes always smelt of vinegar. The cloakroom was upstairs where all the big vats were for making the sauce & the smell from the vegetables they put in was terrible. I was nearly always late getting home as I had a long walk up Park Lane to get the bus home. I always dawdled on the way looking in the shops & on fridays after being paid I would walk up Potters Hill by the Aston Hippodrome to the cooked meat shop & buy a steak and kidney pie which I would eat whilst I was going along, delicious it was & you could smell the cooking for miles, they sold tripe, chitterlings, brawn, faggots & cow heels. (*Letter*, 1991)"**

The founder of HP Sauce was Edwin Sampson Moore. In 1875 he set up the Midland Vinegar Company in Tower Road, Aston and at a later date he paid a Nottingham grocer for the recipe for the sauce which was to make his company famous. His business is owned now by a French company, BSN, which employs around 260 people at Aston Cross. Who else practised their skills in this language by reading the label on the side of a bottle of HP brown sauce? For here were written the words 'Cette sauce de haute qualité est un mélange de fruits orientaux, d'épices et de vinaigre de "Malt"'. Today's HP plant is a highly modern one, including breweries for vinegar and sauce. Because stainless steel closed vats have replaced those which were wooden and open, the works is more hygienic and it gives off less of its distinctive smell. Nonetheless, Brummies know they're in Aston when they see the HP sign and catch a whiff of vinegar and sauce in the making.

A smell which has disappeared from the district is that which came from the Ansells brewery. Like most large Birmingham works, this had developed from small beginnings. In 1857, Joseph Ansell had set up as a maltster and hop merchant and it was not until 24 years later that he became a brewer. Like Edwin Sampson Moore, he was encouraged to do so because Aston had a plentiful supply of water which was ideal for making beer as well as vinegar. At first, Ansell was one of a great number of brewers in Birmingham, many of them publicans producing beer on their own premises. Indeed, in 1873-4, 99% of the city's beer houses and 97% of its public houses had a licence to brew.

This phenomenon has been associated with the predominance of small gaffers in Birmingham. It has been argued that buying a pub or beerhouse was an ideal investment for a successful artisan. If it had its own brewing equipment, it offered the owner the same sort of independence from a large master as did other local occupations. Accordingly, there was a trend into the licensed trade by small manufacturers.

> **Samuel White of the Bellefield (Winson Green) was a graphic example of that progression: having trained as a jeweller, he ran his own business making silver bracelets for six years, and when in c.1881 he bought his first pub, The Yorkshire Grey in Dudley Road, he promptly set about building a brewery behind it. Other landlords featured in the 'Well Known Faces' column of the local trade paper could trace similar careers. Henry Grafton of The Freemason's Arms, Balsall Heath, had been the manager of an electroplating firm; Mr Holt of The Wellington, Gooch Street, after training as a gunmaker, had established a gun factory in New York State; and John Hunt of The Waggon and Horses, Adderley Street, had first gone to work in the button trade. For such men taking a pub, with or without a brewhouse attached, was hardly a main road to respectability, but it was a way of expressing their vigorous self-reliance. (Alan Crawford, Michael Dunn & Robert Thorne, _Birmingham Pubs 1880-1939_, 1986)**

A typical neighbourhood pub, The Olive Branch, Adderley Road, 1930s. (Martin Grealey, Marketing and Services Director, Ansells Ltd)

During the 1880s, the opportunity for such self-reliance declined greatly. Local magistrates were making it more difficult to obtain a new pub licence and so the value of existing premises rose. This meant that purchasers were more likely to take on a mortgage which common brewers were keen to extend in order to secure outlets for their beers. The next step for these businesses was to buy the freehold or leasehold of a pub or beerhouse. Such takeovers were made possible by cash injections which resulted from the flotation of many brewery firms as public companies.

By 1890, the licensed trade locally was dominated by these large brewers, of which the biggest was Holt's of Gosta Green with 155 tied houses. This had grown out of the family business of H. V. Fulford which had been founded as a malting concern in 1819. Next in size came Mitchell's of Cape Hill, Smethwick with 88 licensed premises. In 1898, this firm joined with that of William Butler who had become a common brewer when he began to sell to other licensees the beer he produced at the rear of 'The Crown' in Broad Street. Over the next decades, Mitchells and Butlers swallowed up Homer's Vulcan brewery in Aston; Holder's of Nova Scotia Street; and the large Aston Park concern of Atkinson's. Together with Ansells, Mitchells and Butlers dominates the pub trade in contemporary Birmingham.

At the start of the 1890s, Ansells was third in the list of major breweries with tied houses. Forty years later and following the takeover of Holts, it had moved into pole position in Birmingham. At the same time, it became the leading brewery company in the West Midlands and one of the largest in England. In 1961, Ansells merged with Ind Coope and Tetley's to form Allied Breweries, the first of England's national brewery combines. Twenty years after, following a protracted dispute between management and workers, the Aston Cross Brewery was closed down and production of its famous ales was transferred to Burton-on-Trent. But the company maintains a significant presence in Birmingham and it has developed a commitment to community projects in the city.

The last of Birmingham's major breweries was Davenport's in Bath Row. Like Ansells, its origins lay in malting and dealing in hops - although it began at the earlier date of 1829. The fame of the company lay not so much in the number of its tied houses, even though it took over those of firms like William Dares and Sons of Belgrave Road; rather, Davenport's was celebrated because of its supply of bottled beers to customers in their homes. With a fond smile, Brummies of my generation and older will remember the firm's adverts on television and the song which accompanied them.

The White Horse, an Atkinson's pub, probably in Victoria Road, Aston, about 1935. (Geoff Dowling)

> **"Beer at home means Davenport's,**
> **That's the beer, lots of cheer.**
> **The finest hops with malt and yeast**
> **Turns a snack into a feast.**
> **Straight from brewery to your home**
> **Why collect? We'll deliver.**
> **Then you'll know why folks all say**
> **Beer at home means Davenport's."**

These words used to appear on the screen, with a Davenport's beer bottle hopping above them and following the progress of the tune.

Since its takeover by a larger company, Davenport's has ceased its operations and the Bath Row site is about to be cleared for redevelopment. Only one beer producer now exists in Birmingham, and it is a newer operation set up after Ansells moved to Burton. Aston Manor Brewery in Thimblemill Lane is similar to Davenport's in that it has few tied houses; instead it supplies off-licences with its beer in large plastic bottles.

If Birmingham is now bereft of large brewers, then their licensed premises are significant buildings in the city's landscape - from small back-street beerhouses to large Victorian pubs, and from inter-war buildings to post-modern structures. One of the most magnificent is the 'Barton Arms' in High Street, Aston. Built between 1899 and 1901, it boasts a magnificent staircase, facing which is a tiled hunting scene; and in the Smoke Rooms there are snob-screens, little panes of glass which can be opened to give privacy to a drinker standing at the bar. Other imposing late Victorian pubs are "The Britannia', 'The Swan and Mitre', and 'The Golden Cross' - all on the Lichfield Road, Aston; 'The Fighting Cocks' in Moseley - which has tiled murals of the village as it once was; 'The Rose Villa Tavern' in Warstone Lane in the Jewellery Quarter; 'The Woodman' in Albert Street; and 'The White Swan' in Bradford Street.

CUSTARD, TEA AND COCOA

Near to this latter pub is the prominent structure associated with Alfred Bird. He was an experimental chemist of Bell Street. In 1843 he perfected a substitute for yeast in the making of bread and he followed this with marketing the first custard powder. His son was as inventive. During the 1870s he devised blancmange, and in 1895 he produced jelly crystals. Seven years later, Alfred Bird the younger supervised the move of his firm to the Devonshire Works in Digbeth High Street. Here the 12 year old Florence Hay began work in 1906.

> **"I was not yet old enough to earn the full rate of pay**
> **which was three shillings and sixpence a week payable to**
> **those who had reached the age of fourteen, but was taken**
> **on for the wage of three shillings a week. And it was**
> **sweated labour... we worked from eight o' clock in the**
> **morning until six o' clock at night. We had an hour off for**
> **lunch and ten minutes mid-morning and mid-afternoon for**
> **a cup of tea. Whilst working we were not allowed to talk or**
> **to sing or to whistle. If we were caught doing any of those**
> **things we were told off, though if we were careful and kept**
> **a wary eye out we could chat a little without the forewoman**
> **spotting us... they put me to work in what was called the**
> **'box room'... where the boxes were made which later would**

be filled with the products of the factory... we did not have to wear overalls because we were not actually having anything to do with the food products. Those who worked in the custard powder, blancmange powder and egg powder rooms, had to wear white overalls. (A.E. Hay, *Florence Naylor: Her Story,* unpublished manuscript, no date) **"**

In 1947, Bird's was taken over by General Foods and production was later moved from Birmingham. So too has that of Typhoo Tea.

The drinking of this beverage had gained in popularity during the 1700s. By the early years of the next century, several public houses on the outskirts of Birmingham were celebrated for their tea gardens. Like the 'Angel' on the Stratford Road in Sparkbrook, they became retreats for middle-class people who were able 'to enjoy the delights of the country with a party of friends without having to travel a great distance'. The growing trade in tea stimulated Birmingham manufacturers to produce articles which complemented the drink - urns, caddies, trays and tables; whilst other entrepreneurs retailed the beverage itself.

One of these tea dealers was William Sumner. From 1820, he traded at 97, High Street, Bull Ring and 36 years later, he purchased the shop next door. Until 1894, his son and grandson continued to do business there as tea, wine and Italian warehousemen (suppliers of groceries and fruits from Italy). In that year, they moved further up High Street to Hutton House - built by Birmingham's first historian. The family continued to sell a wide range of goods, but its future lay in specialisation. This was because of the decision of the younger John Sumner to go against the trend for large-leaf tea and to package fannings - smaller leaves. He called his product Typhoo Tipps Tea because this name had an Oriental sound and it was alliterative. One of his employees was R. H. Burton.

"I remember quite well how in 1903 he first introduced the new tea; how everyone concerned was worked up to enthusiasm about it, the assistants pushing it at the counter, and the travellers on their rounds; how one scheme after another was tried to gain the notice of the general public. There was no machinery then, only the hand scales and scoop upon an extemporised counter, and packed at a speed of not a packet a minute. (cited in Kenneth Williams, *The Story of Typhoo and the Birmingham Tea Industry,* 1990. My account of Typhoo is based on this book)**"**

An early advertisement for Bird's Custard. (Thanks to Roy White)

Sumner's brand of tea sold well and he decided to expand this side of his business but his bank was unwilling to finance him to do so. Undeterred, he sold his stock of groceries and he secured backing from friends and relatives during 1905. In the same year, he visited Ceylon and bought 200 chests of tea, mostly fannings. Soon after, he moved to premises in Castle Street (just off High Street) where he employed ten women to pack the tea, three females in the office and Richard Burton as works manager. Another trip to Ceylon followed and whilst he was there, Sumner appointed agents to buy, blend and ship the special leaf-edge tea which he wanted. This beverage was advertised as economical - because one pound of it produced 80 cups more than the drink made from large leaf tea; as tannin-less - which made it have no effect on the nerves; and as a cure for indigestion.

By 1925, Typhoo Tea was so popular that new premises were opened in Bordesley Street. On the first floor was the packing machinery and the despatch department and below it was the bonded warehouse which had a capacity for 20,000 cases of tea. This came from English ports via canals, and it was unloaded on the company's own wharf behind the works. Each week, the canal barges brought up to 3,000 chests of tea from Ceylon. Typhoo's business continued to grow, despite the bombing of its premises in the Second World War, and by the 1960s it was the brand leader in the grocery trade. Each year, it packed over 80 million pounds of tea, much of which went for export.

An early advertisement for Cadbury's. (The Owl, 18 February, 1881)

Towards the end of that decade the firm merged with Schweppes, and shortly after, the new business joined with Cadbury's. The resultant company, Cadbury Schweppes, had an annual turnover of £250 million and was the eighth largest food group in the world. In 1978, because of serious differences between management and unions, the packing of tea at Bordesley Street ended and was transfered to Moreton, on Merseyside. Eight years later, a management buy-out took Typhoo out of Cadbury Schweppes and into Premier Brands Ltd.

Cadbury's has a long history in Birmingham, and like many other leading local firms it traces its origins to a newcomer to the city. After serving his apprenticeship in Gloucester and following his time as a journeyman in London, Richard Tipper Cadbury settled as a silk mercer and draper in Bull Street in 1794. His son, John, was trained as a tea-dealer both in the capital and in Leeds. From 1824 he had his own business in Birmingham opposite his father's shop. Forty-three years later, he moved to larger premises in Bridge Street where he made and sold chocolate and retailed tea and cocoa, the mainstay of his business. The beans for this product were imported from Trinidad and Guyana, and each day two tons of them were roasted in four cylindrical ovens. After this, the husks were taken away in a 'kibbling mill' so as to leave a thick, oily liquid. Strong pressure was exerted to force out the oil which became solid as cocoa butter, whilst the remainder of the liquid hardened into a cake of pure cocoa. Finally, this was ground to powder and sifted through fine silk sieves.

Unfortunately, following the death of his wife and his falling ill with rheumatic fever, John Cadbury's business declined. After his retirement in 1861, it revived under the management of his sons, Richard and George, and within 20 years they had moved their factory to a green field site near to the Bourn Brook. To give the business a continental feel, they named the area around it Bournville. By the inter-war years, the works was surrounded by housing and it was giving jobs to large numbers of local people.

According to Ted Smallbone, 'the main reason for going to work at Cadbury's was that it was an ideal employer as employers go. It was also regarded as a safe job'. In a period when car workers were often laid off at slack times and when much unskilled labour was casual and irregular, 'safe jobs' were appealing to many members of the working class. For this reason, positions were sought with the corporation, the post office and on the railways. Some of them may have been lowly paid, but at least they were regular, and if workers kept out of trouble they had a job for life. Given the reputation which Cadbury's had for security and decent conditions of employment, it is unsurprising that 'it was every mother's dream that her boy and girl would get a job' there. (Howard Williamson, *Toolmaking and Politics. The Life of Ted Smallbone - an oral history,* 1987)

The Cadburys were renowned for their benevolent attitudes towards their employees and for their funding of charities like the Bournville Village Trust which built good-quality houses locally. Their positive actions resulted from their social conscience as Quakers, but their beliefs also meant that they expected their workers to conform to their attitudes to life. Female workers had to leave their jobs once they married; no pubs were allowed on land owned by Cadbury's in Bournville; and employees were discouraged from drinking, betting and indulging in activities frowned upon by their employers - as Ernie Haynes found out. He and two friends, the Banks brothers, played music at 'doos' in licensed premises.

> **Unfortunately, Ernie's employers got to hear about his public house activities, although they took place the other side of town. He was called to a stern interview, and was threatened with the sack if he did not keep away from places offering such temptation. He was very angry, but forced himself to swallow his wrath as he did not dare defy them. However it helped to make his talents known in the factory, and he was often called upon to play for various functions there. The Banks boys did not work at Cadbury's so they were not affected. (Letitia Haynes,** ***The Buried Past in Family History,*** **1993)**

Despite the Cadburys pacifist beliefs, the factory at Bournville went over to war work in the Second World War. Margaret Smith recalled that as a 16 year old, she assembled gas masks there. This job required 'speed and accuracy and was especially suitable for nimble fingered girls'. She was also an auxiliary nurse, and once a week at the Bournville works she and other volunteers entertained 'war-wounded men in a corner of the huge canteen'. (Margaret Smith, *Some Memories of a Northfield Woman,* unpublished manuscript, no date)

The Bull's Head, Stechford early 1900s, with a van from the celebrated firm of Harding's Bread. (Geoff Dowling)

Although Cadbury's is now part of a multi-national concern, members of the family remain prominent in a business which stays committed to Birmingham. This has been shown by the maintenance of chocolate-production at Bournville and by the building of a heritage centre, Cadbury World. One of the key elements of a modern business is bringing goods to the attention of a wide audience. Like Davenports, Typhoo Tea and HP, Cadbury's is a major firm whose products are associated with certain advertisements and slogans. This connection with placarding is long-established. Richard Tipper advertised regularly in *Aris's Birmingham Gazette*. His son, John, had plate glass windows installed in his shop, so that he might be better able to show his products; and he was followed by his friend Thomas Southall, the chemist who founded a sanitary products concern which is now based on the Alum Rock Road and is part of Smith & Nephew.

Advertising was adopted by businesspeople other than shop keepers. In *Wrighton's Directory* of 1813 there are included full page displays of the articles of a number of manufacturers. They include the guns of John Bunney; the metal goods of Brown and Hardman; the wire work of James Busby; the candlesticks of Frederick Homfray; the plated and brass ware of James & Gibbs; and the gimlet and bits of Nicklin and Son. During the early years of the twentieth century, firms like Typhoo recognised that straight-forward advertising could be supplemented by 'give-aways'. In 1914, the company produced a range of 24 cards, each of which had a coloured picture of a certain British bird and its egg. The set proved to be popular as a collectors' item, but each card also had the phrase, 'TYPHOO-TIPPS TEA RELIEVES INDIGESTION'. Ten years later, the business ordered 10½ million cards on the theme of 'Ancient Fables and Customs', whilst another set of 25 was brought out on 'Aesop's Fables'. Each of these had a different slogan, for example, 'TYPHOO TEA may cost more but goes much further'. On the reverse of the card was the moral of the particular fable. Such expensive advertising was beyond the reach of those who were involved in another form of food production - the small-scale producers and retailers of ice cream in Birmingham, most of whom were from Italy.

Working on the BSA motorbike assembly track were left to right: George Croft, Edgar Trueman, Roger Wyman and Eddie Dumbleton. (Birmingham Library Services, names supplied by Geoff Dowling)

NOTES

I should like to thank the following people for their help in the research for this chapter: Garth Luckuck, Head of Distribution Maintenance, MEB; Barbara Shackley and David Shackley, Director-Group Controller, Lucas Industries plc; Pat Lyons, Administration Officer, HP Foods Ltd; Peggy Bamfield; and Roy and Charlotte White for all their assistance and kindness.

FURTHER READING

Anthony Sutcliff &   *History of Birmingham. Volume III. Birmingham 1939-1970*
Roger Smith (1974)

This is another essential work.

Walter Allen   *Black Country* (1946)
Beryl Bainbridge   *English Journey or the Road to Milton Keynes* (1984)
Ian A. Laker   *Typhoo Tea Cards* (1976)
W. Robert Taylor   *Powering Forward. 100 Years of Electricity in Birmingham* (1991)
G. Henry Wright   'A General Survey of the Trades', in, George A. Auden, ed, *A Handbook for Birmingham and the Neighbourhood,* 1913).

An early HP Sauce advertisement. (Thanks to Roy White)

UP THE CROSS

Old Aston Cross, I know it well,
There's the Cross and the clock and the constant smell
Of HP Sauce and Ansells brewing
And the sounds of the little factories doing
Their bit to boost the city's trade,
'Cos there's a million things that's Brummagem made.

The Cross is a lovely place to shop,
There's all kind of stores like the Brum Co-op,
Bird's the tailors to buy your suits,
Timpson's selling shoes and boots,
Randall's could print you a testimonial,
While you cashed your coupons at the Home and Colonial,
A library full of books to be read
And the delicious smell of Baines's bread.

Pawson's was open from early morn,
In case you had anything to pawn,
Bliss's record shop was really great
Where you might buy a seventy-eight
Of Vera Lynne and army men,
Telling us that 'We'll Meet Again'.
On Rocky Lane across the way
We took tea and cakes in Jelf's cafe.

What do you mean it isn't so?
I lived down there not long ago.
I remember Baldwin's fish shop – a famous name –
And Sabin's tha barber's on Park Lane,
The trams all queuing in Park Road
The football supporters to unload.
The Golden Cross on a Saturday night,
Now there was a place to see a fight.

The name has been changed and the clock's been moved.
The whole of the area has been 'improved'.
You can no longer hear the barrow boys shout,
And the folk that shopped here have been moved out.
Oh well, I suppose I can't complain,
'cos HP sauce still smells the same.

(Arthur Wilkes, 1993)

CHAPTER 4
BRUMMIES: THE PEOPLE
OF BIRMINGHAM

Workers leaving Kynoch's in Witton about 1914. (Birmingham Library Services); Inset, shoppers in New Street, 1992.
(Gareth Lewis, Birmingham City Council Department of Planning and Architecture)

A MULTI-CULTURAL CITY

Birmingham has never had a clear-cut identity. It has not been dominated by one industry; it has included within its borders a variety of working and middle-class people; and it is not connected to a particular physical feature. Misconceptions abound about Birmingham. Because of the prominence of families like the Chamberlains and Cadburys, some people believe that it was a city of Non-Conformists. It was not. Its people were mostly Church of England. Others assert that it is a souless and uninteresting place. It is not. Birmingham is a city which throbs with life and is full of surprises. Its excitement and attractiveness lie in its unpredictability and diversity. Both it and its people defy neat lables.

Many Brummies take as much pride in their neighbourhood as they do in their city. This explains the deep rivalry between fans of the two main local football teams. Aston Villa draws much of its support from the north side, from districts like Erdington, Aston, Perry Barr, Handsworth and Sutton Coldfield all of which were once independent boroughs. By contrast, Birmingham City fans are found in the greatest numbers in the south. Formerly called Small Heath Alliance, the club is followed in that district and in most of old Birmingham. But it also has many supporters in Yardley, Kings Norton and Northfield - all three of which were also separate authorities until Birmingham's extension. Some older people remain staunch in their attachment to these older entities. Elaine Harris points out that she was born in Handsworth in 1910, one year before it was annexed by its larger neighbour. As a result, she declares 'I am not a "Brummie" I am a Staffordshire Lass'. (*Letter*, 1992)

It has never been possible to draw a picture of a typical Brummie and today it remains impossible to do so. There are many different people who have loyalty to the city: Afro-Caribbean, Bangla Deshi, Chinese, Cypriot, English, Indian, Irish, Italian, Kashmiri, Pakistani, Polish, Scots, Welsh - the list is endless. Their sense of belonging to Birmingham does not conflict with their attachment to their own culture or beliefs. For the most part, the peoples of the city live comfortably with dual allegiances and they would subscribe to the opinion of Matt Redmond: 'I was born a Dubliner, and I am a Brummie by adoption'. (*Interview,* 1993).

A walk along many Birmingham roads will bring you a medley of languages and accents, from the cries of English butchers to the gentle urgings of Sikh traders, from the patois of Jamaicans to the Celtic lilt of Welsh and Irish people; it will bring you a feast of food to choose from - Cypriot doner kebabs, Indian tandoori chicken, Kashmiri baltis, Chinese dim sung, West Midlands faggots and peas; and it will offer a multitude of colours to clothe you in. In a way that few other towns or cities in Britain can be, Birmingham is the sum of its parts and of its people - wherever they come from.

THE ITALIAN QUARTER

An ethnic minority which has been in Birmingham for over 100 years is that of the Italians. As early as the 1851 Census, a group of musicians from Italy were registered as staying in Park Street. This was a poorer part of Birmingham where there were lodging houses for single men. Also it was close both to the Catholic Church of St. Michael's in Moor Street and to the Bull Ring. Here, in Birmingham's major market place, immigrant musicians could try and earn a living by playing to the crowds of shoppers and traders. Their descendants continued to do so into the 1920s and 1930s, as Clement Albericci brought to mind.

> **" I was born in Bartholomew Street in 1914. I played the Accordion with my friend making Accordion duet partnership. We played in the centre of Birmingham for**

many years competing with the Tamburros, we were called
the Albericci brothers and during the war years we
also played for Ensa in different parts of the country.
My grandfather Clem Albericci made Barrel
Organs for the Italians and also retuned them
and remarked them. He had a small factory
off Bartholomew Street in Banbury Street...
It was a marvellous atmosphere living in Little Italy
everyone knew each other and helped each other
financially and reading and writing as some
Italians could not read or write. (*Letter*, 1992). **99**

*Antonia and Antonio Tavolier
outside their sweet shop in
Duddeston Row. Their
grandaughter, Maria Sartori,
is in the arms of 'Auntie
Theresa', an Irish woman
engaged to Maria's uncle.
(Maria Giansante and John
Sartori)*

The tradition of these musicians has been carried on by Tony Iommi of the international
rock band, Black Sabbath, and by Alan Sartori, a partner in 'Ronnie Scott's' jazz club in
Broad Street.

The Albericcis and Tamburros both came from Sora in central Italy, close to Monte
Cassino. The latter arrived in England via Bristol and they travelled across the country as
accordionists before settling in Birmingham. Similarly, the Mielos arrived in the South
West about 1897. After busking around Devon, they too came to the Midlands 'to try and
find work'. Like their compatriots, they found a home close to Park Street in Duddeston
Row. Together with Bartholomew Street, this neighbourhood became known as The
Italian Quarter - a name it retained until the 1950s when redevelopment and growing
prosperity led to the dispersal of its inhabitants. (Giacomo Tamburro, *Interview,* 1992;
Miss V. Mielo, *Letter,* 1992)

These immigrants from Italy were from rural backgrounds. Despite differences in
language, religion and food, they had much in common with English incomers to
Birmingham from the countryside of Warwickshire and Worcestershire. Like them, they
had few skills for industrial employment and so they had to settle close to sources of
unskilled and irregular work; and like them, too, they could afford only the cheapest form
of housing. In common with the English poor, they sought protection and mutual support
by living amongst their kin.

In the later 1800s, one of the key families in the Italian Quarter was that of Antonio
Tavolier and his wife, Antonia Bove who both came from Sora. They prospered in
Birmingham and became owners of a 'Fried Fish & Chip Saloon', a sweet shop, and a
large house. This became a point of contact and familiarity for their relatives who followed
them to England. Because of this migration of their kin and because of inter-marriage, the
Tavoliers were related to many families in the Italian Quarter. Other 'stop-overs' for
newcomers from Italy were at the Italian grocer's shop of the Ferrarins, and Saracine's
Cafe in Coleshill Street. Like Antonio Tavolier, Guiseppe Saracine was also involved in
making ice cream. (John Sartori and Marie Giansante, *Interview,* 1992; Lyn di Mascio-
Walton, *Letter,* 1992)

This product was a major source of income for many Italian Brummies and the precise
nature of its making was kept a closely guarded secret. Pat Houghton's father was
Francesco Grego, and he:

66wouldn't impart it to anyone who wasn't going to go into
the business. He used to say, 'If you're gonna do it, I'll
show you how to make it'. I remember him doing it at the
back of gran's house in Vauxhall Road. This was a link
detached big three storey house with a big covered yard for
his cart and what they called a brew house (wash house)
which he converted for the ice cream. This was like a mini
dairy and it was subject to health standards. It had six inch
white tiles from floor to ceiling and he did the first boil up
in the stainless steel copper... In the war, instead of butter,

Italian woman selling ice cream in Smithfield Market, about 1901. (Birmingham Library Services)

dad had unsalted margarine and the milk and the sugar and the vanilla flavouring or pods, through government auspices. He used to put this mix into boil to make a custard. Then with great big pan ladles, like bed warming pans with a concave bottom and no top, he used to put it into stainless steel two gallon buckets and leave it to stand overnight to set like egg custard. There'd be muslin cloths over the top to keep out the flies and held down by weights. Then it was churned. It went into a freezer, a deep cylinder, with long opposing blades. It would churn like butter and outside it was electrically cooled. It turned from a pale yellow into an even paler yellow... He would fetch it into a similar container in an ice-cream cart, packed with ice from a place in Shadwell Street and he'd stay out till he sold out. It was the most wonderful ice cream the world has ever known. (*Interview*, 1992)"

Jean Thompson's grandad was Frank Iommi and he made ice cream in a similar way at his house in Buck Street where 'people would turn up with jugs and bowls'. At a later date, larger and better suited premises were used for ice-cream making, like the factory of Vincent Pontone in Park Street. Some families, such as the Verrechias, built up thriving businesses which they still run. They were famous figures in working-class Birmingham. Ron Smith described 'Mr Verrachia' as wearing 'a beautiful white coat' and as having 'brown eyes twinkling, with creases around them, a hooked nose, and beautiful mexican-type moustache, which veered upward when he laughed, and he did laugh a lot showing snowy white big teeth'. (Jean Thompson and R. E. Watt *Letters,* 1992, Ron Smith, *A Paddle Down Hockley Brook,* no date).

Mr Facchino was another ice-cream maker who employed his countrymen to push his carts and sell his product. He also sold hot potatos and chestnuts from portable machines, and he had barrel organs - as did the Secondinis. At one time, Mr Facchino returned to Sora to recruit teenage boys like Anthony Dominic Lombardi to work for him in Birmingham. The enterprising businessman then moved into the manufacture of cones and wafers for his fellow ice-cream sellers. These were sold as 'Facchino's High Class Purity Biscuits' and they were made in premises in Bartholomew Street. (Mrs J. N. Evans, *Letter,* 1992).

Pip Mattiello also supplied the trade from his tinsmith works in Duddeston Row. His speciality was the production of ice-cream conservators and equipment, and he was responsible for designing an ice-cream tricycle. The topboard of this had serving boxes and two 'easily removeable containers' of stainless steel. These were housed in a dust-proof perspex cover. Each container held five gallons of ice cream. In addition, there was storage space for biscuits and 'a special cabinet with hot and cold water supplies', so that 'the whole can be kept spotlessly clean with the minimum of effort'. This machine was awarded prizes and medals at the Dairy Show at Olympia. The Mattiellos also manufactured ice-cream cruisers with a Villiers engine and a speed of 30 m.p.h., and an ice-cream barrow. (J. Mattiello & Sons, *Brochure,* 1950; Mick and Vera Mattiello, Vera Lynoch and Winnie Frances, *Interview,* 1993)

One other business in which Italian Brummies were prominent was that of laying terrazo. Many of the floors of the main buildings in Birmingham were put down by Italians. Giovanni Poalucci's men 'did the terraza for the steps of the old Woolworths in the Bullring'; Giovanni di Mascio and his fellows extended the flooring at the Queen Elizabeth Hospital; whilst Pietro Polsinelli 'worked on the gold masacia work all over the entrance to the Villa Park & the yards & yards of terrazie he laid at Dudley Road Hospital & work on many Birmingham Banks & municipal buildings'. Other Italians were also active in laying the floors in these places and in making walls of mosaic. They included the Volante cousins, both called Ernie, who were employed by a relative called Ernie Bianchi, and

Tony Capucitti. The high-quality work of these men became well-known outside their own city, and they travelled the country to work on major British buildings. (Mrs Hughes, Lyn di Mascio-Walton and Peter Peters, *Letters,* 1992; Micky, Len and Ernie Volante, and Beattie Eastment, *Interview,* 1992)

Not only 'Nobladani' - Neapolitan speakers - were involved in laying floors. At the top of Bradford Street was a small community of Italians from Friuli. This region borders on Austria and Croatia and its people speak a distinct language. Like the district round Sora, it could not provide a living for all its inhabitants and many of them emigrated. One who came to Birmingham was Raffaele Reggio. As a floor layer, 'his pre-war work can be seen in the entrance of the New Street Odeon'; whilst 'after thewar he laid many of the floors in the Birmingham and Aston Universities where the respective Clerk of Works would hold up the job so that they could have him work there, showing the esteem in which his work was held'. (Geoffrey C. Mainwaring, *Mainwaring is My Name. A Personal and Family History,* unpublished manuscript, no date; Evalina Mainwaring, *Letter,* 1992, Santé and Maria Reggio, *Interview,* 1992)

Few terrazo businesses are now run exclusively by Italian Brummies, but there a number of other firms which are associated with them: B & D Public Works, owned by the Boccaioccis; and the shops of the Maturis. These latter were from Venezia in north-east Italy and their father had worked at the court of the Austrian Emperor. When he came to Birmingham, he traded as a cutler, grinder and repairer with premises on the Ladypool Road in Sparkbrook and on the Coventry Road in Small Heath. His descendants continue to operate from this last shop (Eunice Griffin, *Interview,* 1991)

Whilst immigrants from Sora lived in a recognisable part of Birmingham, they were settled amongst large numbers of poorer English people. Outside this quarter, Italians did sometimes encounter racial prejudice, but within it they were treated as neighbours. In

Back Row (left to right), Carlo Mattiello, Joseph Mattiello, Carmen Tamburro; Middle Row, Michael, Joe, Win and Vera Mattiello; Front Row, Stevie Tamburro. (Michael and Vera Mattiello).

the words of Mrs V. Cornfield, the families from Italy whom she knew were 'generous, hard-working and loyal'. Because of shared experiences and mutual attachments to the street and neighbourhood, intermarriage was common between English and Italian people: Micky Volante's mom was Nellie Pursehouse from Newtown Row and his dad was from Sora; Beatrice Verrechia married John Hammond in 1917; both the Phillips and Greens had local fathers and Italian mothers; Musticones and Farinas married into English families; whilst Peter Recci's background was typical of many others in that his dad was an immigrant from Sora whilst his mom was a second-generation Italian Brummie.

THE IRISH IN BIRMINGHAM

The same phenomenon of mixed unions was evident with regard to immigrants from Ireland. In 1894, an Irish Nationalist called John Denvir wrote that 'there are few places where the Irish are more intermixed with and intermarried in the local population than in Birmingham'. He compared this with the situation in Manchester, Liverpool and other towns in the north of England where people from Ireland were 'more homogeneous and rarely marry outside their own creed and nationality'.

Indeed, the great Irish Nationalist leader Patrick Pearse was the son of an English Brummie jeweller's apprentice from Lozells and an Irish mother. This connection has influenced Ian Campbell to write a folk song based on the line, 'Me father knew the man who played the pipes for Patrick Pearse on the night before the fateful day they took his life away'.

> **"When I was an engraver in the jewellery trade, I was sitting chatting at work. An Irish subject came up. And behind us in the room there were four ladies who were solderers and their forelady was a very respectable working-class Birmingham lady, middle aged - May. And her voice suddenly pipes up and she said, 'My dad's uncle was something very big in Irish politics, you know'. So I said, 'Oh, is that right, May?' She said, 'Oh, yes,' she said, 'But we don't talk about him.' 'Oh, why's that?' 'He was executed.' 'Oh, Good Heavens.' So I carried on working, and then as I was working, suddenly I remembered her name. May Pearse! I turned at her and I said, 'May, was your Dad's uncle Patrick Pearse?' 'Yes,' she said, 'But we don't talk about him, they executed him.' And this was such a bizarre situation. I thought, 'Good Heavens, if this woman were in Ireland this would be her proudest claim, "my Dad's uncle was Patrick Pearse", because I actually know a man whose proudest claim is that he piped for Patrick Pearse before he was killed.' (Ian Campbell, on, _Singing The City_, Radio 2, 23 June 1993, producer Sarah Conkey; see also, Gerard Weir, Craobh Phadraig Mac Phiarais [Patrick Pearse Branch] Conradh Na Gaeilige [Gaelic League], in Peter Leather, 'Hidden City', _Metronews_, 18 March 1993).**"

Ellen Moseley was another child of a 'mixed' marriage. As a youngster, she went to the Church of England school of St Alban the Martyr in Dymoke Street because it was 'Anglo Catholic and welcomed troubled children like myself who had Catholic Fathers and Protestant, chapel etc, mothers'. She was not unusual in her parentage, whilst there are many other Brummies like Kathy Tronson whose relationship to Ireland is more distant.

Her dad's 'father was born in Dublin and his mother in County Cork' but her own mom was English 'through and through'. (Ellen Moseley, *Letter,* 1987; Kathy Tronson, *Memories,* unpublished manuscript, no date).

The high number of couples who straddled national and religious divides was the result of the small percentage of Irish immigrants in Birmingham. Like most other industrial centres in Britain, the city had attracted such people from the early nineteenth century and by 1871, they numbered 9,076. Based on this figure, Birmingham ranked seventh in a list of the 'top20' Irish towns in Britain. But in a population of 343,000, emigrants from Ireland made up just 2.6% of the total. As a result, they dominated no large districts as they did in Manchester and Glasgow. Still in the 1860s, the Park Street area was called the 'Irish Quarter' - although it later became associated with Italian Brummies - whilst some other poor neighbourhoods also had significant Irish minorities. These became the site of Catholic churches: St Chad's, Shadwell Street, founded as a mission in 1808; Nechells, around St. Joseph's - opened in 1850 - and with the only Catholic cemetery in the town; Bath Row, near to St. Catherine's, Horsefair - where there was a mission from 1868; and Deritend, by St. Anne's in Alcester Street, which dates from 1849. In its early years this church was served by the Oratory priests, but in 1853 they moved to Hagley Road. Here they established the Oratory Church of the Immaculate Conception which became associated with Cardinal Newman.

Many of the Irish immigrants in Birmingham worked at labouring jobs, but after 1899 a significant minority were employed in the city's police force. In that year, the Watch Committee appointed a new chief constable and it was his presence which led John Rutherford to Birmingham. Later to become a chief inspector, this man was of an Anglo-Irish background.

Italian and Irish Brummie children from St Michael's Roman Catholic School, 1922. Back Row, left to right: Amelia Lanni, of an ice-cream selling family; Leonard Pouzulli; one of the Cunningtons; Frankie Tressine, of another ice-cream selling family; Jimmy Brittle; Mary Reid; not known. Third row: Peggy Hawkins; Nellie Lynoch; Tillie Giles; Chrissie Weston; Vincent Recci, from a terrazo laying family; Bernard Sable; Maggie Brittle; Jimmy Smith. Second row: not known; not known; May Shelley; not known; Kathleen Spencer; Hilda Poole; Vincent Spodute. Front row: Beattie Volante, of a side-car making family; Joey Lanca; not known; Nora Pittock; Annie Devoti, of the sweet shop owners in Digbeth; Hettie Bastianelli, of the newspaper shop owners in Duddeston Row; and May Rogers. (Beattie Eastment)

> ❝I then turned my attention towards the Police service as a career and found that amongst my ancestry on both sides there had been colonial policemen and commisioned officers in the famous Royal Irish Constabulary... I made a detailed study of the subject and found that the two crack outfits which aroused my interest were the Indian Police and the renowned Birmingham City Police. I was sent for by both and the toss of a coin decided that I should go to Birmingham, which at that time was rightly famous as the cream of the service. The Chief Constable was the famous Sir Charles Haughton Rafter and his assistant was Mr Cecil Moriarty, an academic and ex Irish international wing threequarter. They had both come to Birmingham from the Royal Irish Constabulary and had produced a force which was second to none. (John Rutherford, *All Correct Sir. The Memoirs of an Old Policeman*, unpublished manuscript, no date).❞

Rafter and Moriarty recruited a number of officers from Ireland and also Irishmen who had been in the British Army. One of these was W.H. Doughty. He was born in Bangalore, the son of a soldier and when his father died he returned to Dublin where he was sent to the Royal Hibernian Military School. After serving in the army in India, Bill Doughty joined the Birmingham City Police soon after Rafter's appointment. In 1909, he was one of 64 officers from Ireland out of a force of 950 men. This was 6% of the total, a proportion which was two and a half times as great as that of Irish people in Birmingham. Today, the city's police force continues to include a substantial number of men and women of Irish descent. (Stan Doughty, *Interview,* 1985).

People from Ireland were active in other aspects of Birmingham's life: the O'Donnells owned most of the handcarts which the market traders of the Bull Ring hired; and an Irishman founded the *Birmingham Daily Post* in 1857. John Frederick Feeney had come to

Sergeant Bill Doughty, standing front row, a physical training instructor with the City of Birmingham Police until 1919. (Stan Doughty)

the city in 1835 to work on the *Reformer,* and seven years later he bought the *Birmingham Journal.* The sales of this publication had declined to 1,200 a day, but the new owner soon increased this total to 12,000. He did so because of his 'thorough business habits, his tact, his unvarying courtesy, and his capacity for hard work'. (J.A. Langford, *Modern Birmingham and Its Institutions. Volume II, from 1841 to 1871,* 1871)

The *Journal* came out on Saturdays, and Feeney founded the *Post* as a daily paper to complement it. A year after his death in 1869, his son started the *Birmingham Daily Mail* (now the *Evening Mail*) as a late afternoon newspaper. Selling copies of this title was a major source of income for boys from poorer backgrounds. In the 1890s, my great uncle Bill Chinn was one of them.

> **❝No we used to know what it was to rough it. I used to run the Mails from the Mail office in Cannon Street, New Street. A big armful of Mails, sell 'em outside the factories, Birchall Street. And as the people knocked orf at six o' clock, 'Have you got a bit of bread please, bit of bread please.' (*Interview,* 1979).❞**

The *Evening Mail* cost ½d, and if boys sold 12 copies, they would be given a thirteenth paper for free. With their profit of ½d, many of them would walk to Mrs Mountford's cook shop in the Bull Ring. Here they would buy their tea - a piece of bread dipped in the fat of the meat which was roasted on the premises.

By the inter-war years, the Feeney family no longer had any connections with the newspaper founded by John Frederick and it was owned by Sir Charles Hyde. After his death, control passed to Lord Iliffe who formed the Birmingham Post and Mail Ltd. In 1956, this company took over the other newspaper group in the city, the Birmingham Gazette Ltd. This was named after its morning daily, but it also published the *Evening Despatch,* the *Sunday Mercury* and the *Sports Argus.* The firm was one of the oldest in the city, tracing its origins to 1741 and to Thomas Aris and his *Gazette.* Since the merger of the two businesses, the *Birmingham Post* and *Evening Mail* have continued to play a major part in the life of the city. In 1992, following a management buyout, the latter title won the accolade of 'Newspaper of the Year'.

The Feeneys were responsible for a major Birmingham institution and they were leading benefactors of another. In 1880, the Gas Committee of the corporation agreed to fund the building of an Art Gallery above the offices of their department. Five years later it opened, and over its doors was the motto 'By the Gains of Industry we Promote Art'. It was not the first building in the city which had been designed to celebrate painters and their work. As early as 1752 the Graves Gallery, now in Augusta Street, had been set up as a fine art dealers; whilst from 1829 the Birmingham Society of Arts had an exhibition building in New Street. But it was not a public facility as was the municipal Art Gallery.

This was filled with gifts by manufacturers like Joseph H. Nettlefold who gave 26 oil paintings by the Birmingham artist David Cox - the son of a blacksmith. Sir Edward Burne-Jones was another local man and some of his pictures were donated by John T. Middlemore, whilst other deposits were made by Alfred Elkington, Richard and George Tangye, William Kenrick, and Sir John Holder. However, of them all the collection presented by John Feeney was the most substantial. His first gift included 68 pieces of Japanese enamel, 73 of Chinese bronze, 98 examples of Japanese porcelain, 100 of Chinese and Japanese lacquer, and 208 swords from both countries. Numerous additions were made later to this list, and in his will Feeney bequeathed £50,000 to pay for a new art gallery which was opened in 1914.

During the 1930s the proportion of Irish people in Birmingham increased. Many of them were single people, but others were married men who sent for their families once they were established - or thought that they were. Maggie Hughes's dad, Thomas Byrne, was one of these latter.

Maggie Hughes (Byrne) and her sister-in-law Mary McGarry (Hughes) on the front of the motorbike, 1950s. (Maggie Hughes).

"He was a hard worker. He really, really worked. That's what brought him over here - work... Me sister Frances was here first. She just came over with her husband John Devine, 'cus he was in the army. With the letters she used to write to mammy and daddy and with no work back home, me daddy come over. Me daddy was over before me mammy, with one of the triplets. He was supposed to be looking for a place. But when me mammy came over he had nothing. We came over in 1939.

He was in the First World War. He worked in Filleries Toffees, Perry's Chains, The Serck. The last place, Evan and Kitchens, he took his stroke. He was a bloke that always moved around. Because of the army life. He came over to England to get work. He had hundreds of jobs. He was a working man from the day he went into the Irish Army. Then he went to the English Army. (*Interview*, 1993)"

People like Thomas Byrne were pulled from their own country by the lack of employment there. They were attracted to Birmingham by the prospect of jobs in the city's new industries, on its trams and 'on the building'; and they came from Northern Ireland as well as The Republic, from Dublin and Belfast as well as the countryside. Following the outbreak of hostilities with Germany in 1939, more Irish immigrants arrived as servicemen and to find jobs in factories which had gone over to war production. The labour shortage in these plants was so acute that in 1941, I. C. I. and Austin sent agents to sign up workers from Eire, as did the Transport Committee of Birmingham Council. The next year, their example was followed by the British Government when the Ministry of Supply began to organise the large-scale recruitment of Irish people for employment in Birmingham and elsewhere. These operations continued into the post-war period as Pearl Brophy recalled. She came to Birmingham in 1949 from Cork City.

"I was in a factory. I've always been in a factory since I came over here. First job was was just off Browning Street, by the Orthopaedic Hospital, at Baxter's. I was on a capstan, doing little bolts and screws for something. Used to have to put me on a bit of wood. I was that small, I couldn't reach the machine. I was on £3 a week. Then I went to Wilmot Breeden for £7 a week. On a power press, drilling and God knows what. Used to have a laugh. There were loads of jobs going after the war. You could walk into jobs.

Jobs at home were terrible. All my family came after the war. Our Dad was here. Didn't some people say that De Valera (the Irish president) sold us. De Valera got 30 bob for every Irish person that come over. 'Cus they needed all the roads building. The government here was crying out for Irish workers, especially on the roads. (*Interview*, 1993)"

Wilmot-Breeden specialised in making bumpers and door handles for motor vehicles. In 1960, its employees numbered 7,000 and it still operates in Stirchley.

Fisher's was another components company which employed Irish people. In particular, its paint shop became well-known for workers from Dublin, and throughout Birmingham men from The Republic's capital were prominent in the painting trade. Not all of them were trained in this occupation, but then as now, contacts were vital in obtaining employment. Consequently, as with English people, if immigrants had a job they tried to get friends and relatives into their firm once a vacancy occurred. To win the position, the applicants would be told to say that they were able to do the tasks which were needed.

Once signed on, their mates would help them to pick up the skills which were necessary. In this manner, the industrial cleaning firm Brero was celebrated for its Dublin painters. Billy Hughes recalled that like himself, the foreman there was a 'Dub'. Upon the application of yet another of his townsmen for work, he observed dryly that 'Dublin must be a lovely place since I left, with all the painters that live there'. (*Interview, 1993*).

By 1951, there were 36,000 people in Birmingham who had been born in Ireland and ten years later, this figure had risen to 58,000. By this date, there were large numbers of Irish people in all the city's working-class districts, but especially in Sparkhill and Erdington. In 1981, just over one in ten residents in both areas had come from Ireland - as they had in Fox Hollies, Sparkbrook, and Acocks Green. With their compatriots elsewhere in Birmingham, they are part of the city's largest ethnic minority. Catholic Churches with congregations of those who are Irish or of Irish descent are to be found throughout Birmingham, as are Irish clubs and shops; whilst in the Digbeth area there is an Irish Centre, an Irish Welfare Office and Irish pubs like 'The Dubliner'

Elizabeth Coffey working in Deutsch and Brenner Ltd metal merchants, Harford Street, late 1950s. (Birmingham Library Services, 'A Rough Aul Crossing')

JEWISH TRADERS

Along with Italian and Irish immigrants, Birmingham had a small but significant Jewish community. As early as 1766, its members had purchased land in Granville Street for their own cemetery, and a few years later Hutton noted that there was a synagogue in the Froggery. Most of the Jews in Birmingham were pedlars, and they used the town as a base from which to travel around its hinterland with their goods. At the turn of the nineteenth century, they numbered about 130 people and some of them had become involved in manufacturing: Moses Solomon was a jeweller and pencil maker; Eve Solomon made clocks, watch materials and she dealt in pencils, rubbers and slates; whilst Levi Aaron also manfactured watches and was a pawnbroker.

Over the next few decades, the Jewish population in Birmingham rose to an estimated 1,500, and by 1900, it stood at more than 3,200. Part of this growth was provided by long-established families, but much of it was because of the inward movement of Ashkenazi Jews. These people had begun to arrive in England in great numbers during the 1880s. They came because they were fleeing the terrible pogroms which they were suffering in the Russian Empire which at that time included much of Poland. Many of the Ashkenazi immigrants were tailors and so they settled in centres of the textile industry such as the East End of London, Manchester, Leeds and Glasgow. Because of its association with metal-bashing trades, Birmingham was not so popular a destination, but it did provide openings for some Jewish tailors like the grandparents of Ray Rosen. They came to the city about 1910.

“They settled in Ellis Street round where the synagogue was. They were very hard pushed to make a living. They lived in little back houses. My one grandfather had his workshop in the front of the house, they lived in the back, and they slept in the bedroom on top. My grandfather on my mother's side had just an attic and one bedroom with outside sanitation and what they called the brew house down the yard. He worked in Aston. He was what was known as an underpresser. He opened the seams... They lived in this ghetto community. On my mother's side they went to Leeds first, then to Argentina where they were promised land. And there was nothing there and they came back and came to Birmingham. My dad's side, my grandfather was from Warsaw and my great grandfather

Ray Rosen aged about 11 with his prayer book, prayer shawl (tailot) and choir cap for Singer's Hill Synagogue, about 1935. (Ray Rosen)

had a billiard hall in Warsaw. They had to flee. Just lost everything. Finished up in Bristol and worked for Hope Brothers tailors. Then their factory in Bristol stopped working and they moved it all to Birmingham. (*Interview,* 1993) ""

Sidney Rosen was a highly skilled tailor who could make the whole of a garment, and eventually he set up his own business in Masshouse Lane. His son, Walter, also had a tailor's shop in Corporation Street; whilst his grandson, Ray, was the third self-employed member of the family to serve the people of Birmingham by making clothes. Another well-known family of Jewish outfitters is the Zissmans who still have shops in 'town', and I remember that Our Kid and I had our first suits from Moss Zissman's in Sparkhill.

Like most of the Jews in Edwardian Birmingham, the Rosens were Orthodox in their faith and they worshipped at the Singer's Hill synagogue in Blucher Street. But whilst the Jewish community was united in a religious sense there were class and cultural distinctions. The recently-arrived families were working class, their older members spoke Yiddish, and they congregated around Ellis Street. The indigenous Jewish people included many professionals and they lived across the Hagley Road in more prosperous streets.

By the later 1930s, such differences were beginning to break down as many Jewish people began to move away from their quarter of the city. In 1928, the Rosens settled in Small Heath, whilst others were finding homes in Varna Road, Edgbaston. Still, one part of the city continued to have a Jewish feel.

""**Memories of Hurst Street, especially on Sunday mornings are very vivid although I am in my 73rd year. Sunday morning in Hurst Street always seemed quite busy as a child, because quite a few shops opened because they belonged to Jewish people. There was a drapers where I sometimes had a new dress on Sunday mornings if my dad had had a win on Saturdays. They didn't open on that day you see.**
Also Sharpes' the bakers & they sold lovely hot bread with black seed sprinkled all over it. Barney Sharpe their son also kept a theatrical digs, lower down Hurst Street, where the artists from the Hip (Hippodrome) stayed... Joseph's had a fish & chip shop & opposite their daughter kept a hat shop, & another member of the family kept an hairdressers, where I had my first ever perm, in the early 30s for 5/- hung up by my hair to some contraption up above by some sort of electric light cord... I also remember an impressive red bricked building with black iron railings each side of about a dozen steps leading up to a door. I was told it was a synagogue & it was situated about opposite Thorpe Street and I remember seeing gentlemen in long black coats & round hats, nearly always wearing beards going in and out. (Josie Elson, *Letter,* 1993) ""

Another Jewish businessman in Hurst Street was Lazzy Myers. He was an illegal bookmaker who was described by Mrs V. Connor as 'a small dapper man he always wore a (Billy Cock), old Brummie name for Bowler Hat, and he wore a heavy gold watch chain'. (*Letter,* 1990) .

There were Jewish shopkeepers elewhere in Birmingham. Mr Atkins recalled that on the Ladypool Road 'Old Galinsky' 'used to have bargain offers particularly in the way of stockings and gloves'. Nearby in Balsall Heath, Brummies like Les Brown remembered Samuel Goldwyn pushing 'a handcart around', before he went to America and made his fortune making pictures in Hollywood. His name then was Samuel Goldfisch, and his job was to transport the safes made by Charles Henry Whittingham in his workshop in Cox Street West, a manufacturer who later perfected 'steel fire-proof Cinematograph Storage Film Boxes'. (Mr Atkins and Les Brown, *Interviews,* 1984; Gordon Holden, *Letter,* 1993)

Two cinema entrepreneurs were based in Birmingham. One was Oscar Deutsch who built up the chain of Odeon picture houses, and the other was Bertie Samuelson who rented films. He came to the city from Southport in 1910 when he opened the offices of his Royal Film Agency in Corporation Street. From 1913, Samuelson became involved in producing pictures at Elstree when he made 'Sixty Years A Queen' about the life of Queen Victoria. He went on to make many other movies, but his company failed to survive the economic problems of the 1920s. However, his son Sydney is a major figure in the British film industry.

The Birchfield Odeon of Oscar Deutsch, late 1950s. (Birmingham Library Services).

THE EFFECT OF THE WELSH

Birmingham's Jewish community remains small for the size of the city and it has become more dispersed since 1945. Similarly, the large Welsh presence locally has become less noticeable. Close connections were forged between Birmingham and Wales in the 1200s when cattlemen from the Principality began to drive their animals to the Midlands town. Local entrepreneurs like the Holder family of Yardley provided pasture for this livestock to be fattened up before it was sold, and they made a good living by doing so.

It is likely that Welsh people settled in Birmingham from at least the later medieval period, and it is probable that most of them came from the Mid-Wales counties of Brecon, Radnor and Montgomery. It was this last shire which was the ancestral home of the Lloyds, Quaker farmers who established an ironworks in Dolobran. The first of their number to live in Birmingham was Sampson the elder. He arrived in 1699 because the town was unincorporated and gave religious freedom to those who were not members of the Church of England. But his descendants did not forget their Welsh heritage. In the nineteenth century, their home was at The Farm in Sparkbrook and nearby they named Dolobran Road and Montgomery Street. The Unitarian Kenricks, too, were of Welsh ancestry although they originated from the North Wales county of Denbigh.

Apart from these celebrated names, there were countless other immigrants from Wales in Birmingham. One of them was Taffy Lewis. Like the Lloyds, his family were from Radnorshire, athough they hailed from the county town of Presteigne. Before 1914, the Lewises left this place and settled in Small Heath at the house of a sister of Taffy's father. Soon after, they moved into Sydenham Road, Sparkbrook. During the First World War, Taffy worked at the B.S.A. making Lewis guns.

"It was at that time that they began to start treating factory workers as though they were human beings, providing social activities for them, canteens, dances. The B.S.A. took over Lloyd's farm and then opened it up as a recreation ground. Being in the scouts, this Lloyd's farm was a life saver to us. I used to sleep there every night in the summer...
I joined the scouts when the clubroom was at the top of Armoury Road, at the back of the Labour Exchange in the old canteen; and it was there that we met Baden Powell. He visited the works and he shook hands with us, the patrol leaders. I remember him as a little wizened old gentleman with shorts on that were a bit too long, but there you are, I shook hands with Baden Powell.
(Taffy Lewis, 'Any Road'. Pictures of Small Heath, Sparkbrook and further afield 1902- 39, 1979)"

The Old Bank of Lloyds in Dale End, drawn by Thomas Downing. (Kaye Downing)

Like their fellow countrypeople in Birmingham, the Lewises were not separated in a recognisable quarter, but their widespread presence is indicated by the large number of Welsh names in the city as a whole. In *Wrightson's Directory* for 1818, there were listed 68 people who were called Jones. This total was exceeded solely by the entries for those whose surname was Smith. The occupations of those with the Welsh patronym were wide-ranging: shoemakers, bricklayers, butchers, blacksmiths, publicans, shopkeepers, jewellers, brass founders, gunmakers, bakers, merchants and victuallers. There was also an E. Jones who ran a ladies' school, a T. Jones who operated the Soho Hill Academy, and a Hugh Jones who was a schoolmaster in New Meeting Street.

The tradition of these Welsh teachers has carried on into the twentieth century. Throughout Birmingham, people from the Principality are well known for their significant contribution to schooling in the city. I remember well both Mr Ray and Mr Gough who taught me; and at St. Mary's Church of England School in Aston both my Mom and my Nan had 'old Mr Lewis' as teacher. Our Mom knew him as:

> **strong, but a super teacher. But he loved his music and he kept us singing for ever. And it was him who taught us to sing properly in the descant and we were the first lot that had to leave St. Mary's and go to a secondary school, Charles Arthur. And we had assembly every morning and our very first morning at Charles Arthur we had our hymns and 'cus all those that came from St. Mary's sang the descant. And the headmaster Mr Butler and the teachers kept us there to all hours singing. They couldn't believe it. That was all because of Mr Lewis. (Sylvia Chinn, *Interview*, 1993).**

Many of the Welsh came singly to Birmingham, as did Mary Chandler. Her father and brothers were miners in Monmouthshire, and at the age of 13 she arrived in the city to find employment as a general servant for Dr Glass, a member of a Jewish family. After she married, she then worked as a cleaner for people in the Italian Quarter. (Doris Burke, *Letter,* 1991). Other Welsh immigrants came as part of larger parties. In 1832, some were

Birmingham Town Hall, built partly with the labour of Welsh workers, mid 1800s. (Birmingham Library Services, Pershouse Collection)

brought in specifically to work on the building of the Town Hall. This structure was of a classical design and it imitated the temple of Castor and Pollux in Rome. It was made from Anglesey marble and this meant that its construction was dependent upon skilled men from North Wales who knew how to work this material. Ten years later, there was a Welsh Prebyterian congregation in Peck Lane, and by the 1870s there were also chapels for Welsh Baptists, Congregationalists and Wesleyans.

During the 1920s and 1930s, South Wales became a major source of immigrants to Birmingham. The colliery villages of the region were affected badly by the depression and unemployment was rife. In these circumstances, a move to the Midlands was made attractive by proximity and by the presence of new industries as well as older ones which continued to take on workers. One of these was the railways, and as an area dependent on this business Tyseley became associated with a large south Welsh population. This feature was reinforced after the Second World War when Arthur Lloyd, a director of Bakelite, recruited 200 men for his firm from his home area of the Rhondda Valley. (Dr Lew Lloyd, *Interview,* 1993)

Archie Hunter, the Scottish captain of Aston Villa. (The Owl, 21 January 1881)

THE SCOTTISH INFLUENCE

In 1951, there were 12 counties in England and Wales which were of primary importance for sending people to Birmingham. Six of them were in the Principality. At this date, 25,000 people in the city were Welsh born. This total was less than that of the Irish, but it was greater than the number of Scots. In 1824, their settlement in Birmingham was indicated by the opening of the 'Scotch Church' in Islington, and Scottish people like Murdock and Kynoch played important roles in the city's manufacturing businesses. Like many of his fellows, this latter industrialist was involved in local politics and he was also president of Aston Villa.

Other Scots were largely responsible for the rise of this football club to national prominence. George Ramsey was a Glaswegian who joined the Villa in 1876, two years after its formation. He was acclaimed as one of the greatest dribblers of the period, and as a player he was responsible for finding the ground at Wellington Road, Perry Barr. In 1884, he became the secretary of the club - a position he held until 1926 - and with Fred Rinder he negotiated the club's move to its present site at Villa Park. Because of Ramsey's reputation, he attracted fellow Scots like Archie Hunter. As captain, he led a team which

Kynoch's floats in a parade, from an old postcard. (Thanks to Roy White)

was celebrated for its 'Scottish style of play' and which won the F. A. Cup for the first time in 1887. Another Scotsman, William McGregor, was a committee member of Aston Villa. He was a draper in Summer Lane and it was through his vision and planning that the English Football League was organised in 1888.

In spite of the presence of influential Scots in Birmingham, most of their countrypeople did not migrate until the inter-war years. As was the case in South Wales, the heavy industries of Central Scotland were hit hard by the slump, and many men came to Birmingham to earn a living. Amongst them was Bill Hendry. He was a collier from Lanarkshire, and when he and his father lost their jobs they faced a difficult situation. There was no employment in the mines, and the only other main source of work nearby was in the steel plants of Motherwell. Locally it was believed that these hired only Protestants, and as Catholics the Hendrys felt they had no chance of being taken on. As a consequence, they hitched lifts to Birmingham where they had a cousin living in Small Heath. Inexperienced in factory work, Bill Hendry found a job as a blacksmith's striker in the B.S.A., whilst his father was employed at Reynold's Tubes. Once established, Bill's mother came to join the two men, and after living in rooms they took a house in Esme Road, Sparkhill.

The inward movement of Scots continued after the outbreak of hostilities with Germany in 1939, as Cath Shields mentioned.

> **When war was declared I was in service and I was called up. So I had to go into the forces and so I chose Birmingham. Well, ma brother came first and he was, I'll tell you straight, we were worried about him. Ma mother was a widow and he'd sent some letters and some money and then they faded. So I came down to check if he was alright. Then ma mother came and all later on...**
> **In Scotland they were very funny about employing Catholics. I got a lovely job in Burnside in service. When ma first day was over, the woman said 'Well, the kids love you, but Cath, I've got to ask you this, what's your religion?' I said, 'Catholic' and she said, 'Oh, I can't keep you.' I said, 'I'm not going to rob anything'...**
> **Then when I got my first job in Birmingham, I didn't know factory work and I worked on the lathes making shells. Well, I thought this woman was going to ask ma religion after she'd started me. And as I turned away, I thought she would call me back. Never even asked ma religion! And this other woman said, 'They're not like that down here. They're not bothered about your religion.' I really thought that it was great. That really made me look good. I had no regrets at all about coming to Birmingham... I'm more fond of Birmingham than youse. Youse took everything for granted. (Cath Henry, _Interview_, 1993)**

Ironically, although Cath Shields came from the same district as Bill Hendry, it was their separate moves to Birmingham which brought them together and led to their marriage.

LOCAL MIGRATION

Apart from those inhabitants who were Welsh, Scottish, Jewish, Italian and Irish, Birmingham did have a few German residents. In 1881, there were just 295 of them, but their relevance to employment in the city was disproportionate to their small number. Muller's factory in Aston Brook Street was anglicised as Miller's and it made lamps, as did

Powell and Hamner's in Whitehouse Street, Aston. The latter partner was the German and he gave work to many local people. Amongst them were my Nan, my Uncles George and Bill and my Aunts Gladys and Nance. Our Nan recalled Mr Hamner as 'a very big man, a wonderful man. And he never passed you. Every morning he walked through all the shops to say "Good Morning", with his red carnation in his button hole. Never a rose, always a red carnation.' (Lily Perry, *Interview,* 1993)

Despite the presence of ethnic minorities in Birmingham, their collective numbers were relatively small. As late as 1951, 89.1% of the city's inhabitants were born in England. Of course, such statistics do not take into account those who were descended from immigrants, but they do give some indication as to the great size of the English population. This included representatives of all the nation's counties. There were many from Durham - another area which was devastated by the Depression - the East Midlands, and Somerset and the West Country. Migrants from these areas had also been obvious in the nineteenth century, including amongst them people like William Lerwill, a clock-case maker from Braunton in North Devon. (Janet Morris, *Letter,* 1991) Still, these places were of secondary importance in sending people to Birmingham. Along with those Welsh counties which were of primary significance, the shires which gave the city most of its people were Warwick, Worcester, Stafford, Hereford, Oxford and Gloucester. Of these, Warwickshire was pre-eminent. In 1951, 71% of Birmingham's citizens who were listed in the census were born in that county.

Ellen Barwell (Lynn), left Norfolk in 1923 to be a domestic servant in Birmingham and went 'on the buses' as a clippie - conductor - for Birmingham City Transport in the Second World War.
(Ellen Barwell)

These proportions had changed little in several hundred years. The list which exists indicating the origins of almost 700 people who settled in Birmingham between 1686 and 1726 shows that 90% came from within 20 miles of the town. Over 200 had migrated from Warwickshire; a similar number had arrived from Staffordshire; nearly 100 were Worcestershire people; and over 40 belonged to Shropshire. Of the remainder, about 60 in all came from Leicestershire, Cheshire, Derbyshire, Lancashire and Middlesex; and a further 50 were drawn from elsewhere in Britain.

The on-going significance of local migration is emphasised by a detailed investigation of the people of one group of houses in nineteenth-century Birmingham. Linden Terrace lay off Monument Road in Ladywood. It was built in 1860, and the census for the following year records 22 heads of households and spouses: 13 were born in the city, one each came from Northfield and Bromsgrove in Worcestershire, two originated in London, and one each hailed from Ireland, Kent, Essex, Leeds and Bolton. Forty years later, the same headings gave four Birmingham-born people; three from Staffordshire; two each from Worcestershire and Oxfordshire; one from Warwickshire, Leicestershire and Somerset, two from Swansea and Yorkshire; and one each from Ireland, Scotland and Newcastle. (Winifred C. Cheong, *Victorian Terrace, a community study 1860-1960,* 1993)

As a family, the Manlys exemplified the movement of people to Birmingham from the wider West Midlands. They trace their ancestry to John who was born in the late 1600s in Claines, near Worcester. His son was a horse dealer and in the course of his business travels he met and married Susannah Bradstock of Evesham, also in Worcestershire. They settled nearby in Bidford-on-Avon in Warwickshire. Like his father and grandfather, their child was called John. Soon after his birth in 1789 his parents died and he was raised by a local farmer and his wife who were his distant relatives. They had a friend in Birmingham called Henry Adcock, a jeweller in Summer Hill Terrace, and when John Manly was 21 he gave him employment making gilt toys and patent shoe latchets. By 1815, the apprentice worker had set up his own workshop in Newton Street and his descendants ran a brassfoundry. (Gina Manly, *Letter,* 1993)

Not all local migrants became as prosperous. Edna Piper's family lived in a close community in Barker Street, Ladywood but they experienced hard times and bad housing during the 1920s. Her grandfather was a shepherd and farmworker in Little Tew in Oxfordshire. He 'gradually moved up to Staffordshire, eventually reaching Fradley Junction where the Coventry canal & the Trent & Mersey canal met'. His son, who had been born in 1882 in Steeple Barton, Oxfordshire, came to Birmingham to find work as a cabinet maker. He lodged in King Edwards Road, Ladywood where he met his wife who lived nearby in Edward Street. Through her grandmother, she had Irish blood. So did my Mom's family. (*Letter, 1990*)

My Great Granny Wood was born in Worcester, the daughter of a soldier and an Irish woman whom he married whilst stationed at The Curragh. Granny's husband was a bargee from Tewkesbury, and about 1915 after the birth of my uncle Bill and my Nan, they came to Aston in search of a living. They settled in Whitehouse Street where Great Grandad Wood had cousins. After a time of joblessness and poverty in the 1920s, he worked at 'The Met' as a stoker and at Rudder's and Payne's Woodyard. My Nan's husband was Arthur Perry and he was a bandsaw operator. Grandad was raised in Hick Street, but his family were from Tipton in South Staffordshire where they had lived for centuries.

The Chinns were also short-distance migrants to the city. In the early 1800s, they were tenant farmers in Kings Heath which was in Worcestershire until it became part of Birmingham in 1911. My great-great grandad, Henry Chinn, was a bailiff for a local landowning family, the Cartlands, and he married a woman from the nearby district of Northfield. After his death from a fall from a haystack, his wife and children lost their home. In search of work, Mary Anne Chinn moved a couple of miles towards Birmingham, settling in Sparkbrook during the 1870s.

This was a semi-rural suburb on the outskirts of the city, but it did have cheap back-to-back housing. It was also close to Moseley where many middle-class people lived, and women like my great-great grandmother could earn a living by doing their washing. Her eldest son was Richard. After serving in the Coldstream Guards, he married a local woman, Florence Bartlett, whose family were from Somerset and had intermarried with Romanies. Great Grandad Chinn became a blacksmith's striker at the B.S.A. He never

The Gate, Studley Street, Sparkbrook before 1914 when the Bicknells were landlords of this beer house. Studley Street had a high proportion of people who were descended from local migrants. (Mike Tunnicliff)

earned more than 18 shillings a week, but his son, Richard, became prosperous through operating as an illegal street bookie from 1922. My Dad, Buck, followed him and he continued in business along the Ladypool Road until 1984. We still have not moved far as a family, as we are all settled in Hall Green which borders on Kings Heath and Sparkhill.

A famous Romany encampment at the Black Patch, Handsworth, May 1907. (Birmingham Library Services)

Before its legalisation in 1961, the structure of cash betting in Birmingham reflected the city's reputation as a home for independent-minded, small gaffers. In many cities, those who took bets illegally were employed as agents by lawful credit operators or 'turf accountants'. This was not the situation in Birmingham where there were many self-employed bookies like Joe Wheeler of Summer Lane, Horace Foster in Kyrwicks Lane, and Rose Pickering of Highgate. These people provided employment not just for themselves and their families but also for runners - those who took bets for them in factories, pubs and elsewhere.

> 66 **In 1922 when I was 11 years old I used to take a bag of Bets to the local Bookie in Green Lane Small Heath. I was brought up in Wright Street Small Heath where we lived in a terrace. The bets were from the neighbours in the terrace and the Street. I was paid 2/- a week every Saturday Night by the Bookie whose name was (Tucker Wright). I was late for School many times owing to a Copper coming by while I was taking my bag of Bets to the Bookie's & would make a dash to escape the copper. (George W. Langham, *Letter*, 1988)** 99

My family was not alone in escaping from poverty through bookmaking. Nor were they unusual in having farmed in areas which became built-up in the 1920s and 1930s. For if Birmingham was the Workshop of the World, it is only in the recent past that the city's hunger for space has banished agriculture from within its boundaries. Margaret Cutler's grandfather rented land from the Cadburys in Oak Tree Lane, Selly Oak and she has 'memories of the farm, the horses and the work that took place' there before the Second World War.

Similarly, Norah Clift is descended from farmers. (*Letter,* 1993) In 1778, one of her forebears cultivated 84 acres of land in Smethwick. Sixty years later, his son had moved to Sherlock Street in Highgate where he had a house, cowsheds and piggery. The family stayed in this locality as cattle dealers until the 1880s when William Clift took over Trittiford Farm in Yardley Wood. At the turn of the century, his son became tenant of Willow Farm in Stirchley but because he did not own the land, the family had to move on when it was decided to build on it. In 1922, they took the tenancy of Heybarn Farm in Hay Mills, and within a couple of years they had moved again to The Glebe Farm in Yardley.

> 66 **It was very productive and we always managed to get two crops of hay. We usually employed 4 farm workers. It was a mixed farm and Father produced milk and I believe we had about 30 dairy cows. He also kept beef cattle. There were generally a few bullocks and heifers and if a particularly good calf was born he would rear it. He did some cattle dealing visiting various parts of the country buying for customers. Our milking cows were generally of rather mixed breeds, dairy shorthorns, Devons and Lincoln Reds and even Herefords... We had no pasteurising plant and the milk was merely cooled and passed through a filter. All our cows were hand milked twice a day at 5.30 a.m. and then again at 3 p.m. and the milk was sold to a neighbouring farmer named Mr Sandford...We grew kale, swedes and mangolds for the cattle and also some corn. One year we had a load of sewage from the sewage farm in Cole Hall Lane. This was not looked upon very favourably by our neighbours when it was put on the fields and was**

never repeated... but it certainly provided us with wonderful swedes and mangolds and a huge and unexpected crop of tomatoes, which we gave away to friends and relations mainly for making chutney. (*Letter,* 1992) "

In 1931, Glebe Farm was built on with council houses and its buildings disappeared, but Birmingham's agricultural heritage is recalled in farmhouses which remain standing. Amongst them are Cole Hall in Shard End, Malthouse and Bell's Farm in Kings Heath, The Old Farm in Sutton Coldfield where Bishop Vesey was born, and Blakesley Hall. This was erected by Richard Smallbroke in the late 1500s, and its structure indicates the wealth of a family which has given it name to Smallbrook Queensway. Other buildings which remain from this period are the 'Golden Lion Inn' now in Cannon Hill Park; Sheldon Hall; Selly Manor in Bournville; Lifford Hall which is part of the premises of the chemical manufacturers Rhône-Polenc, formerly John and E. Sturge; the Stone House in Sutton Coldfield which was one of 51 dwellings paid for by Bishop Vesey; and Stratford House at Camp Hill built for the Rotton family and 'a remarkable survival of a 2 storey and attic timber-framed and plastered manor house'. Nearby is the 'Old Crown', renowned as the oldest building in Birmingham and with the date of 1368 on its front - although it is probable that it was built 100 years later.

Today this public house is surrounded by factories and busy roads, but some parts of Birmingham still have a rural feel. Kings Norton boasts a village green round which are a number of timber-framed structures, the medieval church of St Nicolas and an 'old grammar school'. The vicinity of St Laurence's in Northfield also appears as a tranquil spot which conjures up romantic images of 'Old England', as do those of St Edburgha in Yardley and St Peter's in Harborne. All four places lie just a short way from main roads, but this small distance gives them a certain seclusion and separateness from modern Birmingham. This feature is not shared by Kings Heath, Erdington and Moseley Villages which are cut through by major thoroughfares so that the buildings of a distant past are almost overwhelmed by noise, bustle and new developments.

EUROPEAN REFUGEES AND MIGRANTS

The 1920s and 1930s were the decades in which the localised nature of Birmingham's people began to be affected by a stronger Celtic influence. During the same period, the city became home to an increasing number of Europeans. Some of these arrived in small family groups and were not part of a larger migration. One such family was that of Nora Olgiati. She was from Poschiavo in Switzerland, and after a short stay in Tunbridge Wells she came to Birmingham in the early 1920s when her father obtained a job in the Grand Hotel as a patissier. He gained his position because his brother-in-law, Maurice Semadeni, was the manager there, as he was of the Midland Hotel. The Olgiatis lived in 'a very poor but friendly district' where 'Mother was addressed as "Madam" and Father as "The Count"'. Like many immigrants to Birmingham, Nora was brought up to respect her English neighbours but she was also encouraged to remember her heritage and her father taught her 'to be proud of being Swiss'. Today, although Nora has been settled in Birmingham for over 60 years, Poschiavo 'still means home'. (Nora Angelina Olgiati, now Nora Davis, *Little Foreigner,* unpublished manuscript, 1982)

Unlike the Olgiatis, there were other newcomers to Birmingham who had no choice but to leave their homeland. During the First World War, 30 Serbian children were brought to the city and away from the attacks of the Austro-Hungarian forces. Their benefactor was Dame Elizabeth Cadbury and they were looked after in Bournville. In the years following the Second World War, adult Serb exiles followed them to Birmingham. They disagreed with the Communist rule of Marshal Tito, and as a focal point for their community they have paid for and built themselves a church. St Lazar's is in Cobb Lane, not far from the Cadbury's factory, and it is a beautiful Byzantine-style structure.

During the 1930s, a significant number of other refugees had made their way to Birmingham. Zoe Josephs has written about how Hitler and the Nazis inflicted terror and violence on German Jews, and she has detailed how the Simmons family were in the forefront of helping some of them. They had a large Victorian house in Edgbaston, and the spare rooms were 'occupied by people staying sometimes a night or two, sometimes longer'. Many of them moved on to the United States of America and elsewhere, others stayed.

> **"Of all the immigrants to Birmingham in the 1930s, Dr Kossi Strauss, in co-operation with his partner, Eric Weiss, was perhaps the greatest benefactor to his adopted city. Together they founded the firm of Foseco which rendered outstanding help in the war effort and later gave employment to thousands. (Zoe Josephs, *Survivors. Jewish refugees in Birmingham 1933-1945*, 1988)"**

Kossi Strauss had a degree in organic chemistry and a doctorate in engineering. In Germany he had worked as the Chief Industrial Chemist for Halle, a firm which was run by the uncle of Eric Weiss. The company made compounds for the foundry industry, and the two men established a similar business in Birmingham after their flight to safety. Today, Foseco is a leading international operation which is based in Nechells.

After the defeat of Germany in 1945, national boundaries were re-drawn throughout Europe and there was a massive movement of people. Many became displaced persons, and in particular large numbers of Poles found themselves stateless. Some were allowed into England to work in a few basic industries. One of them was Bruno Plauszewski. At the age of 14, he had been taken from his family by the Nazis and with other Poles he was sent to Austria as part of a slave labour force. Upon the war ending, his part of Poland was annexed to the Soviet Union because of the insistence of Joseph Stalin. Unable to return to his own country, Bruno came to England to work as a miner in Stoke-on-Trent. Soon after, a friend in Birmingham suggested that he come to the city. He did so and found a job at the M.E.M. in Tyseley. As he recalled, 'at that time it was very easy, you can change jobs, you could go from one factory to another'. (*Interview*, 1993)

Mary and George (on left) Christoforou, Greek Cypriots from Mazotos, in their Fish Net fish and chip shop on Shaftmoor Lane, Tyseley, 1993. (Richard Albutt, Birmingham Library Services)

People like Bruno Plauszewski were not the first Poles to settle in Birmingham. They were preceded in the nineteenth century by the Muntz family who came from Minsk. In England, George Frederick Muntz became a manufacturer of metals and from 1840 until his death in 1857 he was one of Birmingham's MPs. His son Philip also represented the borough in Parliament, but he is best known for the important part he played in ensuring that Birmingham was granted a Charter of Incorporation in 1838. This allowed a town council to be set up, and 50 years later the actions of Muntz were acknowledged when he became an honorary freeman. On this occasion he was praised by the mayor 'as one of the founders of our municipal liberty'. The family is remembered by Muntz Street in Small Heath and by the Muntz Trust. This was set up in 1890 with a sum of £21,000, the income of which was distributed between Birmingham's voluntary hospitals.

Today, Polish Brummies are not gathered in one area of the city. But if their homes are scattered, they do have a community centre in Bordesley Street. Nearby, a Polish Mass takes place each Sunday in St Michael's - formerly the focal point of Birmingham's Italian Quarter. Similarly, the Greek Cypriots of the city are spread out, although they have two social clubs in Erdington as well as a church. However, the community's main place of worship is in Summer Hill at St Andrew's and St Mary's and it is here that the Greek Orthodox Bishop of Birmingham is based.

Greek Cypriots came to Birmingham from the late 1930s. At first, men came on their own to sell the lace which was made by their wives in the district around Paphos. When they had sold their stock, they returned home to obtain more. In the 1950s, some of them ceased this movement to and fro and they brought their wives and children to settle with them in Birmingham. During the same decade, there was a migration to the city by a few men from the villages of Mazotos and Ardpou in the area of Larnaca. They worked in the Burlington Restaurant, just off New Street, and then in other dining places. Mirroring the earlier coming of Italians from Sora, these pioneers set out the path for others to follow. In the words of Bambous Charalambous, 'if one person from one village comes then he brings his relatives and his friends and one brings another.' Through hard work and saving their money, these catering industry workers moved into self-employment. Today, they own a large number of fish and chip shops in Birmingham, whilst in the city centre there are restaurants owned by other Greek Cypriots and those from Greece itself such as 'Bambos's, in Station Street. (*Interview, 1993*)

Following the Second World War, there was a labour shortage in many sectors of the British economy. Needing more people to help in the task of rebuilding the country, the government actively sought immigrants for this purpose. Not only were recruiting agencies set up in The Republic of Ireland, but also they were established in Italy. As with most of his countrypeople who came to Birmingham, Santé Mizzoni is from Sora; but unlike the great majority of them he arrived at the later date of 1952. He remembers seeing a poster in his town which advertised for workers to come to England, and with many others he did so. His fare was paid by the British government and he was directed to employment on the railways in the West Midlands. Once he had acommodation in Birmingham, he sent for his immediate family to join him. (*Interview, 1992; Carla Lloyd, Letter, 1992*)

BLACK BRUMMIES

In addition to Italians and Irish people, the government encouraged West Indians to move to England. As a major centre of population and industry, Birmingham was a place which became home to many of them. Here they settled in Handsworth, Birchfield and East Sparkbrook where large Victorian houses had been turned into premises for multi-occupation. It was this last district in which Winston Bennett lived first.

" I came here in July twenty first 1960. I came from Barbados, I was living in St John's, Barbados. Well actually, not knowing about the country I had relatives who had come over in 1955 and who lived at 50, Grantham Road, and I came to lodge with them. At that time in Barbados things was not that easy, work was not that easy to come by, although I did work for the transport as a bus conductor and I was learning carpentry. But I came to England to find steady work... When I came over her I worked for a firm in Tyseley as a grinder, then Bywaters on the Coventry Road, I was a butcher there for three years. Then I left and I been working on the building and other jobs. It depends on where the money was, I decide to follow it, especially after I settled down and had a family, I was looking for better finances. You could afford to leave from one job to get another, then, but after the late 1960s it was more difficult. (*Interview*, 1993) **"**

An Afro-Caribbean transport worker, 1950s. (Birmingham Library Services, Dyche Collection)

Just as Winston's cousin, Zelda Holditt, had put him up when he arrived in Birmingham, so too did he provide a base for his younger sister and niece when they emigrated.

By 1961, the population of Afro-Caribbeans in Birmingham had increased to 16,000, compared to just 500 ten years before. Most historians attribute this rise to a convergence of factors. They point out that there was a growing population in Jamaica, Barbados and other islands and that this put pressure on employment opportunities in these places. Given that the United States restricted immigration from the West Indies in 1952, they argue that the search for work led many Afro-Caribbeans to Britain where jobs were plentiful. This reasoning should not be dismissed, but there are flaws in it. Many emigrants were not out of work. Some were students, whilst others left secure and skilled employment to come to places like Birmingham. As Tommy White put it, he gave up his position in Montserrat's water department because 'you see, as young people... as you know living with your father and mother, you want to be independent'. Along with other young adults, he saw emigration to Britain as a means to achieve that objective. He had two brothers and a sister already in Birmingham, and he came here as 'that's the only place I know, really'. (*Interview, 1993*)

Tommy White had a wide-range of jobs. Shortly after his arrival in 1960, he painted the gas holders in Windsor Street; then he was employed for 13 years at the Morris Commercial, until the Adderley Park plant closed down in 1974; after that he did a few years spot-welding; and finally, he worked at the Land Rover. Many of his fellows from the West Indies also went into factories. Others took vital positions in the National Health Service and on the buses. They were welcomed by most employers who required their services, whilst the city's Trades Council was opposed strongly to any discrimination. In pursuit of this policy, it urged unions to recruit Afro-Caribbean workers and to ensure that they were not paid lower wages than those White people who did the same jobs. Still, there were instances of racial prejudice. In the late 1940s, there was a strong feeling that Black people should not work in the bakery trade; and in 1954, their employment by Birmingham Transport Department was objected to by a majority of bus workers. This prejudice was overcome so that by the end of that year, 257 Black and South Asian people were employed on public transport in the city.

. An Afro-Caribbean National Health Service nurse, 1950s. (Birmingham Library Services, Dyche Collection)

It would be foolish to believe that bigotry has disappeared; equally, it would be wrong to think that people from the West Indies have not encountered friendship and kindness from their fellow citizens who are White. Carl Thorpe has experienced both reactions. His uncle came to Britain at an early date and he settled in Gloucester because he had a friend there. Carl's father and one of his brothers joined him. Together, they moved on to Birmingham where they found work in the B.S.A., and as a younger son, Carl came to be with his dad in 1962. He travelled from Kingston, Jamaica on a Spanish ship, and after his arrival he went through a depressing period of joblessness.

Andy Hamilton, the famed jazz musician, at 'Ronnie Scott's' club. (Endboard Productions for Central Television)

> **I used to work back home constantly. And when I came over here I made lots of applications for jobs. I used to walk about days and days looking for work. In the end, I was really desperate. I saw two applications in the Mail, one for a gardener in that hospital in Moseley, the Sorrento, and one was for P. J. Evans. I wrote off to both and I got a reply from both and I took the job of motor mechanic at P. J. Evans. I learned my trade partly in Jamaica plus in England I attended college three nights a week for seven years, at Handsworth Tec.**
> **Well there was some racial discrimination. When I started at P. J. Evans in 1962, there was racial discrimination from the guys, but not as far as the management was concerned. The gaffer was Scotch and he was a very nice guy. And he helped to smooth things out. I was 19 then and you know young boys, they used to take the micky. (*Interview*, 1993)**

Through hard work, talent and determination, Carl Thorpe has become a highly-skilled mechanic with sought-after qualifications to repair Rolls Royce cars. Along with many immigrants, he came to England, 'just as everybody used to say, for five years, but somehow I'm still here'. And in common with other West Indians, he has married in Birmingham and with his wife he has raised children who are Black British.

There are 44,000 Afro-Caribbeans in Birmingham, as well as nearly 3,000 Black Africans from countries like Nigeria. Collectively, these Black Brummies have contributed greatly to the well-being of the city and to its life. Their numbers include educationalists such as Carlton Duncan, footballers like Mark Walters and Tony Daley, athletes such as Sonia Lanaman, community workers like Bert Carless, Gus Williams and Roger Bethune, and musicians of the talent of Joan Armatrading, Ruby Turner and Andy Hamilton. A jazz saxophonist, this Jamaican played on Errol Flynn's yacht before he emigrated to England in the late 1940s. Since then, he has been an active trade unionist and a cult figure on the music scene in Birmingham. In recognition of his services to the city, Andy Hamilton was awarded an honorary degree by The University of Birmingham in 1992.

Carl Thorpe of P.J. Evans after passing the course to become a Rolls Royce mechanic, 1967. (Carl Thorpe)

Black music has affected many bands locally. South Asian Brummies like Apache Indian sing a mixture of Jamaican influenced Ragga and Punjabi Bhangra, whilst Aswad and UB40 have found fame through another sound from Jamaica - reggae. This last group is made up of eight men from Balsall Heath and Moseley. They grew up in the 1960s and 1970s, as part of the first generation in Birmingham which lived in a society that was fully multi-racial. Their own backgrounds highlight this phenomenon: Afro-Caribbean, Scots, Egyptian, Welsh, Irish and English.

Today, the records of UB40 are outselling those of 'monster groups' like U2; but like John Taylor, Sampson Lloyd and other successful businesspeople in Birmingham's history, the band members remain committed to their city. They live in the districts in which they were raised; they sponsor a youth boxing club, 'The Cauliflower Ear', in Digbeth; and they are bringing jobs to Birmingham. This is because they employ local people in their recording studios in Deritend. Called the Slaughter House, the premises backs on to a canal, and was once a brewery which received its supply of hops from barges. (Joe Travers, *Interview*, 1993)

Yemenis at prayer in a Balsall Heath house, early 1960s. (Badr Kahya)

YEMENI WORKERS

Although the large-scale immigration of Afro-Caribbeans did not take place until the late 1940s onwards, there were a few Black people in Birmingham before that. Some settled in the city soon after the Second World War, when they were demobbed from service in the Royal Air Force and they joined isolated men like 'Old Joe'. He had a stable in Long Street, Sparkbrook and he used to 'come round the local roads with a pony and float'. The two wheels of this vehicle 'were imitations of the lids of cherry blossom boot polish and Old Joe used to deliver the consignments of shoe polish to all the hucksters' shops (little general stores) and shoe repairers'. (Mr Atkins, *Interview*, 1984)

If there was a small Black presence in the city in the interwar years, there were also a few Arabs. In 1939, it was reported that a family of these people had died through suffocation when a wall of sandbags had collapsed on them in an air-raid shelter in Holloway Head. Soon after this sad event, Arabs in Birmingham formed an association called Zania Islamia Allonia which set up a mosque in Edward Road, Balsall Heath; and by 1952, their community totalled 400 people, the great majority of them from the British colony of Aden in South Yemen. In the following years, the Arab population increased in the same way as did that of the Greek Cypriots, and for the same reasons. The main figure amongst the Yemenis locally was a man called Zindane who was from a well-off family. After he arrived in Birmingham, he wrote back saying that 'it was good' and 'he brought the rest over', close and distant relatives, friends and associates. In their turn, they encouraged their contacts to emigrate.

Along with most unskilled immigrants, many of the Yemenis found work in factories. Later, again in common with the Greek Cypriots and others, some of them bought their own businesses as did Mohamed Mockble. He came to Birmingham in 1955. At first he worked at the Chrysler, but after he had saved enough money he bought a small general store on the corner of Fulham Road and Stoney Lane which he still runs. Nearby in Taunton Road is the carpet warehouse of Abdullah and Son. The business of these North Yemenis has become well known in Birmingham, not just for its products but also for its adverts on local radio. (Carmen and Gamal Mockble, *Interview*, 1993)

THE CHINESE QUARTER

The kitchen of the Noble House Chinese Restaurant in Sutton Coldfield. (Birmingham City Council)

The Yemenis of the city are gathered in Small Heath, Sparkbrook and Sparkhill. They number an estimated 3,000 people - a comparable figure to that of the Chinese. Similarly, a few members of this ethnic minority were present in Birmingham before 1939 and they were involved in the laundry trade around Gosta Green. But the majority of Chinese in the city arrived more recently, during the 1960s and 1970s. Their roots lie in the farming communities of the New Territories of Hong Kong, particulary in the villages of Paipo and Yuen Long. Along with so many other rural immigrants to Birmingham, they were lacking in the skills for well-paid industrial work and as a consequence, a few families decided to open take-aways. They did so because they were Cantonese, and as Geoff Yap put it, people from this province 'are well known for their food'. Working as teams of either husbands and wives or brothers, some of these entrepreneurs moved into the restaurant trade. They employed waiters and waitresses from their own villages, and in turn, many of these started their own businesses. (Geoff Yap, Kitts Green Linen Services, *Interview*, 1993)

Chinese take-ways and restaurants are found throughout Birmingham now, and their owners and workers are also scattered in their homes. However, several large restaurants are situated in the Hurst Street area. With names like Heaven Bridge and Chung Ying Gardens, they have become the focal point of a vibrant and colourful Chinese Quarter. Few people live here, but there is a community association in the aptly-named Cathay Street; and when it is the Chinese New Year, the streets are full of processions with imitation dragons and they sound to the noise of cymbals and firecrackers.

A number of businesses have been set up to supply the Chinese catering trade. They include Kwok Hing in Sherlock Street and Wing Yip, situated in Nechells away from the Chinese Quarter. This sells food:

> "mostly from the Orient, the spices, the rice. We do sell a lot of frozen food, partly from abroad like prawns, shrimps, king prawn, pancake roll, vegetable pastry, dim sung, dumpling, only from abroad. But in the meantime, we sell a lot of pork, chicken, beef, duck. You name it, we have it. And food and food accessory, like wok... anything go into the kitchen. (Mr Wing Yip, City Sound Archive Birmingham Museums and Art Gallery, *Take Heart Birmingham. People, History & Change in Birmingham's Heartland*, oral history compilation cassette, 1992)"

THE SOUTH ASIAN MUSLIMS OF BIRMINGHAM

Another distinctive ethnic food is the balti. Although its origins lie in the North-West Frontier of Pakistan, this dish is most associated with the Kashmiris of Birmingham. It is like a stew and it is the speciality of a number of simple and unpretentious restaurants. A balti is served in a metal karahi (wok) and it is made with chicken, lamb, fish or vegetables, whilst each balti house has a secret combination of ingredients which includes coriander, cardamon, ginger, garam masala, fennel and cummin. The interest in this food has become great since the late 1970s, and Birmingham has become well-known in the West Midlands for the restaurants which specialise in it. As a result, visitors flock to the city to enjoy 'a uniquely Brummie phenomenon'.

The popularity of baltis is partly because of their cheapness: a starter and a main course costs about £5, and as most balti houses are unlicensed, diners can buy their own drinks from a nearby outdoor (off licence). But affordability and value-for-money are not the only reasons why these restaurants attract so many customers.

> **"The balti house experience can mean many things -
> glass top tables, appetising counter displays, kebabs
> and tikkas cooking on an open flame, moist and freshly
> baked nans and chapattis, but most of all, sizzling balti
> bowls hissing their messages of spicy freshness.**
> **(Andy Munro, *The Essential Street Balti Guide*, 1993)"**

Preparing a Balti. (Gareth Lewis, Birmingham City Council Department of Planning and Architecture)

Birmingham's 'balti-house belt' is concentrated on three roads in the south-east of the city. On the Ladypool Road in Sparkbrook are restaurants like 'I Am The King Balti' and 'Imran's'; nearby on the Stratford Road in Sparkhill are 'Sher Khan' and others; whilst on the Stoney Lane are the famous 'Adil's' and 'The Royal Al Faisal'. These latter premises are owned by Mr Ajaib who claims to be the first balti restaurateur in Birmingham. Elsewhere in the city, there are concentrations of balti-houses in Moseley Village and on the Moseley Road in Balsall Heath; on the Alum Rock Road in Saltley; on the Lozells Road; and on the Bristol Road in Bournbrook. Apart from this last location, these neighbourhoods are characterised by their large numbers of Kashmiris, a Muslim people whose land is divided between India and Pakistan.

There were South Asian Muslims in the city before the Second World War, and in 1944 they opened a mosque in Speedwell Road, Edgbaston - not far from where the Central Mosque stands now on Belgrave Road in Highgate. Still, the large-scale migration of these people to Birmingham did not begin begin until the late 1950s when the British government was seeking labour from across the Commonwealth. In particular, it made arrangements with the Pakistani authorities to send over male workers. Mostly, they came from what were then poorer and neglected rural areas such as Mirpur in Azad Kashmir. The social structure here is the same as that of the other predominantly agricultural districts which have sent immigrants to Birmingham from across the world. It is a place where the emotional and physical support of kin is valued and needed; and there is 'a chain linkage of family right across the region', whilst 'close neighbours tend to be called family'. (Safdar Hussein and Sharif Mohammed, *Interview,* 1993)

As a result of these intimate connections within villages and the closeness of extended kinhip ties, the Kashmiri men who came to Birmingham were mainly from certain 'tehsirs' (districts) such as Khadanvad and Dhadyal. Like many West Indians, some of them emigrated for reasons other than a search for work. As Khawaja Khan remembers, he left Dhadyal because 'everybody was going and I had my passport'. As with other men, he came to stay with a relative, a brother who rented one room in a house on the Dudley Road. However, their maternal uncle lived in Saltley and 'he asked us to move over here'. They still live in this neighbourhood, and like many men, they were joined by their families during the late 1960s and early 1970s. (*Interview,* 1993).

Lacking manufacturing skills, most Kashmiri workers were employed in factories as machinists and labourers. Since the recession of the early 1980s, this kind of work has been affected badly by lay-offs and younger Kashmiri men are now finding employment with the council, in the catering trade, as retailers of groceries and textiles, and as taxi-drivers. So are those Pakistanis who come from Gujar Khan, Gujar and Rawalpindi in the Punjab. Like the Kashmiris from Mirpur, these people speak a Punjabi dialect, and as family groups they have gathered in Saltley, Alum Rock and Small Heath. In the same manner, some of them have bought businesses with the help of relatives and friends who are involved in 'savings committees': each week or month, the members of these deposit a sum of money with a holder and on a rotating basis one person collects the pool of cash. Generally, these committees are run by women, some of whom work in their own homes for textile manufacturers.

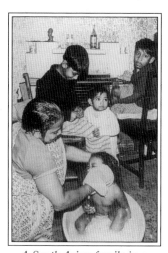

A South Asian family in a Birmingham house before it was renovated and improved by Urban Renewal, early 1970s. (Birmingham City Council Urban Renewal)

During the late 1950s, the Pakistani government also directed workers to Britain from East Bengal, now the independent state of Bangla Desh. The majority of these people came from the north-eastern district of Sylhet, as did Mohfizin Rahman.

> **❝I came here in 1960, third of February. Some of my relatives were here. I found it very good. I didn't get homesick as I had a lot of relations. After six months I bought a house in College Road, now demolished. A lot more Bengali people came and more are coming to Saltley because Bengali people like to stay by their own countrypeople. (*Interview*, 1993)❞**

Mohfizin Rahman worked for British Steel, and since his retirement he has been an active community worker and governor of Shawhill School. However, many Bangla Deshi men are employed not in factories but in the catering trade. Apart from the balti houses, most of the 'Indian' restaurants of Birmingham are actually owned by families like the Chaudrys. They were amongst the first Bangla Deshi restaurateurs with the 'Shah Bagh' on Bristol Street, and they now own 'The Purple Rooms' on the Stratford Road in Hall Green.

Not all South Asian Muslims in Birmingham are from Mirpur, Gujar Khan and Sylhet. Some are from East Africa, and like Ahmed Youssef Barekh a few originate from the Indian province of Gujrat. In 1986 he went from India to work in Panama, and he came to Birmingham three years later when he married. His wife, Amina, arrived in England in the late 1970s when she and her mother followed her father to Blackburn. He was a religious teacher in a mosque whose committee included Gujrati Muslims and which had sent for him. He and his family then moved to Birmingham where he continues to teach the Muslim faith in Saltley. In addition to Amina's relatives who live locally, Ahmed has a first cousin whose house is close by. As a consequence, he wants to stay in the neighbourhood because it has South Asian shops as well as those who speak his own language. (*Interview*, 1993)

Similarly, Campblepuris have gathered in Sparkhill where they are involved in the ownership of lodging houses and the retailing of carpets and textiles. They are from the north west of Pakistan, as are the Pakhtoons (Pathans) who are concentrated in Saltley, Alum Rock, Sparkhill and Small Heath. Most of these come from the Swat area or from the district surrounding Peshawar. Many of them have close connections with the British Army and before they came to Birmingham they operated canteens and shops on miltary bases in Cyprus, Northern Ireland and elsewhere. Now they work in factories, they own shops and taxis, and in common with other Muslims, their children are becoming involved in higher education. Indeed for many Pakhtoons, 'we do not think about making money, but we want to make a high grade in life'. (Mr. A. Rahman, *Interview*, 1993)

If most South Asian Muslims have come from agricultural backgrounds, it should not be presumed that all of them were without qualifications or emigrated as part of village-based groups. Manzoor Ellahi is a Hinku-speaking person from northern Pakistan who lived in the southern state of Sind from when he was a young boy. As a consequence, he is fluent not only in his native language but in Sindi, Urdu and English. Although he had no relatives in Birmingham, he arrived here in 1960 and obtained skilled work as an electrical tester. Because he wanted to gain more experience, he took jobs at four different places which included the G.E.C., Rubery Hospital and Tucker Trucks in Hall Green. In 1970, he moved to Saltley and he opened a radio and television repair business in Wright Road. He is now retired, but he has motivated his children into professional positions with the teaching of the Koran that 'this is your duty - to keep gaining knowledge until you die'. (*Interview*, 1993)

SOUTH ASIAN HINDU AND SIKH BRUMMIES

After the Irish, Pakistanis make up the third largest ethnic minority in Birmingham with a population of 66,000, compared to nearly 13,000 Bangla Deshis and 51,000 Indians. This latter heading includes Sikhs from the eastern part of the Punjab, and again contrary to popular belief, the presence of these people in Birmingham pre-dates the Second World War. In 1938, the press noted that three Sikhs, who wore turbans, found it difficult to put on the gas masks which were to be supplied in case of attacks by German warplanes. Elsewhere in the city there were Indian doctors who had trained in England and settled locally after obtaining their qualifications. Along with students and businessmen, they were members of the Birmingham Indian Association. In the early 1940s, this organisation was joined by one for Indian workers. It was set up by Dr Dhani Prem for those non-professionals who had came to Birmingham during the war and who were living in cheap accommodation in Balsall Heath, Aston and Saltley.

After 1945, these workers sent for their families to join them, as did some ex-servicemen who had fought in the Indian Divisions of the British Army. Seven years later, it was estimated that the city had a population of 2,500 Pakistanis and 500 Sikhs and Indians. However, the large-scale migration of these latter people did not begin until the early 1970s. Many of them were shopkeepers and traders from East Africa where some of them had been settled for over fifty years. They fled this region because their businesses and lives were threatened by the 'Africanisation' campaign of Idi Amin in Uganda, and because of a worry that their position was insecure in Tanzania and Kenya.

Large numbers of Sikhs and Indians had been encouraged to move to East Africa by the British authorities and they held United Kingdom passports. They had been away from India for one and more generations, and as a result when they left their homes many of them came to places like Birmingham rather than to cities like Bombay. An example of this migration is the Gosai family. Its head, Rajbharthi, was 14 when he left his village of Modpur in the Indian province of Gujrat to go to Dar-es-Salaam where he joined his brother. Later he acquired a restaurant, but in December 1972, he and his family left Tanzania and settled in Leicester where his sons, Pravin and Chandrkant, worked as machine operators. With the money Rajbharti Gosai had earned in Dar-es-Salaam and with the savings made in England, he came to Sparkbrook in 1976. He rented a shop on the Ladypool Road and he opened it for the sale of Indian sweets and vegetable savouries like samosas and bhajis. (Pravin and Chandrkant Gosai, *Interview*, 1993)

Other Gujrati Hindus are established as leather traders, pharmacists, newsagents and retailers of materials for sarees and clothing in general. They are concentrated on the Soho Road in Handsworth and along the Stratford Road in Sparkhill. Here there is a small South Asian Jewellery Quarter which includes premises owned by Mohanlal Bhimji Pattni and others. The Soho and Stratford Roads are also the focus for Sikh traders. Like the Gujratis, many of them come from Kenya, Tanzania and Uganda. Some of them trace their origins to labourers who were brought over by the British to build railways and who

Young South Asian Brummie dancers in Centenary Square.
(Post Studios, Birmingham)

South Asian shops on the Soho Road, 1993. (Richard Albutt, Birmingham Library Services)

were followed by their families. Because their children had the benefit of schooling, they were able to open up businesses and to move into better jobs.

Later, Sikhs arrived in East Africa as professional people like teachers or as skilled builders and carpenters. The father of Ranjit Singh Burmi was one of these latter workers. In common with many Sikhs he was from Jalendhur in the Indian Punjab and he set up in Nairobi as a building contractor. Ranjit himself was in the Kenyan Police, but after independence he kept his British passport and so lost his job. Because of apartheid he was unable to follow his White colleagues to Rhodesia and South Africa, and he decided to come to England in 1965. He joined his brother in Evelyn Road, Sparkhill and after he went to the Labour Exchange he was sent to work as a clerical officer in a government agency. Unfortunately, he had to leave that job because of racial discrimination and he later joined the Royal Mail where he is now a supervisor. *(Interview,* 1993)

Along with Gujratis, Sikhs are prominent in professional positions as dentists, solicitors and architects, whilst the chairman of the British Medical Association (Birmingham Division) is Dr Surinderjit Singh Bakhshi who was brought up in Dar-es-Salaam. Other Sikhs are notable as shopkeepers, off-licence proprietors and dry-cleaners, and they are well known in the building trade with firms like Pannessar Construction. In particular, they are renowned for their skill as carpenters, and like Newton Kitchens of Sparkhill a number of businesses have grown up which are related to this craft. Many Sikh women are also active in the life of Birmingham. Some have entered higher education, others have taken clerical jobs, and some are machinists for textile manufacturers.

Despite the discrimination which he faced when he first lived in England, Ranjit Singh Burmi is keen to emphasise that he has no regrets at leaving Kenya and coming to Birmingham. He believes that now relations between the races are good; similarly, Pravin Gosai is proud to be 'a good British citizen and a British Asian'. He and his brother are raising their children to respect 'the majority of people' but to remain loyal to their heritage. One way in which South Asian Brummies maintain their identity is through Bhangra. This is based on the music played at harvest time in the Punjab when dancers tell the story of a farmer who sows his seeds, gathers in the crop, and then sells it at the market. In the urban and industrial setting of Birmingham, Bhangra has been influenced

Pravin and Chandrkant Gosai in the Sona Sweet Mart, Ladypool Road, Sparkbrook, 1993. (Richard Albutt, Birmingham Library Services)

by other rhythms and sounds and it has evolved into a distinctive British Asian sound which is very popular. Groups which play in this style regularly sell more records than those of bands which have hits on 'Top of the Pops'.

THE PEOPLE OF BIRMINGHAM

It would be folly to argue that there is no racial tension in Birmingham. There are attacks on members of ethnic minorities and in 1985 there were serious civil disturbances on the Lozells Road when the shops of South Asians were attacked by some White and Afro-Caribbean youths. But overall, relationships between the various peoples of the city are distinguished by tolerance and a wish for everybody to get on. It is these features which impress most citizens.

Most immigrants are like Winston Bennett: although they miss their homelands and their friends, they have no regrets about coming to Birmingham. They have made lives for themselves here and they are Brummies. Wherever they come from, the people of Birmingham belong to this city and have given something to it.

" Ranjit
Ideally you become part of the country: you have relationships with people, you start to acclimatise yourself, you become part of the structures of society... In some respects you almost begin to think you were born in the country. It used to come to me as a surprise, - 'Oh, I'm Indian!' - from time to time... there was a slow and steady shift into the English way of life; and by English way of life I don't mean the white way of life because English way of life is a white and black way of life. I know that Enoch Powell says that the Black man simply by living in this country, or even born in this country, does not become an English man, but I think he is wrong. An English man can be black or white or what ever he can be; an ex Anglo-Saxon or a Viking or a Hun, but now is English. (Birmingham Black Oral History Project, *Brochure and Cassette*, 1992) "

Children at Clifton Road School, Sparkbrook, about 1974. (Mike Tunnicliff)

NOTES

I should like to thank the following people for their help in the research for this chapter: Mrs C. Hands and Chief Superintendent C. W. Lloyd of West Midlands Police; Sydney Samuelson for sight of *Bertie - The Life and Times of G. B. Samuelson,* 1991; Martin Flynn, Head of Faculty, Birmingham Library Services; Dr Margaret Gelling; Jenny York, Area Librarian, Birmingham Library Services; Nahid Moselhuddin, Officer Urban Renewal; Gulzarina Khan, Officer Urban Renewal; Howard Pidd, External Relations Officer, Urban Renewal; Frank Baker; Eric Rolls; Anne Roach, Birmingham Museums and Art Gallery; Micky Volante for his contacts with Brummies of Italian descent; and for their information on the Italian Quarter, Albert Albericci, Eileen Kenny, Madelaine Green, Mr R. Phillips, Miss Albericci, D. J. Albericci, Neil Cassin, Mr Secondini, Mrs P. Arnold, Mrs Musticone, and Sadie Horton.

FURTHER READING

Walter Allen	*All in a Lifetime* (1959)
Vivian Bird	*Streetwise. Street names in and around Birmingham* (1991)
Birmingham Jewish Historical Group	*Birmingham Jewry: 1749-1914* (1980)
Mildred Boulton	*As I Remember* (1993)
Vanley Burke	*Voices of Handsworth. Photographic images of Handsworth from 100 years ago to the present* (1992)
W. H. B. Court,	*The Rise of the Midland Industries, 1600-1838* (1938)
Jack Crawford	*Jack's Patch* (1992)
Jack Francis (Jim McGovery)	*Pawnshops and Lard* (1989)
Syd F. Garrett	*I Remember… Tales of Old Ladywood* (no date)
Mike Green	*Brummie Boy 'Go Home!'* (1991)
Valerie M. Hart	*Balsall Heath. A History* (1992)
George Hill	*To Live It Again…* (1983)
Win Heywood	*My Mother's Story* (1986)
Win Holt	*Up The Hill to Harborne* (1992)
Denis Howell	*Made in Birmingham* (1990)
Douglas V. Jones	*Edgbaston As It Was* (1986)
Helen and Keith Kelsall	*Diary of a Victorian Miss on Holiday* (1992)
Julia Larden (ed)	*Three Brummie Lives* (1991)
Joseph McKenna	*Birmingham Street Names* (1986)
Ann Madden	*From Paradise to Motherland. A reminiscence pack to assist Birmingham's Post-War Caribbean Immigrants in recalling their pasts* (1993)
Leslie Mayell	*The Birmingham I Remember* (1980)
Hilda Mleczko	*My Book of Memories. Picking Up The Pieces* (no date)
Ronald K. Moore	*Up The Terrace Down Aston and Lozells* (1988)
Dave Reeves (ed)	*Brummies All Write* (1991)
Malc Stent	*Go and Play Up Your Own End* (1992)
Simon Taylor	*A Land of Dreams. A study of Jewish and Caribbean migrant communities in England* (1993)
Keith Thomas	*The Poems, Prayers and Writings of Keith Thomas* (1991)

CHAPTER 5
INTERNATIONAL CITY

Centenary Square, with The Hall of Memory in the foreground and the ICC in the background.
(Post Studios, Birmingham)

THE NEW BIRMINGHAM

Sounds tell the story of Birmingham. The clamour of manufacture, the clatter of horses, the rattle of trains, the crescendo of lorries, buses and cars, the banging of building, the roar of aeroplanes and the rhythm of music. The level of these noises indicates the direction in which the city and its people have gone and in which they will travel. Birmingham remains a great manufacturing centre and the crash of machinery still echoes through many of its streets. It continues to be motor city, and the sound of engines hums day and night across its length and breadth. But it is becoming known for the rock beats and classical melodies which are drawing people to its concert halls. It is achieving fame for the facilities of its conference centres. And it is finding renown in the throb of crowds who throng its exhibition halls.

A new Birmingham has emerged which boasts major developments like the International Convention Centre, Symphony Hall, the National Indoor Arena, Birmingham International Airport and the National Exhibition Centre. These facilities are drawing an increasing number of visitors to the city. Once here they discover a place which bears little relation to the caricature drawn by the critics of industry. They are able to listen to the internationally acclaimed City of Birmingham Symphony Orchestra; they can watch the celebrated Birmingham Royal Ballet (formerly Sadlers Wells) and the Welsh National Opera at the Hippodrome Theatre, or else see the D'Oyly Carte - now based in Birmingham largely because of the enthusiasm of Councillor Bryan Bird; they can look at the world's largest collection of pre-Raphaelite paintings in the City Art Gallery or view special exhibitions in the Gas Hall, the foremost show place of its kind in England; they are able to walk in Centenary Square, the biggest public open space built in Europe since 1945; they have the facilities of the Birmingham Repertory, Alexandra and Crescent

Victoria Square, showing the Council House and 'The River' by sculptor Dhruva Mistry, 1993. (Gareth Lewis, Birmingham City Council Department of Planning and Architecture)

Theatres; and in the newly-pedestrianised Victoria Square they can gaze at one of the largest fountains in any European city centre.

The Birmingham of the 1990s is re-defining its role and carving out a new reputation as a cultural centre and meeting place. In 1991, it hosted the delegates of the 97th session of the International Olympic Committee - thanks greatly to the efforts of Denis Howell, formerly Labour MP for Small Heath; the next year it became the United Kingdom's City of Music and it entertained the Council of Ministers of the European Community; and in 1993 it has drawn travellers to the largest gathering of Canaletto's works which has been mounted in Britain. Each year, its Readers' and Writers' Festival is the largest literary event in the country; it has an annual Film and TV Festival which premières movies from across the world; and its yearly Jazz Festival provides the opportunity to listen to celebrated musicians.

The speed with which Birmingham has embraced the concept of conferences and the accessibility of art has astonished many observers and given them cause to re-assess their image of the city.

Gas Street Basin: photographer Roy Peters' insightful portrait of old and new Birmingham. The canal barges are overlooked by the glass works of Abraham Cutler – now a pub – as well as the Hyatt Regency Hotel and the ICC.

The Broad Street area in 1977, just before the recession which battered Birmingham's manufacturing base. (Darryl Chinn)

> **❝Last week, art-lovers met in the shadow of Birmingham's International Convention Centre set on searching out and acknowledging the existence of quality public art in the second city's underpasses and arcades. The event was part of Birmingham city council's concerted effort to prove that the city is no longer a smoke-filled cultural desert. The city's new pride is reflected in the Convention Centre itself. To many locals it is visual art at its most functional. It illustrates a new confidence in the economy of the city and affirms that art is clearly visible to all those who wish to look for it. Our guide... Ranger Bird began with worthy praise of the Convention Centre and Centenary Square, the site of almost £1m-worth of public art. The building itself is adorned by Ron Hasledon's *Neon Birds*. The moulded strips of light give the impressions of birds in flight...**
>
> **Dominating the square, an enormous and impressive redbrick Italian-style piazza designed by Tessa Jaray, is *Forward*, Raymond Mason's monument to Birmingham. The glassfibre sculptured tableau combines vast creams with red highlights and patches of brown: it illustrates the development of the city from industrial production to the service era. (Haydn Price, 'A Magical History Tour', *Independent*, 27 May 1992)❞**

Birmingham's move into the service industries and its building of prestige structures in the city centre has been part of a co-ordinated policy by its local government. This has been adopted enthusiastically by most councillors as a means to counter the ravages of recent recessions on employment and businesses.

RECESSION

Throughout their history, Birmingham's people have responded swiftly and effectively to changes wrought by technology and fashion. As one trade has declined, then the city's workers have moved into another; as one technique has been superseded, so they have taken up innovations. But in the early 1980s, the ability both to react to change and to found new industries was challenged by a slump in the economy. In particular, this had a serious and adverse effect on British manufacturers. Many firms closed down, and a large number of workers lost their jobs.

This decline in manufacturing was the result of a combination of factors: depressed world market conditions which had followed the oil crisis; competition from newly-industrialising nations in South-East Asia where labour and productivity costs were lower than those in Britain; a lack of investment and modern plant in some businesses; problems between management and workforces in others; and a government which seemed uninterested in supporting those who made things and which appeared to want British society to become a centre of services.

As the country's major centre of manufacturing, Birmingham was hit hard by recession, and between 1978 and 1989 local employers had to lay off 107,205 workers. This was an enormous and almost catastrophic fall of 43% of the employment in the making of things - the most vital part of the city's economy. Job losses were spread across the field, from the old-established metal-bashing firms to the newer producers of cars and electrical engineering goods, and many well-known firms disappeared. Birmingham's rise as a manufacturing centre had begun in the llOOs, and in just a decade it appeared that centuries of development would be destroyed.

This has not happened. Not because of government policy but because the surviving manufacturers and their workers have determined that they will continue to make good-quality products which are competitively priced. Despite numerous business closures and in spite of huge job losses, 30.1% of local workers still make things. This total is greater than that of any other sector of business in Birmingham and it is bigger than that of anywhere else in the country.

Aston Science Park, Dartmouth Street, 1992. (Gareth Lewis, Birmingham City Council Department of Planning and Architecture)

Resilience and commitment have maintained the city's position as the manufacturing heartland of the United Kingdom, but employers are no longer able to provide work for all those who once depended on them for a living. By the early 1980s, the city had many jobless people for the first time in its history. As recently as 1966, less than 2% of Birmingham's workforce was registered as unemployed, but by 1981 this proportion had soared to 21%. This global statistic failed to emphasise the huge numbers of men and women who were out of work in certain parts of the city. By the end of the 1980s, the Small Heath inner-city parliamentary constituency had a jobless rate of 30.1%., whilst on the outer-city Cockhill Council Estate in Rubery, unemployment reached a dismal and depressing 70%. At the same time, job losses were associated with a fall in wages: in the two years from 1979 to 1981 average incomes in the West Midlands plunged from second place in the national league table to the bottom position.

HIGH TECHNOLOGY

If long-term mass unemployment was an unwelcome arrival to Birmingham in the early 1980s, then another unwanted first was the limited presence of new industries which could provide work. During the 1980s a major growth area of the British economy was the high technology industry; but most businesses in this field were concentrated in England's Silicon Valley along the M4 and in Scotland's Silicon Glen. Two leading exceptions to these locations were Kalamazoo and Apricot Computers. The former firm is based in Northfield and it expanded into computers from its production of manual book-keeping systems; whilst the latter business was begun in 1965 as Applied Computer Techniques. It was founded by Roger Foster as a mainframe computer bureau, and although it later moved into distributing software it was not until the early 1980s that it began to make computers itself.

> **❝In an industry dominated by the large, functional boxes and low price/performance of the IBM-PC, the Apricot PC was little short of a revolution in personal computer design. It immediately positioned ACT as a British equivalent of Apple, being innovative and non-IBM compatible. The Apricot PC was powerful, compact, ergonomically designed and transportable. Innovative features included the Microscreen - a small LCD panel in the keyboard which provided a programmable function key template to support different applications. This enabled users to identify and select key functions without learning complex commands. Incidentally, the original Apricot was also the first major commercial PC to use 3.5" disk format, predating IBM's eventual move to this format by four years. (Jes Dorrell, 'Apricot Computers: A Case Study for Information**

Technology in Birmingham', in, Barbara Tilson, ed, *Made in Birmingham. Design and Industry 1889-1989,* 1989. My account of Apricot is based on this article.)**"**

The Apricot PC was developed by a research team in Birmingham, but the company has based its main factory in Silicon Glen in Fifeshire. This was because of the financial advantages offered by the Scottish Development Agency and the presence of both suppliers of electronics components and workers who were experienced and skilled in high technology. However, Apricot Financial Systems has remained in Birmingham and it is the market leader in investment management systems in the United Kingdom; whilst Apricot Research and Development is also based locally, at The University of Birmingham Research Park.

This has proved a beneficial siting which has allowed an exchange of staff, knowledge and resources between the company and the university, and it has led to collaborative ventures such as that on voice input technology. The Research Park itself was set up by The University of Birmingham and the City Council to encourage this kind of movement of skills and knowledge. In particular, this is achieved through Birmingham Research and Development Ltd, the university's technology transfer company. Its brief is to help companies develop links with the Faculties of Science, Engineering and Medicine, the local authority's Business Development Service, and sources of venture capital.

Aston University is also involved in encouraging the growth of high technology industry in the city. In 1983 it went into partnership with Birmingham City Council and Lloyds Bank to set up Birmingham Technology Ltd which manages the 22 acre Aston Science Park where over 1,000 people are employed by 80 firms. Amongst them are Deltacam Systems which provides CADCAM systems, and Sagem Lucas. This is a joint venture between Lucas Industries and the French company Sagem and it is developing a new engine management system. Near to the Aston Science Park is the Hoskyns Technology Park, a £3 million research and development centre set up by Hoskyns Group Ltd. This is one of the leading systems houses in the country, and its investment in the infrastructure of Birmingham has been matched by an injection of £3 million into training.

Chamberlain Square from the Central Library looking towards New Street, showing the Town Hall and the Council House with the Rotunda in the background. (Gareth Lewis, Birmingham City Council Department of Planning and Architecture)

AN ENTERPRISING COUNCIL

It is no surprise that the City Council has been an active force in trying to bring high technology industry to Birmingham. In the late 1970s, confronted by the depressing loss of jobs in manufacturing, councillors recognised that local government had to take a positive approach if new employment opportunities were to be provided. Based on a political consensus, their strategy has been to encourage inward investment, to work with employers, and to provide the facilities which will bring those with spending power to the city. This vigorous involvement in the economic well being of Birmingham has been recognised nationally. In 1991 Paul Cheeseright of the *Financial Times* wrote that:

> "This financial year Birmingham city council will spend a gross £1.47bn. It has more than 42,000 employees. It needs to raise nearly £860m from the community charge. It is the largest metropolitan authority in England. It is conscious of its own importance: prickly even about its fiefdom.
>
> The council has a tradition of energy, of intervention. This, coupled with its size, means it has a finger in every pie. It embodies a strain of municipal activism which, in the Thatcher years, was acceptable to central government only if it came from the private sector. In Birmingham, for the past 120 years, the main thrust of activism has come from the council. (Paul Cheeseright, 'The inheritors of Chamberlain', *Financial Times*, 18 October 1991)"

Birmingham Central Library, 1992. (Birmingham Library Services)

The entrance to the National Exhibition Centre. (Post Studios, Birmingham)

A performance of the City of Birmingham Symphony Orchestra, conducted by Simon Rattle, at Symphony Hall, Birmingham. (Post Studios, Birmingham)

The actions of the council since the 1970s are in keeping with well-established traditions both of municipal socialism and municipal entrepreneurship. One hundred years previously, under the leadership of Joseph Chamberlain, an authority dominated by Liberal businessmen and capitalists took over for the city its supplies of water and gas and laid out the impressive Parisian-style boulevard of Corporation Street. In the succeeding years the council acquired its own electricity supply, it built libraries and schools, it set up a Municipal Bank with the main objective of helping working-class people to save, it built more council houses than any other local authority in Britain, and it maintained parks and recreation grounds. In addition to these functions, its committees supervised the local police force, fire brigade, transport system, markets, public baths, salvage and veterinary departments, drainage board, allotments, hospitals for the mentally ill, and public health services.

With one million people and with councillors determined to act on their behalf, Birmingham resembled a small state. Jealous and wary of the power and influence of local authorities, national government has stripped them of many of their responsibilities. In defiance of this centralisation of control, Birmingham City Council has continued to play a decisive role with its leadership, initiatives and job creations. One of its crucial decisions was to build a municipal airport.

As early as 1928, it was recognised that air traffic might stimulate 'the present and future trade of the city' and 11 years later Elmdon Airport was opened for flying. For a long time it remained a small operation, but the recession of the early 1980s alerted the council to the need to develop the city's transport links. Since 1972 and the building of Spaghetti Junction (the Gravelly Hill Interchange), Birmingham has been the focus of Britain's motorway system, but it was acknowledged that this position needed to be complemented by major connections with European countries and elsewhere. These were crucial for the export and import of goods, for the provision of new employment, and for the inflow of capital to the West Midlands. In partnership with the region's six other metropolitan councils, Birmingham decided to upgrade its air links. Together, they constructed Birmingham International Airport which opened in 1984 with a revolutionary 'hover-train' called Maglev leading to the nearby specially-built Birmingham International Railway Station.

In 1991, a second terminal was opened at the cost of £60 million. It was Europe's first purpose built hub and spoke operation, a facility which was pioneered in the United States of America. Euro Hub has established Birmingham International as an airway interchange centre, a position which has been enhanced by its proximity to five motorways. Its location, facilities and determined management have meant that it now carries 5½ million passengers each year, a total which is expected to double by the year 2000. If this happens, another 5,000 people could find work at the airport. This will be in addition to its present total of 4,500 employees and the 2,000 workers who are indirectly dependent on its success.

PARTNERSHIP: MUNICIPAL AND PRIVATE ENTERPRISE

Birmingham International Airport is situated next to the National Exhibition Centre, a facility which is the result of a company set up in 1970 by the City Council and Birmingham Chamber of Industry and Commerce. In the words of Sir Robert Booth, a director of the latter body, this historic event led to a 'unique partnership of civic and private enterprise, with bi-partisan support given by the Conservative and Labour leaders'.

The first phase of the NEC was opened in 1976 with 981,350 square feet of halls. This doubled the exhibition space in Britain, and the national importance of the facility was recognised by the government with grants to assist in its building. Since then there have been large additions to the NEC: in 1980, the Arena was opened; four years later, the Forum was ready for public use; and in 1989, 20,000 square metres were added to the display space. The European Community played a significant role in this latter development, giving a grant of £12.25 million towards its cost of £41 million. It did so because the NEC has created long-term employment in an area which has been recognised as in need of assistance because of the devastation of manufacturing industry and the subsequent loss of jobs.

Interior of the International Convention Centre. (Gareth Lewis, Birmingham City Council Department of Planning and Architecture)

The expansion of exhibition halls has continued in 1993 with the addition of 33,000 square metres of space. Because of this and its favourable location, the NEC hosts the 'top 12 international trade fairs' which are held in Britain. These include the British International Motor Show which recently attracted 650,000 people, and exhibitions for a variety of trades: building, packaging, giltware, machine tools, plastics, electronics, gardens and leisure, furniture, and giftware. The NEC has also hosted public events like Crufts Dog Show and BBC Clothes Show Live.

In all, each year the NEC attracts six million people who spend money on accommodation, food and travel and whose presence has led to the building of leading hotels like the Metropole. It cannot be doubted that the NEC has boosted the local economy and employment: there are almost 1,000 workers on the 580 acres site; it has led to a large number of indirect jobs; and over the last ten years, its profitability has meant that it makes a direct financial contribution to the City Council's funds.

The success of the NEC led the council to realise that there was a demand for a purpose-built conference centre in Britain. Accordingly, in 1984 it approved plans for the erection of the International Convention Centre in the heart of the city. This has 11 halls - one of which has accommodation for 1,500 people - and ten executive rooms for smaller meetings. In keeping with the collaboration which distinguishes relationships between the local authority and business, the ICC is managed by the NEC and the Birmingham

An athletics event in the National Indoor Arena. (Gareth Lewis, Birmingham City Council Department of Planning and Architecture)

Chamber of Industry and Commerce. This last body is one of the most dynamic of its kind in the country as it is also involved in urban regeneration in the Heartlands Scheme, and with the Institute of Asian Business. Its actions are matched by those of 'Birmingham – City 2000', a private sector association of financial, professional and commercial firms which aims to change the city's image and to help its development as a business centre of national and international standing. (Much of my information on this section has been provided by Councillor Paul Tilsley, M.B.E., and Bob Moore, Chief Executive, Birmingham - City 2000).

Close to the ICC is the Symphony Hall which has seating for 2,200 visitors and is the only place in Britain which is designed to modern specifications for orchestral concerts; and also nearby is the National Indoor Arena another facility constructed to clear designations. Before the NIA was opened in 1991, Britain's main indoor sporting centre was an old aircraft hangar in Shropshire. The ICC itself cost £180 million to build. This sum was provided by a £50 million grant from the European Community's Regional Development Fund and by the City Council. Despite its prestige, the ICC has attracted criticism both for its cost and its effect on nearby communities. Some residents are like Pamela Edwards and feel that their small council estate in Ladywood is 'sandwiched' between high-profile projects which have not benefited local people. (*Letter,* 1989)

In the same way, many people disapproved of the Super Prix which ran from 1986 to 1990 and was the result of the enthusiasm of Councillor Peter Barwell and Martin Hone. Welcomed by the council as a publicity venture which would draw attention to Birmingham's new image, the race attracted huge crowds as much as it gave rise to opponents who disliked its high expenditure and its disruption of the lives of those with homes near the circuit. The balance between spending on prestigious developments and events and the provision of basic services is a difficult one to maintain. It is essential that Birmingham draws in investors and new companies who will provide jobs, but equally it is crucial that ordinary people do not feel that their views are irrelevant. The major task which councillors now face is to reconcile these objectives and to bring conflicting opinions into harmony.

Still the ICC is a major example of positive 'pump-priming' by the city council. By its presence, it is aimed to raise Birmingham's reputation internationally, to create direct jobs, and to attract private sector investment into the city - which will result in more employment. In these respects, the facility has been a success. It has focused media attraction on Birmingham and forced many commentators to change their negative opinions of the place; in its first year of operations, it brought in one million visitors and helped to inject £26 million into the local economy; and it has led to the creation of 7,500 jobs and the construction of 25 new hotels. Amongst them is the £34 million Hyatt Regency, and within a five-mile radius of the ICC there are now 6,780 bed spaces in major hotels like the Swallow, Copthorne, Campanille, Plough and Harrow, Novotel, Belfry - which has a golf course where the Ryder Cup was played in 1993 - and the New Hall Country House - a Medieval moated manor in Sutton Coldfield. Birmingham is now the fourth most popular British city for the visit of international tourists and businesspeople, and it has also become a leading European financial centre.

Martineau & Smith, Brass Cock Founders and General Factors. (William Hawkes Smith, Birmingham and its Vicinity, 1836)

FINANCIAL AND BUSINESS SERVICES

The provision of financial and business services is not a new phenomenon in Birmingham. D.E.C. Eversley has argued that in the fifteenth and sixteenth centuries 'there was a certain amount of lending by those who owned land to those who worked in trade'. Further, 'the merchants to whom the final product was sold might act as bankers to the small man'. (D. E. C. Eversley, 'Industry and Trade 1500-1880', in, The Victoria History of the Counties of England, *A History of the County of Warwick. Volume VII. The City of Birmingham,* 1964)

A similar situation prevailed 200 years later as is indicated by the history of the Scholefield Goodman Group. This traces its origins to 1780 and Clement Cotterill, a merchant of Old Square whose business was taken over by his son-in-law, Joshua Scholefield. Later he also became a banker and in partnership with Mr Goodman, he acted as a factor in the American trade. Many Birmingham merchants were like these two in that they sold the goods of other manufacturers on a commission basis, and it was this business which led Scholefield Goodman into confirming.

> **"You would have a buyer's book and a list of products and wares which you were purchasing. Now in confirming, the overseas customer writes to the confirming house and tells you to order 100 guns, or in my day 100 motorcycles from B.S.A.. You would get the quotations, send them out to the customer and when one was acceptable the customer would place the order with the confirming house which would then place an order with the UK supplier. The supplier would prepare the goods and make them available to the confirming house which would arrange a shipping date and packing and the confirming house would pay the UK supplier. The confirming house would then send out appropriate bills of lading. The financial arrangements with the customer varied. Sometimes they would pay when they sold the goods, or else they would pay every six months or yearly and interest would be charged. But if the overseas customer defaulted that would not affect the UK supplier.**
> **(J.H. Ruston, *Interview*, 1993, former buyer 1964-65 with Scholefield, Goodman and Sons Ltd)."**

Since the Middle Ages, merchant families like the Holtes and Clodshales of Saltley had been active in the political and social life of Birmingham as much as they were in its economic affairs. This all-round involvement was as apparent with their successors like the Scholefields. Joshua was one of those who founded the Birmingham Chamber of Commerce in 1813, an organisation which was based on the Commercial Committee formed 30 years before; and in 1832, he and Thomas Attwood were elected as Birmingham's first MPs since the thirteenth century. His son William also represented the electorate in Parliament, and in 1838 he became the town's first mayor. He was followed in this office by many distinguished people, from Albert Bradbeer who was a prominent Labour lord mayor, to Denis Martineau who was the fifth member of his family to serve the city in this way.

The Martineaus exemplify the important and close interplay between manufacturers and those who provided them with financial and business services in Birmingham. They were descended from a Huguenot who fled religious persecution in France and settled in Norwich. In 1828 his descendant, Robert Martineau, came to the Midlands after he married Jane Smith - daughter of the man who owned the Eagle Foundry where George

Birmingham Fire Office, 1808, forerunner of Royal Insurance (UK) Ltd. (J. Bisset, Magnificent and Grand National Directory, 1808)

Holyoake worked. He went into business with Mr Brooke Smith as a manufacturer and factor, whilst his son Sir Wilfred became a solicitor and a partner in the practice of Arthur Ryland. Today it continues as Martineau Johnson.

Other law firms are as well established in Birmingham: Tyndalwoods & Millichip was started in 1792 by Thomas Webb; Rigbey Springthorpes began eight years later; and Wragge & Co. opened in 1834 with the partnership of Henry Wragge and Clement Ingleby. The firm now employs over 250 people and has 25 partners; whilst a competitor, Edge Ellison formed in 1870, has 55 partners and offices in London and Brussels. Another large concern is Pinsent & Co. which advertises itself as 'lawyers to the business community since 1877'. However, the significance of the legal profession in the city was recognised long before this when the Birmingham Law Society was set up in 1818. It was not the only body which indicated the growing relevance of financial and business services. In 1845 the Stock Exchange began its operations locally with members like N. Lea & Son whose business was founded 11 years before. It now trades as Harris Allday Lea & Brookes, along with 13 other stockbrokers in an exchange which did not merge with its London counterpart until 1972.

Birmingham was also a major centre for insurers, and it remains so. The Sun Insurance Company was founded at 10, Bennetts Hill in 1710; Royal Insurance (UK) Ltd has its origins in the Birmingham Fire Office started in 1805; Wesleyan Assurance Society began 36 years later with members of the local Wesleyan Methodist Church; and Britannic Assurance dates its formation to 1866 and the British Workman's Mutual Assurance Co. Ltd of Great Francis Street. One of its chairmen was Joseph Patrick whose son, Albert, began the Patrick Motor Group with the purchase of a garage in 1929. Since then the family has expanded into dealership and has set up a 'purpose-built motor museum' in Kings Norton. (For a discussion of Sun Insurance Company policies see Eric Hopkins, *Birmingham, The First Manufacturing Town in the World*, 1760-1840, 1989)

Many working-class people were as interested in saving money to buy property as they were in assuring their lives against death.

> **The trades which set up the Birmingham Trades Council in 1866 were skilled groups like the cordwainers and the mill sawyers, proud of their traditions and not unlike the gilds of the middle ages. There was pride in skill and in accomplishment, and Bunce in 1865 remarked on the large number of artisans in Birmingham who owned their own houses. It was not accidental that Birmingham was the home of the building-society movement. The artisans 'earn good wages, and by moderate thrift can afford to lay something by. That they do so is abundantly proved by the large deposits in the savings bank; by the existence of innumerable sick and benefit clubs, in connection with numerous churches and chapels, with various "Orders" such as Odd Fellows and Foresters, and, unfortunately, in connection with almost every public house.'**
> **(Asa Briggs, *History of Birmingham. Volume II. Borough and City 1865-1938*, 1952, quoting Samuel Timmins.)**

The Birmingham Freehold Land Society led the way in providing mortgages in the nineteenth century, and it is one of the predecessors of the Birmingham Midshires Building Society.

As a manufacturing centre, Birmingham was marked out by the multiplicity of its trades and this phenomenon was matched by the wide range of financial and business services which the city offered its people. These included chartered patent agents such as Luke Hebert who started the present firm of Shaw, Bowker & Folkes in 1835; bailiffs like John

Crilley who began work in 1869 and whose business remains active; and chartered accountants like A. Daniells who opened his company in 1827. It is now part of Coopers & Lybrand, many of whose competitors also have well-established backgrounds. They include Wenham Major founded in 1867, and Price Waterhouse which includes the business of Howard Smith started in the same year.

INTERNATIONAL FINANCIAL CENTRE

The Iron Man Statue in Victoria Square, paid for by TSB as a gift to the city and sculpted by Anthony Gormley, 1993. (Gareth Lewis, Birmingham City Council Department of Planning and Architecture)

Today, Birmingham is the regional focus of a great number of large accountancy concerns like KPMG Peat Marwick. In its local office it has 51 partners, 800 staff and in 1989 it had a fee income of £40 million. These figures emphasise the major difference between such firms and their nineteenth-century forerunners who operated on a smaller, local basis.

> **London can offer very few services that cannot be provided equally as well, and probably more cost effectively, in Birmingham.**
> **Take, for example, accounting and business advisory services. All the major firms are here in strength, including Price Waterhouse. During the 1980s we expanded rapidly, with the result that our operations spread into four separate buildings. Recently, however as the culmination of several years planning, we took possession of Cornwall Court, one of the finest and most prestigious of the new buildings in the heart of the commercial sector. With approaching 500 people our Birmingham office would, if standing alone, be in the top 20 accounting firms in the country. (George Carter, senior partner Price Waterhouse, *Communiqué. Birmingham City 2000. The Working Capital*, 1992)**

The rapid rise of Birmingham as a major financial centre is evident in other areas such as banking. It has branches of European financial institutions like Societé Géneralé, Credit Lyonnaise, Bank of Cyprus (London) and ABN; it is a focus for the Bank of Ireland and Allied Irish Bank as well as the Royal Bank of Scotland; and it has leading Asian banks like the Mitsubishi Bank, Bank of India, the Bank of China, the Baroda Bank, the Bank of Tokyo International, and Habib Bank. Significantly, a leading British bank, TSB, has transferred its headquarters to Birmingham where it employs 1,000 people. It main building, formerly Birmingham's General Post Office, is on Victoria Square where it has sponsored a piece of public art known locally as 'the iron man'.

TSB's move indicates a clear shift in Birmingham's economy. Between 1978 and 1989 there was an increase of 22,487 jobs in the area of financial and business services, a gain of 54.1%. In this period, the only other rise in employment was that of 5.3% in public and personal services. Together these growth sectors were now giving work to 286,804 people, nearly 40,000 more than had jobs in manufacturing. Unfortunately, the emergence of positions in the service industries has not matched the fall of employment in the making of things; and most of those who have lost work in this field do not have the skills to move into banking, accountancy and similar jobs. A crucial contemporary task is to provide the training which will enable young Brummies to obtain this work.

FURTHER READING

| Birmingham City Council | *Celebration of a Centenary. Commemorative Book and Calendar of Events in Birminham 1989* (1989) |
| Birmingham Post | *Birmingham. The European City* (1992) |

'The Spirit of Enterprise' by Tom Lomax in Centenary Square, symbolising the three forces which have motivated the people of Birmingham and led to the city's greatness - commerce, industry and enterprise. (Gareth Lewis, Birmingham City Council Department of Planning and Architecture)

CHAPTER 6
SERVING BIRMINGHAM

The Bull Ring, about 1950. The barrow boys are on the right-hand side leading to Spiceal Street, and under Richard Westmacott's statue of Lord Nelson - unveiled in 1809 - are gathered crowds watching two Bull Ring 'performers'. (Birmingham Library Services, Warwickshire Photographic Survey).

High Street, Birmingham and The Bull Ring by David Cox, 1827.

PRIVATE SERVICES

Birmingham has always been more than a manufacturing city. As a great centre of population, it has encouraged the growth of private businesses and public bodies which have served the needs of those who have been involved in making things. Shops, hospitals, council departments and markets all emphasise that Birmingham is a place for trading and caring as much as it is the site of production and investment.

In 1993, *The Birmingham Post & Mail Year Book and Who's Who* listed 202 firms which were carrying on business in the city and which had been established for 100 years or more. Not surprisingly, the majority were manufacturers of a wide variety of goods, but the largest single category of occupations was that of solicitors which numbered 12 companies. This was followed by property services which had seven firms and funeral directors which had six. Of these undertakers, the oldest are Bach and Barker which began to offer its services in New Street in 1824, and N. Wheatley & Sons which started in 1856 in Hill Street.

The history of businesses such as these has been neglected, but their role was a vital one not only in the removal of the dead but also in the manner in which they did so. Dignified funerals were desired by working-class people as much as they were by those who were affluent, and the wish for 'a proper send-off' was instrumental in the emergence of burial clubs and life assurance companies. 'Doing the right thing' for the deceased extended even to the funeral of babies.

      ❝Referring to the old days I have never seen the printing of any remarks giving the details how Child Bearers carried the coffins of Babies who had died into the cemetery. I was one who did this often, a white dress and black sash for the occasion, the undertaker brought you the white gloves to wear. There were no tears from me for I didn't know who

Wheatley & Sons Funeral Directors, probably their old premises in Hill Street, late 1890s. (Maxwell E. Taylor, Grimley J.R. Eve, chartered surveyors)

the Babies were. I received the cane the next day at school
when asked where I was and I replied I went to a funeral,
my feelings today are why ever did they allow this
kind of thing to take place. (Mrs E. Muckler, *Letter*, 1990) 99

Funeral directors were one of a number of businesses which offered private services to the people of Birmingham. They ranged from arms auctioneers such as Weller & Dufty founded in 1835, to Schultzky & Co. picture framers which began 10 years later and now trades as Gale & Co. Other services were provided by photographic artists like Joseph William Pickering who started his operations in 1857 and whose firm was a forerunner of John Whybrow Ltd; by dealers in motor accessories like A.B. Fletcher who began his firm in Great Lister Street in 1914; and by people such as Charles Keay who collected rags, bottles and metal from 1864. His business is now based in Leopold Street, but perhaps the best known of Birmingham's modern scrap metal merchants is Henry Taroni of Aston Church Road.

Descended from immigrants from southern Italy, this entrepreneur began his business after doing his National Service in the 1950s. 'At that time there were so many scrap cars in Birmingham' that the council paid him to take them away. Within a short time, Henry Taroni was collecting over 400 vehicles each week and was chopping them up with axes. This laborious and heavy task is now done by automatic car crushers, and Taronis were the first scrap metal merchants in the Midlands to import one of these machines from Germany. (Paul Taroni, *Interview,* 1993)

PUBLIC SERVICES

If Birmingham is becoming a leading international centre of finance, then it is also emerging as a major focus of the communications industry. One of the landmarks of the city is the Post Office Tower in Newhall Street where BT is now based, whilst another is Central House in Broad Street. This is the headquarters of 'the largest seven-day' independent television company in Britain. It provides a variety of local and regional shows, it is a leading supplier of 'top-rated network' programmes, and in 1987 it gained the Queen's Award for Export Achievement for its success in marketing its products across the world.

Outside the city centre, BBC has a major base at Pebble Mill in Edgbaston.

66 Television output includes Top Gear, now the most
popular indigenous programme on BBC-2, the Clothes
Show, and this autumn the entire weekly morning sequence
on BBC-1 from Kilroy through Good Morning with Anne and
Nick to Pebble Mill at One. But it is for its drama that
Pebble Mill has built up a richly deserved reputation over
the years; this year sees the screening of A Year in
Provence starring John Thaw as well as Ken Russell's
production of Lady Chatterley's Lover.
As well as being the home of the Archers, Pebble Mill's
Radio Studios have a long tradition of producing highly-
acclaimed drama and documentary programmes for Radio
4... Regional Television output from Pebble Mill and a
network of studios throughought the Midlands provides
regular daily news bulletins on BBC-1. A team of
correspondents specialising in local government, business,
environment and community affairs contribute to the
nightly news programme Midlands Today...

City of Birmingham Weights and Measures Department, before 1914, and probably the offices in St Martin's Lane. (Birmingham Library Services)

The roots of BBC broadcasting lie in its local radio stations, however, and BBC Radio WM based at Pebble Mill is one of 39 stations covering the country providing lively, topical and entertaining speech-based programming reflecting the communities they serve. (Jerry Johns, manager, Press and Public Relations, BBC Pebble Mill, in, *Communiqué. Birmingham City 2000. The Working Capital,* **issue 8, spring 1993).** "

Public services are of increasing significance to the economy of Birmingham and its largest employer, the city council, belongs to this sector. Although it has been forced to make many workers redundant recently, the corporation still gives full-time jobs to over 40,000 people, or one in eleven of the working population in Birmingham. If part-timers are added to the total of employees, then it rises to over 50,000. As a consequence of these figures, the council's significance as a source of employment cannot be underestimated.

This role as a provider of work effectively dates to 1851 when councillors set up a number of committees: Finance; Assessment, Rate and Appeal; Estates and Public Buildings; Watch (Police); Public Works; Markets and Fairs; Lunatic Asylum; Baths and Wash-houses; and General Purposes. Some of these committees necessitated the employment of senior officers or professionals like T.H. Fiddian the Superintendent of the Rate Department and J. Pigot Smith the Borough Surveyor; others required the taking on of manual workers; and all needed the services of clerks.

The Public Works Department was one of the most extensive in the municipality. By the 1890s it was headed by a City Surveyor and it was split into eight sub-departments: Secretarial; Accountant's; Drawing and Surveying; Building and Surveyor's; Sewerage and Rivers; Roads and Scavenging; Public Lighting; and Mechanical and Electrical. The majority of employees were involved in the physical labour of improving streets and watercourses, in building public conveniences and sewers, and in erecting public lamps; but a few were needed to administer these tasks. Archie Mann was one of them. He joined the PWD in January 1880 as an office boy and he rose to become Chief Accountant. In his early years, he was paid six shillings (30p) a week for working from 9.00 a.m. to 6 p.m. Monday to Friday, and until 1.00 p.m. on a Saturday; and it was not until 1890 that he and the other administrative staff were provided with a typewriter. (Information supplied by Ian Heard, Principal Administration Officer, and Sue Cook, Public Liason and Administration, Birmingham City Council Department of Planning and Architecture).

When the Public Works Department disappeared in 1974 it employed about 3,000 people, of whom one third were non-manual workers. Today with the inclusion of part-timers, the largest departments within the council are Education which has over 23,000 employees; Social Services with about 9,000 workers; and the Direct Service Organisation with a staff of over 6,000 people. Some of these are responsible for the 6 million trees in Birmingham as well as its parks, of which there are more than in any other European city. Other departments include Community Affairs; Economic Development - a committee which emphasises the council's active role in the creation of jobs and economic regeneration; Housing; Leisure - which includes Recreation and Community Services, Library Services, and Museums

Sergeant Daniel Long, in the background, at a fire probably in Nechells Park Road, late 1890s. (Miss Sheppey)

and Art Gallery; Planning; Policy and Support - which embraces Finance and Management, General Purposes, and Personnel; Public Health and Environmental Protection; Technical Services; Trading - which ranges from Commercial Services to the NEC and ICC and to the Direct Labour Organisation; and Urban Renewal.

For over 100 years, Birmingham has been led by determined and forceful councillors who have followed coherent and thoughtful strategies. Prominent amongst them have been Joseph Chamberlain (Liberal), Sir Theodore Pritchett and Sir Frank Griffin (Conservative), Harry Watton and Sir Frank Price (Labour), Sir Neville Bosworth (Conservative), and Clive Wilkinson and Sir Dick Knowles (Labour). Despite their political differences, these men have been distinguished by their over-riding priority - the well-being of their city. However, the ability of the council to act independently has been affected by the increasing power of national governments. They have sought to weaken the influence of local authorities by stripping them of significant functions relating to the supplies of water, gas and electricity and to the provision of fire and police officers. Even so, Birmingham City Council remains of major importance because of its great size, wide services and large number of employees. Brought up in a tradition of municipal activism and cross-party initiatives, most Brummies would not welcome the further weakening of local government, nor would they greet the increase of quangos which are not accountable to the electorate.

Souvenir of the opening of The University of Birmingham, 1909. (Sheila Jackson)

Men such as Joseph Chamberlain have been influential inside and outside the council chamber. It was through the vision and commitment of this former mayor that Mason College became The University of Birmingham in 1900. Nine years later, this educational establishment began its move from Edmund Street – where the buildings had been paid for by Josiah Mason - to its present site in Edgbaston. This transfer was not completed until 1961, and Les Davies could remember working at the old premises during the Second World War.

66 **Looking back, I wonder what I let myself in for when accepting the position of Junior Clerk (salary 15s plus 2s bonus) at the City's only seat of higher education in the heart of the city centre. A sloping desk was the main furniture unit in the main office... A prompt start at 9.00 a.m. (Mondays to Saturdays) was a must, and a finish, when the last piece of mail was brought in for despatch. It was not long before one became an expert in knowing when Woolworth's in New Street would be selling its small ration of biscuits or sweets, or when Etams disposed of its limited stock of fully fashioned stockings. How popular I was when I brought back a pair for the office girls...**
Fire watching was obligatory for academics, students and staff alike and what a thrill to see Sir Raymond Priestley [the Vice Chancellor] - to sign on the same as myself. The duty also enabled me to (a) meet the students of whom Norman Painting (of BBC fame) and Ted Downes, the world famous were just two and (b) to improve my skills on table-tennis.
(Les Davies, 'A War-Time Office Boy', in, *Shard End Library, On the Street Where You Live. Memories of Old Birmingham* unpublished manuscript, 1992) 99

The University of Birmingham is now recognised as one of Britain's leading centres of higher education. In addition to its students, it has a staff of approximately 4,600 people ranging from cleaners, porters, caterers and security personnel to lecturers and researchers. As a result, the institution is a major employer locally, as are the newer University of Aston and the University of Central England.

Another forerunner of higher education in the city was The Royal School of Medicine and Surgery in Birmingham which became Queen's College in 1843. This change of name signalled its association with the Queen's Hospital which had opened two years before in Bath Row. It was built largely because of the vision of William Sands Cox and the financial generosity of the Reverend Dr Warneford; it had 130 beds; and medical services were given voluntarily by three consultants and six physicians and surgeons. The hospital catered for large numbers of people, situated as it was in a poorer part of Birmingham: in 1860 alone, its staff treated 1,200 in-patients and 10,500 out-patients.

The Queen's was the first English teaching hospital outside London, and some of its doctors achieved international fame for their practices and innovations.

> " The ready availability in every developed society of two common dresing materials, absorbent cotton wool and absorbent gauze, is probably taken for granted. They were partly invented and certainly popularised just over 100 years ago by a Birmingham Surgeon, Joseph Sampson Gamgee... (he) was always very much concerned with wound care, his principles being described in a lecture delivered in 1876... Cotton wool comprised the wound contact layer, Gamgee recommended that used by jewellers: it was non-absorbent and cost 2s 9d (14p) for a llb (454g) parcel. Picked oakum provided absorbency; manufacture of this material being supervised by HM Prisons... Gamgee not only insisted on antiseptic methods for dressing production... but also made available dressings medicated with substances such as iodene, phenol and tannic acid. (Dr J.C. Lawrence, MRC Burns Research Group, Birmingham Accident Hospital, 'A Century after Gamgee', paper presented at the British Burn Association Meeting in Birmingham, 1986). "

In 1938, the Queen's moved to a site donated by the Cadburys close to The University of Birmingham. It was re-named the Queen Elizabeth, and three years later its former buildings became the Accident Hospital and Rehabilitation Centre. This was the first establishment of its kind in Britain and also the last charity hospital set up in the country. It was known affectionately by Brummies as 'The Acci' and its doctors, nurses and auxilliary staff performed vital services within the heart of the city especially with regard to injuries caused by burns. In 1993 the people of Birmingham were outraged when 'The Acci' was closed down by the Regional Health Authority.

The Queen's was preceded by the General Hospital in Summer Lane. This was completed in 1779 and its building owed much to the endeavours of Dr John Ash who has given his name to Ashted Row in Duddeston. In 1897, the General moved to Steelhouse Lane to 'one of the finest buildings of the kind in the kingdom, and is supplied with every appliance which can contribute to the comfort of patients and their recovery to health'. Its architect was William Henman and he designed the hospital on a system whereby pavilions radiated from main corridors. This gave 'ready access to each floor and more plentiful supply of air and light'. (John Henry Lloyd, 'The Hospitals', in, J.H. Muirhead, ed, *Birmingham Institutions,* 1911)

One of the most remarkable doctors to work at the General was J.F. Hall Edwards who was responsible in the late 1890s for the first operation in Britain which was performed from an X Ray. His research into this form of photography was pioneering and he devised a means of protection from the radiation which X Rays gave out. Sadly, this came too late to save him from contracting skin cancer. So badly was he affected by this disease that his colleagues were compelled to amputate his left arm and the fingers on his right arm. Despite this, Hall Edwards declared that once he was over his operation and was well he would return to work.

Like the Queens, the General was a voluntary institution which was supported by subscriptions, donations, and organised charities such as the Birmingham Saturday Hospital Fund. Although it began officially in 1873, this organisation was based on the Hospital Sunday Fund which was started in 1859 by Dr Miller, the rector of St Martin's in the Bull Ring. Both relied on the small sums of money given by working-class people and they contributed greatly to the finances of hospitals such as 'the Orthopaedic' (1817), 'the Ear and Throat' (1844), 'the Dental' (1859), 'the Women's' (1871), and the Birmingham and Midland Hospital for Skin and Urinary Diseases (1881).

Local businesspeople were also active in providing money for the city's hospitals. One of the most prominent of these benefactors was Christian Kunzle. He was born in Switzerland, and after a time as a chef at The House of Commons he came to Birmingham in 1903 when he opened a bakery at Snow Hill and a café and shop in the Midland Arcade. Over the next few years his business expanded and it became well known for its distinctive cakes. By the 1930s, Kunzle had premises in Leicester and London, but his base remained a factory at Five Ways, Birmingham and he was committed to the well-being of the people of the city. In 1932 he was elected president of the Childrens' Hospital, as a result of which he opened his family home in Switzerland to some of its patients. The Chateau Brusselle was in Davos and it was surrounded by 200 acres of 'park and mountain lands'. This feature and the local climate made it suitable for the care of 'debilitated and pre-tuberculous children', and until the outbreak of the Second World War scores of young Brummies benefited from visits to Kunzle's home. Trips resumed in 1947 when groups of 25-30 children went there 'on a six months rotation basis'. This connection ended eight years later upon the sale of Chateau Brusselle, following the death of the Swiss-born confectioner. His firm was later absorbed by the Lyons chain. (Information supplied by Joe Hunt, President, The Birmingham and Midland Institute)

Other hospitals in Birmingham were at Little Bromwich where medical attention was given to people suffering from T.B. and infectious diseases, and Dudley Road. It is ironic that such a beneficial institution grew out of the infirmary of a hated establishment - the workhouse. This had been built in Winson Green in 1852, and like other workhouses throughout Britain its prison-like appearance and regime were aimed at dissuading the desperately poor from applying for help from the authorities. Despite the coming of the Welfare State in 1947, the workhouse lingered on for a few years as a hangover from the time when the poor were punished for their poverty.

> ❝It was the winter of 1948, (yes as late as that) I was 23yrs of age, a mother of two young girls and expecting my third baby. We were homeless my husband, my children and myself were hungry, tired and cold so police advised us to go to Weston Road. I'd no idea what the place was & where. We trudged there pretty late at night. After stating our situation my husband and I were parted, my children were dragged away from me. I can still imagine their screams. I'd no idea where they'd been taken to, and I was not to see or hear from them for nearly six months.
> I was taken to a bathroom scrubbed with some evil smelling substance and given a uniform (like a prisoner's) to put on and then taken to a dormitory...
> When we explained we were man and wife we were told we could see each other and talk on visiting which was for two hours once every month... My husband was put to work in the laundry, I had to bump and clean the wards. I often wondered how I endured and lived through this time, never knowing when I would see my babies again and living as a family ought to. The only way we achieved this was because my husband 'jumped the wall', stayed away a couple of weeks then came back and said his friend would put us up. It was not until I walked through the

archway of tears my husband told me he had lied, we were still homeless. I didn't care we were free and were determined we would never go back there again. (Muriel Duff, *Letter to the MetroNews*, 1991) "

Elsewhere in Birmingham there were buildings which were constructed because of compassionate motives. In 1824, the Eye Hospital was founded because of the urgings of Dr Joseph Hodgson, a distinguished medical practioner who became a Fellow of the Royal Society and a member of the Royal College of Surgeons. One of his 'pupil-dressers' was Richard Middlemore whose ancestors had been lords of the manor of Edgbaston and devout Catholics after the Reformation. Middlemore later became a surgeon at the Eye Hospital where he 'desired to alleviate as far as he could the pain and misery which is caused by diseases of the eye', and he was also concerned for the general welfare of those who were blind. To this end he supported the efforts of Mary Badger and Elizabeth Harold - the daughter of a local merchant - who opened a school for sightless children in Ruston Street in 1846. Within three years this became the Birmingham Royal Institute for the Blind with large premises at its present situation in Carpenter Road, Edgbaston.

Women from prosperous families were prime movers in the establishment of another philanthropic venture - the Birmingham Womens's Settlement which opened in 1899 in the working-class neighbourhood of Summer Lane. Amongst those involved in its operations were Edyth Lloyd; Alice Beale - wife of a Lord Mayor and herself a Kenrick; Mrs Ellen Pinsent; Mrs Muirhead - whose husband was a professor at The University of Birmingham; Dame Elizabeth Cadbury; Lily Sturge - daughter of Joseph Sturge who had sought to extend the vote to working men; and Mrs Agnes Barrow - whose family owned a store in the city centre.

Under the guidance of these and other women, the Settlement bought a house from which voluntary helpers made Provident collections and at which they established a Medical Care Committee, a Crippled Children's Union, and clubs for girls. Many of these volunteers became social workers and the Settlement had close links to The University of Birmingham and the Selly Oak Colleges. Under the presidency of Christine Kenrick, it continues to help the local community with employment training sessions for women and advice bureaux on debts and how to escape from the cycle of debt.

Floodgate Street Infant Welfare Centre, set up before 1914 by Mrs Caswell and Miss Jessie Lloyd, helped by Joel Cadbury, Dr Robertson, Birmingham's Medical Officer of Health, Drs Pooler and Savage and Councillor Jackson. Southall Brothers gave 'cod liver oil, many Medicals (helps), Cow and Gate crate dried milk and Glaxo'. (Ivy Caswell)

COMMUNITY ACTION

Rocky Lane Chapel Youth Club, March 1942, meeting in Charles Arthur Street School because the chapel had been badly damaged by bombs in April 1941. (Dot Leroux)

The urge to do good was not restricted to wealthy women. Many lower middle-class citizens were active in missions like that in Hatchett Street. This was part of a Wesleyan Chapel which had a Sunday School, Boys' and Girls' Brigades, facilities for gymnastics and drill, and which arranged summer camps. Nearby in William Street North was a mission of St George's C. of E. where Mr and Mrs Bentley 'organised games for children and the odd day out at Sutton Park'; whilst St Edward's Hall in Theodore Street was supervised by Mr Wilson who had a furniture shop in Newtown Row. At this mission, children could attend a lantern lecture after which 'everyone received a mug of cocoa and a jam sandwich'. In the same street was a Salvation Army Hall, ' a very small place that did excellent work among the poor', especially in the sale of second-hand clothes, furniture and household goods. (Pauline and Bernard Mannion, *The Summer Lane and Newtown of the Years Between the Wars 1918-1939,* 1985)

Away from missions and their workers, other lower middle-class people were involved in more irregular acts of charity. In harsh winters, the hungry could get food at soup kitchens which were set up by butchers and greengrocers, whilst coal dealers like the Fawkes' of Studley Street were well-known for giving fuel to those who could not pay for it. But working-class people were not passive recipients of the aid of more prosperous citizens. In a multitude of ways they helped each other to combat the ravages of poverty. Their self-help extended from formal organisations like friendly societies and trade unions to informal 'didlum' savings clubs which were operated by women in factories and streets; and it included the daily and unrecorded acts of kindness showed by those who lived in the close-knit communities of the back streets. This might be the neighbourly giving of a cup of sugar or 'a piece' (of bread) to those who were in hardship, or it might be the constant advice and support provided by someone like Percy Shurmer.

During the inter-war years this man was a Labour councillor and he later became M.P. for Sparkbrook, but his fame was achieved on a local rather than a national level. He arranged day trips for children known as 'Shurmer's Sparrows' and he was determined to improve living conditions for the people of the districts of Gooch Street and Balsall Heath. Through his efforts, pavements were slabbed properly and gas lighting was laid on to homes which had lacked it. Because of his success in down-to-earth matters he was acclaimed as 'The Miskin King'. The miskin was the name given to a communal lean-to in a back-to-back courtyard where the dustbins were kept, and it was usually in a dilapidated condition so that the rubbish overflowed to create a health hazard. Shurmer was celebrated because 'he used to smash them, he used to make the landlords change them even though they didn't want to'. (Alan Mahar, ed, *Memories of Balsall Heath, Highgate and Sparkbrook. Local History from Conversations,* 1983)

The public service of those who have striven for the well-being of the citizens of Birmingham has been matched by the dedication of people who were concerned with the welfare of animals. In 1861 the long-established 'Birmingham Society for the Prevention of Cruelty to Animals' became a branch of the RSPCA, and one of its first suporters was Lord Calthorpe whose family, the Goughs, still owns most of Edgbaston. For much of the nineteenth century the members of the RSPCA were concerned with the condition of horses, cattle and sheep which were driven along the streets of the city: in 1871 they provided a trough and water supply in Stephenson Place; and they successfully campaigned for a steam roller to push down the rough road surfaces which led to 'horrific injuries to hoofs and lower limbs, and consequent pain and lameness'. At this time, the headquarters of the branch were in Cherry Street, but today they are at Barnes Hill where there is an animal sanctuary and hospital and a base for seven RSPCA inspectors. (Margaret Jones, Assistant Branch Secretary RSPCA Birmingham and District Branch, *Letter,* 1992)

These officers are concerned with helping all animals, but they are not alone in their actions. In New Bartholomew Street there is the Birmingham Dogs' Home where strays

Tommy Tudor, from Belgrave Road, and his Co-op coal wagon in Balsall Heath in 1947 when he won first prize for his turnout in the May Day Parade; his daughters Eunice and Maureen are on the pavement beside him. (Albert Judd, information supplied by Mrs Eunice Phillips and Lily Millard)

are cared for. These premises were constructed between 1986 and 1989 at a cost of nearly £2 million and they replaced those in New Canal Street which opened in 1892 for the sum of £532. The impetus for this facility came from Sir Alfred Sherlock Gooch, a wealthy landowner whose name is remembered in several streets in Birmingham. He called a meeting of four friends 'to discuss the serious problem of dogs roaming the streets of Birmingham, apparently abandoned' and his family remains associated with the Dogs' Home which:

> **is administered by a committee of business people who offer their time and expertise on an entirely voluntary basis. One of them is Derek Lea, grandson of Montague Percy Lea who was the land agent of Sir Alfred Gooch and present at that historic meeting in 1892. The Lea family and the Gooch family have maintained their connection with the Home ever since, for it was Sir John Gooch, great-grandson of Sir Alfred, who provided the freehold site for the present building in 1983. ('A Home from Home for Man's Best Friend', press cutting on the release of Noel Blackham, *It's a Dog's Life: the story of Birmingham Dog's Home*, 1992)**

PROPERTY SERVICES AND BUILDING

Derek Lea's son is the fifth generation of his family to work for 'the only firm of chartered surveyors in Birmingham associated with the original founder and with the original name'. The business, James and Lister Lea, dates to 1846 and the partnership of two brothers, but it is not the only property consultants in the city which is long established: DTZ Debenham Thorpe is connected to the business of Chesshire, Gibson and Co. which began in 1784; whilst Grimley J.R. Eve started about 1830 with the operations of Horatio Nelson Grimley. (Norman C. Wright, *History of Grimley and Son, 1830-1957*, unpublished manuscript, 1957)

Like its fellows, this firm has grown with the city and it received a major impetus in the 1840s and 1850s when Edwin Grimley acted for a number of claimants who lost their properties for the construction of New Street Station. This was just one of a number of high-profile buildings which transformed the city centre of Birmingham in the mid nineteenth century. Others included King Edward's School in New Street (1833) erected to the plans of Sir Charles Barry who later became the architect for the Houses of Parliament; the Market Hall (1834) designed by Charles Edge; the Town Hall (1835) planned by Hansom and Welch; Curzon Street Station (1842) of which Philip Hardwick was the architect; Kent Street Baths (1852); Snow Hill Station (1854); the Birmingham Library (now the Birmingham and Midland Institute) in Margaret Street (1858); Woodcock Street Baths (1860); the Exchange Building in Stephenson Place (1865); and the Central Lending Library (1868).

These were not the first public buildings in the city. Between 1709 and 1715, St Philip's Church (now Cathedral) was erected to the designs of Thomas Archer on land owned by Robert Phillips - an ancestor of the Inge family; in 1749, St Bartholomew's opened for worship on the east side of the town on a site provided by John Jennens; to the north, St Mary's was built in 1774 on a plot donated by Dorothy and Mary Weaman and the Lench's Trust; whilst on the west, St Paul's was erected five years later thanks to the generosity of Charles Colmore.

All of these places of worship were raised on open land, and their construction preceded the expansion of Birmingham into their neighbourhoods. In this respect as much as in their function they differed from the great structures erected in the central area of the city in the nineteenth century. These necessitated the destruction of property and the disappearance of streets and familiar landmarks, as Ellen Hampshire recalled. When she was a child in the 1860s she lived near Five Ways and she regularly visited town with her older brother and sister.

James Harrison, auctioneers of New Street. (William Hawkes Smith, Birmingham and its Vicinity, 1836)

"On our way home we often called somewhere for refreshment, sometimes at 'Joe Hillman's Tea Room' where the G.P.O. now stands (Hillman's was also a licensed restaurant). In the tea room we had cheese cakes and milk... Or we bought cakes from Bryan's confectioners (their shop was on the corner of Ann Street where the entrance to the Council House now stands), or to Bosley's Pie Shop - hot kidney pies 2d each in Congreve Street (where the Norwich Union Offices were built later). Then we sometimes stood for a while on the waste ground at the back of the Town Hall (now Chamberlain Square) to watch the different entertainers on Sunday afternoons... A little way down Worcester Street on the left, Alfred Bird (of custard powder fame) had a fountain of coloured water playing in his shop window.
Barrow's Tea Shop in Bull Street had the figure of a Chinaman standing in the doorway, before their Corporation Street corner shop was built... In Lower Temple Street, Welsh's were noted for their pork pies... Hot baked potatos were sold at the top of Stephenson Place, from a portable oven... Also at many street corners in the town, hot sheep's trotters did a good trade, customers taking their own vessels to hold the broth. (Ellen Hampshire, *Memories of Birmingham in the 1880s*, 1977)"

New Street, looking down from Victoria Square with Christ Church on the left and Corbett's Temperance Hotel on the right, about 1875. The statue of Sir Robert Peel by Peter Hollins and cast by Elkington and Mason is now in front of the Police Training College on the Pershore Road. (Birmingham Library Services, Poulton Series)

The shopping thoroughfare of Coventry Road, Small Heath, early 1900s. (Geoff Dowling)

But rebuilding was not a new phenomenon in Birmingham. If change is the only constant in the city's industrial history, then transformation seems to be the over-riding force influencing its physical appearance. As early as 1828, James Dobbs was so affected by the loss of Pudding Brook, Newhall Hill and half of Spiceal Street that he wrote the song 'I Can't Find Brummagem' which he performed at the Theatre Royal.

> **Full twenty years and more have passed**
> **Since I left Brummagem,**
> **But I set out for home at last**
> **To good old Brummagem;**
> **But every place is altered so.**
> **There's hardly a single place I know,**
> **Which fills my heart with grief and woe,**
> **For I can't find Brummagem.**

The power of this song lies in its continuing relevance, but whilst Brummies today would share Dobbs' regret at the destruction of well-known places, the growth and continual rebuilding of Birmingham has created jobs.

During the first half of the nineteenth century, the town's population rose spectacularly from 71,000 to 233,000. Such a huge increase led to a need for more houses and it encouraged the building of factories, workshops, railway stations, shops and offices. This meant employment for many people, and not only in property consultancy and chartered surveying. A great number of small-scale building firms emerged, as did some large ones which continue to operate in Birmingham: William Sapcote and Sons Ltd, started in 1853; Moffatt and Whittall, begun ten years later; and Elvins Construction Group Ltd, which followed in 1865.

The city's modern building industry includes other firms which are well-established: the Osborne Partnership of chartered architects which was started by John P. Osborne in 1872, and the similar operation of Crouch Butler Savage Ltd which began 12 years later; Bigwood Bros (Birmingham) Ltd, architectural metalworkers and builders' engineers which dates to 1879; Bryon & Co. Ltd, ceramic wall and floor tiling specialists which opened for business in 1888; and the builders' merchants Derringtons & Sons Ltd. This firm was founded in 1856 as a manufacturer of bricks and quarries - two materials which were essential for the development of Birmingham. Throughout the city and its environs there were brick fields and clay pits, like Bonds Brick and Tile Works in Bordesley where Will Thorne worked as a child of eight or nine. He gained this job because of his uncle.

> **"The place was three miles from our home, and each day a six-mile walk was added to the day's work of twelve hours. I think the Birmingham Football Ground is now on the site of these brick works. My work was to carry away the bricks from my uncle. Each brickmaker had a shed to himself, and the bricks had to be laid out on a hot floor. In this way I had to handle four to five hundred bricks a day. As my uncle made the bricks from two moulds I took them and laid them out on the floor, and generally it was almost impossible to work with my boots and stockings on, so I didn't wear any at all. The work was hard for a lad of my age. Each brick weighed about nine pounds, and in the course of the day I carried several tons of clay bricks. We usually started work at six in the morning, when I would pick up the bricks from the floor of the shed that had been dried from the previous day and night to make room for the new ones. Sometimes we would finish work at five o' clock, but it was generally later. It would depend on the supply of clay from the clay-grinding mill. (Will Thorne, My Life's Story, 1925)"**

Brick fields like this were built on when they were worked out, and in this manner they heralded the outward movement of Birmingham's boundaries.

The great buildings of the mid 1800s were followed by others later in the century: the Council House constructed between 1874 and 1879 under the supervision of the architect H.R. Yeoville Thomason; Highbury, the home of Joseph Chamberlain erected in 1879; schools like Ladypool Junior and Infant, built in 1885 to plans drawn by Martin and Chamberlain, as was the College of Arts and Crafts in Margaret Street; and the Victoria Law Courts in Corporation Street, finished in 1891 to the design of Sir Aston Webb and Ingress Bell. This street itself was an example of the continual redevelopment of Birmingham. It was conceived by Joseph Chamberlain and its building swept away the alleys, gullets and insanitary properties which lay between New Street and Old Square. Unfortunately, there was no provision to rehouse those who were made homeless by a project which improved the image of Birmingham and gave it new facilities. The same lack of thought was evident in the rebuilding of the Newhall Street area which became the city's commercial sector with the construction of offices and structures like the Central Telephone Exchange.

'Late afternoon kick off, children playing football outside condemned houses in Ladywood, late 1960s. (Peter Donnelly)

For the first half of the twentieth century, 'town' remained Victorian in its look - although in the 1920s and 1930s, Broad Street was the site of new buildings like Baskerville House, the Birmingham Municipal Bank and the Hall of Memory. However, a number of suburbs changed drastically as council and private dwellings covered what was formerly farm land. One of the biggest builders was Dares whose 'Distinctive Houses' were sold for £375 in places like Hall Green. F. Hill worked for this firm when he was a teenager.

> **"You were expected to lay the complete flooring downstairs in a day and the next day the upstairs floors. Cut your boards to size, fetch them from the stack of timber and cramp them up tight, then nail them down with two nails (floorboards) per joist, per board and woe betide you if you put any hammer marks on the face of them boards. You bought all your own tools and no one stole anyone else's tools, an unwritten law, for they always said you were stealing another man's bread and butter. Yet in this affluent society stealing tools is rife.**
> **By sixteen years of age I was expected to help put the roofing timbers on, hang doors, skirting, architrave, in fact do a man's job, the wages rising to about 16/- a week. But no bonus, you just had to work as hard as you could otherwise someone else took your job. When the time came the foreman would come round the job on a Friday afternoon to sack the ones he didn't want... (Letter, 1992)"**

Following the Second World War, a massive redevelopment programme also altered the older parts of Birmingham. It obliterated whole streets and destroyed long-established and well-regarded buildings, places and neighbourhoods. In the city centre, property developers like Jack Cotton and Charles Clore recognised the potential offered by this sweeping modernisation, but their speculation in new structures did have a positive effect on Birmingham's economy. As Maxwell E. Taylor of Grimley J.R. Eve emphasised, the office space they provided was cheap to rent compared to that in London, whilst it was more accessible than similar facilities in Manchester because Birmingham was the hub of the nation's motorway network. As a consequence, firms which provided financial and business services were drawn to the Midlands from the 1950s. This trend was helped by solicitors like John Wardle of Edge and Ellison who 'stole a march on other cities by doing flotations' of private companies into public liability concerns. Today, Birmingham city centre has 17 million square feet of office space which gives work to 110,000 people. (Maxwell E. Taylor, *Interview,* 1993)

Both council-led and private enterprise inspired building projects led to a thorough change in the appearance of 'town' in the 1960s. The comprehensive victory of the new

Workers of Birmingham City Council Urban Renewal improving houses, streets and the environment in the 1980s. (Birmingham City Council Urban Renewal)

over the old was symbolised by the disappearance of the old Bull Ring and the erection of the Rotunda. Although it is disliked by older Brummies, for my generation this circular structure symbolises our Birmingham. Yet it too might be knocked down as part of another plan to improve the city centre on its south side. Such a project would complement those in the vicinities of Centenary Square and The Chinese Quarter, and it would keep people working in the building trade.

Between 1978 and 1989, Birmingham lost nearly 9,000 jobs in energy, water and construction - almost 28% of the total in this sector. It is important to realise that the ICC, NIA and Symphony Hall were conceived in response to these depressing figures as much as they were to the need to create employment in services. The building industry plays a vital role in the local economy and it gives employment to members of all ethnic communities. Harry Gillan is typical of many of them. He came to Birmingham from Belfast in 1949 and from then until his retirement he was employed by General Asphalt. He is proud to 'have worked on all the new estates, Chelmsley Wood and all them and I worked on the Lloyds Bank beside the Council House where we done the roof, we stripped the roof and re-done it; and we done a lot of work by Dale End... I've built a lot of buildings in Birmingham'. (*Interview*, 1993)

A significant number of local firms have benefited from the high-profile projects of the 1980s and early l990s, and some of the largest of them are now involved in the regeneration of Nechells, Duddeston, Aston and Bordesley. This initiative is coordinated by an Urban Development Agency called Birmingham Heartlands, a body epitomising the theme of co-operation which runs throughout the city's history. It is chaired by Sir Reginald Eyre a former Conservative MP for Hall Green, and it includes representatives of the Labour-controlled council, the Birmingham Chamber of Industry and Commerce, and five private building companies - Bryant, Tilbury Douglas, Galliford, Tarmac and Wimpey. The aims of Birmingham Heartlands are fourfold: the building of new houses with developments like Bordesley Village; the creation of jobs; the construction of better road links; and the improvement of the environment with programmes like Waterlinks which will restore canals as a local amenity.

SHOPPING IN BIRMINGHAM

Until its move to Solihull in the late 1970s, the Bryant Group 'was a well known Small Heath company, with its builders yard, offices and joinery shops in Whitmore Road, off Coventry Road'. It was founded about 1885 by Christopher Bryant, but its growth into a large concern was stimulated by the post-war re-development of Birmingham. So too was that of the Douglas Group. Lately, this company has also been active in the Elim Pentecostal Church Development in the Sandpits, the construction of both the M40 and the ICC, and the erection of the City Plaza indoor shopping centre. Similar facilities are provided at the Pallisades and Pavilions, 'Birmingham's £75 million showcase, which occupies one of the prime locations in High Street' and draws 200,000 shoppers each week. Together with 'traditional' outlets like Marks and Spencers, Littlewoods, British Homes Stores and other smaller shops they provide 2.3 million square feet of net-retail floor space in the city centre. (Information on Bryants from Bob Marsden, *A.B.C. of Small Heath and Bordesley Green*, 1987)

Most shops and stores are found in a small area which has recently been pedestrianised. This embraces the long-established shopping thoroughfares of New Street, Bull Street, and High Street as well as the more recent cutting of Corporation Street along which were erected major structures from the 1880s. They included the Cobden Hotel which was founded as a coffee house to combat the 'national vice' of drinking and which has now moved to the Hagley Road; and the draper's of Rackhams and Mathews, today trading solely on its first name as part of the House of Fraser.

Rackhams is recognised as Birmingham's leading department store, but for many years it was rivalled by the nearby businesses of Grey's in Bull Street - now the site of an office block - and Lewis's which was on the corner of Corporation Street. This store opened for business in 1885 and:

> **❝All around are signs of an extraordinary trade. At first one might fancy himself in a huge bazaar where everything useful and ornamental was being offered for sale. But Lewis's surpasses any bazaar for the variety of articles on sale. On one side we see all kinds of fancy goods for ladies' wear; opposite, there is a department for the sale of ladies' and gentlemen's hosiery. Almost adjoining are hundreds of toys; within a few yards from this department the sale of music is taking place. It is impossible to mention the various departments in this large establishment. From the basement to the top of the building there are goods of every description. Clothing, ironmongery, boots, grocery, tobacco, music, ribbons, lace, everything that can be wished for; yet there is remarkable order. (J.G. Hammond, ed, _Birmingham Faces and Places. An Illustrated Local Magazine. Volume IV,_ 1892)❞**

The recent closure of Lewis's was regretted greatly by Brummies. Other well-known premises on Corporation Street have also disappeared including the Midland Educational Co., Barrows Stores and the Grand Theatre. Still, the lower part of this street remains busy with shoppers drawn to large retailers like C.and A. and shoe shops such as Manfield's which traded on New Street over 100 years ago.

Leading from Corporation Street towards St Philip's Cathedral is the attractive Great Western Arcade, built over the tunnel of the railway which named it. This enclosed space opened in 1875 with 42 shops on the ground floor and the same number of offices on the balcony where 'nearly every artistic trade is represented therein'. The shop fronts 'are in ebony and gold, as are also the railings of the balcony, and other fittings, and the roof is of etched glass, with a dome in the centre of the building'. From this was suspended a massive chandelier, whilst further 'mellow light' was given by 350 lamps. One effect of developments such as this was to give work to shop fitters like A.E. Edmonds & Co, and F. & G. Smart both of which began business in 1870. (Contemporary quote on the Great Western Arcade cited in Ian Heard, _Developing Birmingham. 1889-1989,_ 1989).

Colmore Row, looking from the Grand Hotel toward Greys, 1930s. (Geoff Dowling)

The Great Western Arcade. (Post Studios, Birmingham)

Day & Co. shoe shop, New Street, 1950. (Birmingham Library Services, Warwickshire Photographic Survey)

As youngsters, my brother Darryl and I were fascinated by the Great Western Arcade. It was unusual, and it seemed quieter and its pace appeared slower than Corporation Street with its heaving, rushing crowds of shoppers. In the school holidays, Our Nan and Aunt Win would take us to the arcade for sausage and chips in the Midland Counties Dairy coffee house. Afterwards we would walk down to look at the toys in Barnby's on Colmore Row and from there we went to browse at Hudson's book shop in New Street. This was a rabbit-warren of rooms above and below ground, stretching across the enclosed Stephenson Place. It was a shop where you could readily lose yourself in the worlds of different authors, and for many Brummies of my age Hudson's was synonomous with books. It now trades as Dillons, but a few old retailers survive in town. One of them is the cigar and tobacco shop of John Hollingsworth and Son Ltd, which began in 1821 and which holds a Royal Warrant for supplying Prince Albert.

The Piccadilly Arcade in New Street also has its attractions, one of which is a branch of Drucker's Vienna Patisserie where shoppers can eat continental cakes and drink coffee. This business was founded by an Austrian Jew who fled persecution by the Nazis in 1938. André Drucker came to Birmingham because his sister lived here, and he found work as a commercial artist with Jacey Cinemas whose director was Joseph Cohen. However in the late 1950s, Drucker was struck by the thought that:

> **"there must be people in Birmingham who would appreciate the Viennese cafés where you could sit down, read the newspapers and talk over really good coffee or schlagobers (coffee with whipped cream) and eat something small but delicious.**
> **We opened La Boheme in Aston Street, next to a secondhand book shop. The café must have satisfied a need for it went like a bomb. I used to go to London to collect cakes each week from a Greek baker. People thought they were Viennese, and certainly they were different from anything produced in Birmingham.**
> **We started a small bakery of our own in Moseley, and then a patisserie in town. This didn't take on at all. Then, in the sixties, the tourist trade exploded. Everyone was going abroad on package holidays. People would look in the window and say 'that's just the same as we had in Austria and only one shilling and sixpence (8p)!'. This completely changed the public attitude. We advertised and found a wonderful German patissier who taught us how to make his exquisite confections'. (Zoe Josephs, *Survivors. Jewish Refugees in Birmingham 1933-1945*, 1988)"**

Drucker's now has a bakery in Hall Green and 10 branches.

Birmingham's central retail district is a small one considering the great size of the city and its population. For the last 30 years its space has been limited by the stranglehold of the Inner Ring Road, but 'town' has also had to contend with shopping thoroughfares nearby such as Broad Street where 'the privately owned independent family business of Lee Longlands' was set up to sell furniture in 1903. A longer-established furnishers is Alfred Allen which has traded on Bristol Street since 1865, and close to their premises is Frank Starkey Ltd which first sold bread and cakes in 1888.

Another focus of shops was High Street Digbeth and High Street Deritend which run into each other below the Bull Ring. Starting from Alcester Street, Lance Tudor recalled Wright's corn shop, Harding's the newsagents, Nutting's the pork butchers, Bishop's the ironmongers, a sweet shop, and his own father's gramophone and records shop - 'not forgetting the needles!'. Mr Tudor also made 'beautiful cabinets to house the gramophones of the day' and framed pictures. Next to his premises was Bott's home brewery, followed by a magneto factory, William's lamp shop, Bannock's the marble masons, Probert's transfer printers, Russell's the hairdresser and tattoo artist, and Wilday's rag and bone yard. (Lance Tudor, *Looking Back Over the Century. A trip up the hill to St. Martin's in the Bull Ring*, 1989).

Competition to the retailers of town was also provided by the major shopping thoroughfares in the suburbs of Birmingham. In Duddeston and Nechells there were Great Lister Street and Nechells Park Road where Bullivant's Drapery Stores has been in business from 1890; whilst on the Pershore Road in Cotteridge, John Skinner & Son Ltd have been selling shoes since 1868. Other main local shopping roads were 'The Rock', Alum Rock Road in Saltley; 'The Lane', Ladypool Road in Sparkbrook; 'The Bend' in Gooch Street; 'The Mo', the Moseley Road in Balsall Heath; 'The Cov', Coventry Road in Small Heath; High Streets in Kings Heath and Erdington; Newtown Row for the Summer Lane area; Lodge Road in Winson Green; Monument Road in Ladywood; and the Aston Road where C. Aldridge's dad had a motor enamelling garage in the 1920s.

The shopping centre of Cotteridge, Pershore Road near Midland Road, early 1900s. (Geoff Dowling)

66 In those days Aston Road, Aston Road North, Aston Street, in fact from Gosta Green to Salford Bridge, Lichfield Road was one continuous shopping & business area, many or most living over the shop. From our place going past the undertakers we had Edens, the tailors, Myers gas fitters... Past Myers was an old fashioned ironmongers its ceiling festooned with every item imaginable. Then the grocers and vegetable, a chip shop, cabinet-maker, secondhand furniture, with Lloyds Bank on the corner of Miller Street... We had our coal from Eggersons in Miller Street, who had a line of two wheel trucks outside, many could only afford a $\frac{1}{4}$ cwt (28lbs) and fetched it themselves. They also kept hens and chickens which ran around in the coal. One of my favourite shops was here, it sold Pop loose, this was called Vantus, CO_2 being passed through water in a spherical glass dome and what ever flavour you wished added... Going back to Aston Road, you name it we'd got it. Post Office, ladies-children dress shop, Butchers, two businesses never heard of now, the Tripe and Chitterling shop and the Faggot & Pea shop. This brought us to the crossroads, with Premier Motor Co on the corner of Dartmouth Street, next to which in Dartmouth Street was the hucksters shop that hired out basket carriages in which we fetched coke from Windsor Street. Other corners had Bell's the drysalters, a pub the White Hart and Walkers newsagents and barbers. This still had the old overhead shafts and pulleys that once worked the clippers and brushes (*Letter*, 1993) 99

Shopping thoroughfares such as the Aston Road gave vitality and unity to the districts which they served. They connected all the neighbourhoods which straggled off them, and they brought to their pavements shoppers as well as those out for a walk, adults as well as children. It was these roads which were the local monkey runs, the places along which teenage boys and girls paraded in their 'glad rags' hoping 'to click' with a partner; and on a Saturday night these thoroughfares had a market-like air as butchers shouted out the prices for the last of their meat, competing with the cries of hawkers.

THE BULL RING

Birmingham grew because it was a market town. Without the market, traders and dealers, smiths and metal bashers would not have come here and it would have remained an insignificant hamlet. The Toyshop of Europe, the Workshop of the World, Motor City, International City - all the titles which Birmingham has gained are due to the granting of the right to hold a market in 1166.

The importance of the buying and selling of goods was recognised by Leland when he passed through Birmingham in 1538 and called it 'a good market town'. Fifteen years later, it was noted that along its streets there were stalls for fishmongers, butchers and tanners, whilst there were separate Corn, Welsh and English Markets. Almost 250 years afterwards, William Hutton also commented on the dispersal of traders in Birmingham.

> **“Corn is sold by sample in the Bull Ring; the eatable productions of the garden in the same place. Butchers' stalls occupy Spiceal Street... Flowers, shrubs &c., at the ends of Philip Street and Moor Street; beds of earthenware lie in the middle of the foot ways; and a double range of insignificant stalls, in front of the shambles, choke up the passage. The beast market is kept in Dale End; that for pigs, sheep, and horses, in New Street; cheese issued from one of our principal inns, but now from an open yard in Dale End; fruit, fowls, and butter are sold at the Old Cross; nay, it is difficult to mention a place where they are not. (William Hutton, *History of Birmingham*, 1795)”**

Within 10 years of Hutton writing this piece, a hay and straw market was set up each Tuesday in Ann Street - now Colmore Row - and a fish market was begun in Dale End.
By the turn of the nineteenth century, High Street was so congested with stall holders on market and other days that 'many accidents' were caused 'to the great annoyance of passengers'. As Birmingham lacked a town council at that time, it fell to the street commissioners to resolve this situation. They did so in 1806 when they declared that no stalls should be set up between Welsh Cross and Philip Street. Instead market traders were to gather in the Bull Ring where there was ample room 'for every purpose of that kind'. (John Alfred Langford, *A Century of Birmingham Life from 1741 to 1841. Volume II*, 1868).

The Market Hall viewed from Worcester Street, mid 1800s.
(Birmingham Library Services, Pershouse Collection)

This injunction heralded the gathering of Birmingham's other markets in the Bull Ring area and under the shadow of St Martin's, the church which was at the heart of the medieval town. In 1817 the street commissioners opened a 'new beast market' at Smithfield on the site of the moated manor house of the de Birminghams. It was used for the sale of cattle, horses, sheep, and pigs, as well as hay and straw. Eighteen years later a Market Hall was built in its vicinity. This was located between Bell Street and Philip Street and it had two main entrances which led into the Bull Ring and Worcester Street respectively. These were supported by 'massive Doric colums', whilst the hall itself was 365 feet in length, 180 feet wide, and 60 feet high. It provided accommodation for 600 stalls 'fitted up for the sale of fruit, game and poultry, fish, butcher's meat, fancy articles, live pets, etc.', and it cost about £67,261 to build. (Robert K. Dent, *Old and New Birmingham. A History of the Town and its People,* 1880)

Birmingham's Fish Market, early 1990s. (Post Studios, Birmingham)

In 1869, a proper fish market was opened in Bell Street, giving shelter to firms such as J. Vickerstaffe & Co. which was established in 1827 as a wholesale fish, poultry and game merchants. This market was familar to Bob Holyoak whose dad had a fish and chip shop and wet-fish business 'on the edge of Coleshill Street' in the 1940s.

> 66 **It was going down the fish market at five, closing the shop at midnight, scrubbing down and going back down the fish market at five. So when I got to the age of 10 or 11 I was either scrubbing out on a Saturday morning... at about two in the morning because you didn't have the modern labour-saving devices getting the grease off, cookers and things like that, so you actually got the soda and you scrubbed everything down. I would do that, or I'd go and pay his bills, or I'd actually do some work in the fish market for him on a very temporary basis, somebody would just give you some money if you did some work basically...**
>
> **I remember quite a lot of the characters in the centre of Birmingham too... In Carrs Lane by the side of Marks and Spencers, there used to be a guy serving the newspapers named Frank and Frank had had diptheria before the First World War and he'd lost a leg and an eye. And he used to serve newspapers with a dwarf. The dwarf's name was Horace, 'Little Hoss', and they stood outside the bookmaker's Tom Sheldon's... Frank used to have a stool which he sat on and an old brown suit which he never discarded, a brown cap and a crutch, in fact, didn't have a false leg, he had a crutch. It was a thick piece of hard timber and the top of it was just a cross piece. And I remember him all of my life like that until he died in the Fifties. (*Interview,* 1993)** 99

Although the sale of corn was moved from the Bull Ring to an Exchange in Carrs Lane in 1847, the general trend remained to consolidate the town's markets round St. Martin's and in 1851 a 'dead meat market' was opened in Jamaica Row. This trade was stimulated by the gradual decline in the number of butchers who slaughtered livestock on their premises, and by the rising imports of American and Australian meat in the 1880s. As a consequence, the number of animals sold at Smithfield dropped, from almost 41,000 cattle at the start of that decade to nearly 20,000 at its end. This led to the use of part of the site as a wholesale vegetable market, a takeover which was completed by 1900 by which date the cattle market had moved to Montague Street.

The huge increase in sales of dead meat led to the 'serious inconvenience and discomfort' of everybody other than butchers in Jamaica Row. So bad was the situation that it was reported that any pedestrian who used the thoroughfare was at 'imminent risk of having carcasses of sheep or quarters of beef poked into his eye, or a butcher's cart made

View of the Bull Ring from High Street, probably 1840s, with Dakin's tea dealers on the left. (Birmingham Library Services, Pershouse Collection)

View of Birmingham from Camp Hill end of Bradford Street; showing the driving of cattle to the Bull Ring market and the toll gate, probably turn of the 1800s. (Birmingham Library Services, Pershouse Collection)

uncomfortably familiar with the small of his back'. In response to this over-crowding, the council built a new meat market in Bradford Street at which there were also slaughterhouses. (J. G. Hammond, ed, *Birmingham Faces and Places. An Illustrated Local Magazine. Volume III,* 1891)

Well into the twentieth century, livestock was unloaded from rail carriages at Upper Trinity Street in Bordesley and driven to this place. However some butchers continued to specialise in 'home killed meat' as Jim Bennet recalled. He worked at Marsh and Baxter's slaughterhouse in Smallbrook Street where his father was foreman.

> **❝I remember one instance whilst working in the Slaughterhouse we had to sart electrocuting the pigs. We used what they called Calipers they were like a big pair of Pinchers with on the end was metal Pads what you clamped on the Pigs neck behind the ears & pressed a button that stunned the Pig. Well one day I was chaining the Pig's Leg while my brother Bill was using the calipers. It was a Big Sow. Bill had his leg across the Sows back and me stooping down behind, he said ready I shouted right and as it was only 60volts instead of knocking her out she reared up. Bill on top of me, the Sow on top of him and he'd still got his finger on the button with the Caliper on my neck it put me out. When I came to my Dad said what you been pissing about at. (my brother Bill was 20 stone in weight). (*Letter,* 1990)❞**

In 1940, the Market Hall was gutted by a fire caused by a German bombing raid, but the Bull Ring and its markets continued to be the focal point of Birmingham for most of its inhabitants. The Bull Ring seemed to have everything. It had well known shops like Chapman's which sold birds, the Army and Navy Store, Woolworth's, and the Misfits' outfitters which had bespoke clothes made to the wrong size. It had hawkers and barrow boys who were quick with their patter and who were keen to sell their stock. It had a Rag market where the 'wardrobe dealers' laid out their clothing on hessian bags. It had people selling food from roast chestnuts to cockles. It had entertainers like the escapologist, quacks who touted cures for corns, and the destitute like the ragged old lady who sang 'Glory for Me' as she dragged her one foot in the gutter. It had its speakers such as Holy Joe who stood on a box and shouted 'Feed my lambs' so that shoppers would fill his pram with bread for the poor. And it had preachers like Jimmy Jesus outside and Canon Brian Green inside St Martin's Church.

> **❝He drew crowds from all parts of the city and it was difficult to get a seat after 6.00pm. At 6.10pm. he would go into the pulpit in his cassock and get his congregation to sing Mission type choruses and hymns before going to robe for evening service. He had a shoppers service every Saturday afternoon which packed the church and was relayed outside. He also had a Sunday Epilogue Service from 9.00 pm. until 9.30pm. which was very evangelistic and drew vast numbers especially Nurses from Hospitals in the area who had worked all day came to this service with their different coloured scarves looking very colourful... He was really respected by the Market People and Traders. (Stan Millard, *Letter,* 1992)❞**

The Old Bull Ring with its cobblestones and hand carts has gone, swept away by the redevelopment of the 1960s. In its place stands a new Bull Ring which in turn seems likely to be cleared and redesigned. Only St Martin's remains a familiar sight, but if the look of the Bull Ring has changed its meaning has not. It is still the emotional heart of

Birmingham. Markets drew people to the city and it is the people who have made Birmingham. We recognise that vital connection. More than anywhere else in our city, the Bull Ring symbolises Birmingham's past, its present and its future. The Bull Ring is Birmingham.

The modern Bull Ring overlooked by the Rotunda, 1992. (Gareth Lewis, Birmingham City Council Department of Planning and Architecture)

NOTES

I should like to thank the following people for their help in writing this chapter: Helen Taylor, Grimley J.R. Eve; Baroness Doris Fisher of Rednal; Joan Hammerton; and Sheila Jackson for the reference to Emma Hampshire.

FURTHER READING

Birmingham City Council	*Architecture Through the Ages. The Grand & the Ordinary in Birmingham* (1993)
Birmingham City Council	*Annual Reports and Accounts 1991-92* (1992)
Wilfred C. Mathews (introduced)	*1847-1947. The Story of the Birmingham Royal Institution for the Blind* (1947)
Brian Pearce and Maureen Alcott	*The Chequered History of the Birmingham Super Prix* (1993)
Joyce Rimmer	*Troubles Shared. The Story of a Settlement 1899-1979* (1980)

It is well worth readers looking at the monthly editions of *Bygone Birmingham,* a newspaper which looks at the city's past; at the local history journal, *The Birmingham Historian;* and at the nostalgia issues of the *Evening Mail,* entitled 'Old Brum'.

WHERE TO GO NEXT

Libraries

Birmingham Central Library in Chamberlain Square is home to probably the largest collection of local studies material in the United Kingdom. The librarians there are expert and helpful about this marvellous resource. Those who are interested in Birmingham and its people ought to make a visit there to look at the records, books and photographs which are kept in two departments: Local Studies and History; and Archives. Information: **021-235-4549.**

There are a large number of community libraries in Birmingham whose librarians are keen to help with queries on their locality. Additionally, most local history societies are based at the relevant community library. Information: **021-235-4511.**

Admission is free to the Central Library and all community libraries in Birmingham.

Museums

The city is fortunate in having a fine Museum and Art Gallery in Chamberlain Square, and a Museum of Science and Industry in Newhall Street. This is home to a Social History Section focusing on Birmingham, the only working James Watt engine which survives, the City of Birmingham locomotive, and much else.

There are also a number of working museums throughout the city: Aston Hall in Witton Lane, Aston; Blakesley Hall in Blakesley Road, Yardley; The Jewellery Quarter Discovery Centre in Vyse Street, Hockley; Sarehole Mill in Colebank Road, Moseley; and Weoley (pronounced Weeley) Castle, in Alwold Road, Weoley Castle. Soho House, the home of Mathew Boulton, is in the process of restoration and will be open to visitors from late 1994.
Information: **021-235-2834.**
Admission is free to all museums in Birmingham.

Trails

Brum Trails: There a number of booklets which describe walking trips around parts of Birmingham and which indicate places of interest. They are called Brum Trails and they are available for purchase in the Library Shop, Central Library, Chamberlain Square. Amongst them are trails covering the City Centre, The Jewellery Quarter and Moseley. Information: 021-235-4511.

Canals: There is a leaflet called 'Canals in Birmingham' which details a walk along canals in the central area of Birmingham. Information: British Waterways Board, 021-633-3666.

City Centre: Peter Groves, *Exploring Birmingham* (1992), an excellent booklet guiding people on a four and half mile walk around the city centre and its outskirts. Edmund Bealby-Wright, *A Sketchbook Guide to the City of Birmingham* (1993), another very good trail covering the shorter area between Centenary Square and the Great Western Arcade. Both publications are available from local bookstores.

The Digbeth Slice of Life Trail: an evocative and instructive tour through one of the former working-class heartlands of Birmingham. Information: Birmingham Museums and Art Gallery, 021-235-2834.

The Heartland Ring: A trail which covers the ring of canals going through Bordesley, Duddeston, Nechells, Aston, Digbeth and Deritend. Information: Birmingham Heartlands Community Trust, 021-333-3060.

Kings Norton Trail: a two-part trail covering (a) Kings Norton Green, St Nicolas's Church and other buildings, and (b) the local canalside. Information: Kings Norton Community Library, 021-458-1532

Open-decked bus tours of Birmingham are also available, as are barge trips on local canals. For further information ring City of Birmingham Information Centre on 021-643-2514. This is located at 2, City Arcade, just off Corporation Street.
There is also an Information Office in the entrance to Birmingham Central Library, Chamberlain Square; and another in the Mall of the ICC.

Independent Visits

For those people who might wish to arrange their own tours, the following books are recommended:
Sue Cooke   *The Child's Vanishing Landscape. A Storybook about*
Sue Fenoughty   *Listed Buildings* (1993)
Erica Pounce (compilers)
This also includes a comprehensive list of Birmigham's listed buildings and gives information about them.
Simon Berry   *101 Things to see and do in Birmingham* (no date)
Birmingham   *The Triangular Guide to Birmingham* (1990)
Birmingham Post & Mail   *Year Book and Who's Who* (1994)
This has a particularly useful section on 'The City's Principal Buildings',

BIRMINGHAM
(I LOVE DEARLY)

There's a place called Birmingham that I love dearly,
It nestles in the Midlands as you know,
Where the people speak a very funny language,
They say aint, daint, wont and ere yo.

Just again to hear the rumble of the tram cars,
The buses as they journey on their way,
To watch the liners berth in Saltley Dock yards,
And see the ships go down the River Rea.

The breezes blowing from Summer Lane to Nechells,
Are perfumed by the gas works on their course,
And if the wind is not in that direction,
Perhaps you'll get a whiff of Holbrook's Sauce.

And again to hear the hawkers in the Bull Ring,
They hawk their wares from barrow and from stall,
And now that building has gone off the permit,
Perhaps we'll get a roof on the Market Hall.

I have tried to show you Brum in all her glory,
You know as much as me I must confess,
And now I am at the ending of my story,
I wish you all goodnight and God Bless.

(Words by Bert Whittick, 1912-1976, sung to the air of
'Galway Bay'. Thanks to John Whittick, and 'Big' Fred
Titley)

*(A Birmingham Skyline: the Post Office Tower in the
background with St. Chad's on the right.
Post Studios, Birmingham)*

SUBJECT INDEX

Printed by H.E. Jones Limited, Seeleys Road, Birmingham B11 2LA